Minding Minds

Minding Minds   Radu J. Bogdan

Evolving a Reflexive Mind
by Interpreting Others

A Bradford Book
The MIT Press
Cambridge, Massachusetts
London, England

This book was set in Times Roman by Wellington Graphics and was printed and bound in the United States of America.

First printing, 2000.

Library of Congress Cataloging-in-Publication Data
Bogdan, Radu J.
  Minding minds : evolving a reflexive mind by interpreting others / Radu J. Bogdan.
      p.   cm.
  "A Bradford book."
  Includes bibliographical references and index.
  ISBN 0-262-02467-5 (hardcover : alk. paper)
  1. Philosophy of mind. 2. Self-knowledge, Theory of. 3. Other minds (Theory of knowledge) 4. Metacognition. I. Title.
  BD418.3.B63   2000
  128'.2—dc21   99-30174
                                                                      CIP

We need to conceptualize how the development of a child's own mind is bound up with her increasingly sophisticated awareness of other minds. . . . The very structure and functioning of the mind may alter as a result of new understandings about the mind itself.

Hobson, *Autism and the Development of Mind*

Contents

Contents

Preface

This is a book about mental reflexivity or metamentation, which is the ability to think about thoughts. Metamentation may be rightly regarded as the crown jewel of the human mind, underpinning reflexive consciousness, deliberation, moral judgment, self-evaluation, the ability to think ahead by judging hypotheses and possible scenarios, and much more. Aside from various hints and insights found in works on consciousness and propositional attitudes, relatively little in philosophy or psychology has been written specifically about what metamentation actually consists in and even less about how it came about and why. So I decided to take a closer look. But the decision was largely predetermined. Some years ago I became intrigued by commonsense psychology and sensed that much more is at stake than transpired from the philosophical debates around its truth or falsity or mere utility. I thought that the best way to understand commonsense psychology was to explore its evolutionary roots and rationale. Anticipated by a few papers, the result was a book called *Interpreting Minds* (Bogdan 1997). My interest in the subject overlapped in time with a remarkable explosion of psychological and evolutionary research in this area, sampled in that book and to some extent in this one. While working on the earlier book and assimilating the growing interdisciplinary literature, I begun to suspect that commonsense psychology or the naive theory of mind, which I prefer to abbreviate as *interpretation,* not only organizes and lubricates the social life of primates but might be essentially involved in the design of their minds.

The present book is the fruit of that suspicion. For some time it has been apparent to some developmental psychologists that interpretation designs several mental abilities, such as understanding word reference, communication, cultural learning, and more. This book adds mental reflexivity to that list. It should thus come as no surprise that my thinking on these matters is heavily indebted to the psychological and evolutionary work on animal and child interpretation and to some of the distinguished workers in these fields who commented on my work, privately or publicly, or with whom I had the privilege to talk or correspond. No matter how fragmentary or extended, these contacts have been enormously helpful. So it is with great pleasure and gratitude that I thank Sue Leekam, Paul Harris, Josef Perner, Anne-Nelly Perret-Clermont, Danny Povinelli, and Mike Tomasello.

With the same pleasure and gratitude I turn to my philosophical friends and colleagues who shared my interest in the multifaceted story of interpretation and metamentation and took time to hear me out and voice their reactions. In the hope that I do not omit too many, I would like to thank Martin Davies, Dan Dennett, Pascal Engel, Alvin Goldman, Harvey Green, Pierre Jacob, Keith Lehrer, Carolyn Morillo, Norton Nelkin, François Recanati, Dan Sperber, Sorin Vieru, and Ping Tian. Bits and pieces of this essay have been tried out on various audiences, which must be thanked collectively but no less warmly: philosophers gathered in Caen at the 1997 colloquium of the European Society for Analytic Philosophy; members of the philosophy departments at the universities of Bern (Gerhard Seel in particular), Geneve (Kevin Mulligan in particular); Neuchâtel (Daniel Schulthess in particular); the theory-of-mind group at the University of Kent at Canterbury (Sue Leekam in particular); and my regular and faithful audiences for many years, students and colleagues alike, at the University of Bucharest, Tulane University, and the University of New Orleans.

Finally, my heartfelt debts are to those who got directly and substantially involved with this manuscript. As always, Carolyn Morillo read every chapter and verse, left no suspicious-looking stone unturned, voiced skepticism when skepticism was due, and all the while cheered me on. As always, saying "Thanks, Carolyn!" is saying too little. So is saying "Thanks, Dan!" Aside from being a constant and lively inspiration for and discussant of my meta-evolutionary ruminations about the mind, Dan Dennett took a good look at an early version and provided timely observations and suggestions for the next versions, and for that and for his unfailing encouragement I am immensely grateful. Warm thanks also to my former doctoral student and now a college professor in Beijing, Ping Tian, who shared my preoccupations for several years. Her own dissertation (Tian 1996) tackled some of the issues I was thinking about and that was very stimulative, as were her remarks on this text. I am indebted to Eric Schwitzbegel for a much appreciated blend of philosophical and psychological sophistication in detailed and helpful comments and to several anonymous reviewers for their hard work and keen observations, and to one in particular whose call for intuitive props led to Mom and Mim, the real heroes of the second part of this essay.

The MIT Press team once again did a terrific job. A good division of labor between two Amys made the editorial sailing smooth and efficient. Constant in her interest in my work, Dr. Amy Brand encouraged this book project and provided guidance and support during its gestation, as she did during past collaborations. Amy Yeager handled well and cheerfully the interim details of a laborious process. Warmest thanks to you, Amy, and to you, Amy! Thanks also to Alan Thwaits for his fine editing and excellent suggestions.

Catalina minded my mind in more ways than one, and so did her art. One of her works, sampled on the cover, illustrates that, as do my love and deepest gratitude.

Minding Minds

Introduction

1 The Theme

The theme of this essay is rather simple, though its demonstration is not. It is that humans think reflexively or metamentally *because*—and often *in the forms* in which—they interpret each other. In this essay 'metamental' means 'about mental', and 'reflexive mind' means 'a mind thinking about its own thoughts.' To think reflexively or metamentally is to think about one's thoughts deliberately and explicitly, as in my thinking that my current thoughts about metamentation are right. Thinking about thoughts requires understanding thoughts as thoughts, as mental structures that represent; it also requires an ability to relate thoughts to other thoughts and to recognize such interthought relations. Since metamentation is essential to and uniquely distinctive of human minds, the idea that it originates in interpreting other minds can be encapsulated in the slogan that minds are minded because minds mind minds. This word play translates thus: minds evolve into reflexive minds because they mind other minds—where 'minding other minds' means interacting and bonding with other minds, being concerned or curious about them, representing their relations to the world, manipulating and using these relations for some purpose, and the like. All of this amounts (in my terminology) to *interpreting* other minds in social contexts of cooperation, communication, education, politics, and so on. It follows that *inter*mental relations among individuals, handled by a distinct competence for interpretation, are essential to the evolution of abilities to represent the *intra*mental relations among thoughts typical of a reflexive mind.

I take 'interpretation' to be a convenient, short, and grammatically flexible label for what is known in philosophy as commonsense or folk psychology and in psychology as theory of mind, mindreading, or naive psychology. Interpreting is a cognitive rapport between an interpreter (she, in this book) and a subject (he), whereby she represents his mind-world relations from the simplest, such as seeing or wanting, to complex propositional attitudes, such as desiring, believing, or intending, and factors these representations into her goal policies and strategies for action. Interpretation first evolved by natural selection to enable such factoring, thereby promoting the biological interests of the interpreter. So construed, interpretation was naturally selected among primates as a battery of practical skills that precede language and advanced thinking by a long evolutionary shot. In human ontogenesis the grip of natural selection gradually weakens and is replaced by forces of culture, whose grip on the mind may nevertheless be as universal and coercive as that of nature. This means that the emergence of mental reflexivity out of interpretation (and other enabling factors) should be understood as both evolution by natural selection (in early phylogenetic and ontogenetic stages) *and* development under cultural constraints (in later ontogenetic stages).

The idea that metamentation evolved out of interpretation is an exaggeration but not an extravagant one. It is an exaggeration because interpretation is not the sole reason for, and not the sole designer of, metamentation. Language is also a key player, although its mastery owes much to interpretation. It is an exaggeration also because the metamentation indebted to interpretation need not be all the metamentation there is. There are forms of thinking about pictures and sentences that may approximate reflexivity without interpretation, or without much of it, as the case of intelligent autism suggests. More important, the idea that reflexivity evolved out of interpretation is an exaggeration because also involved, crucially, were the abilities to pursue goals by imagining, planning, and solving problems—in short, mental advance work or mental rehearsal. Indeed, I will argue that metamentation begins as *interpretation mentally rehearsed.* Interpretation and mental rehearsal are thus the two pillars on which rests the construction of the primate mind and of its upper metamental floors in particular. A third pillar, equally vital, originates in a mutual physiological regulation between human infants and mothers and soon takes the form of comment-topic protoconversation or topical predication, as I will call it. This is a human development that moves interpretation from its earlier and narrower subject-world focus to a new triangular mind-world-mind pattern of mental sharing in which two individuals (interpreter and subject) share attitudes and information about items of common interest. It is in this pattern of mental sharing that interpretation conspires with mental rehearsal to develop metamentation. Soon after its emergence out of mutual regulation, topical predication is absorbed into communication with and interpretation of others. This is why, for all practical purposes, this third pillar will be counted here as part of interpretation.

Yet the notion that metamentation evolved out of interpretation is not extravagant, because the basic skills needed to think explicitly about or in terms of other thoughts could not have emerged from any source or cognitive ability other than interpretation and can actually be reliably traced back to it both in primate evolution and child development. The patterns required for metamentation can be found solely in the domain of interpretation and are intelligible only as tasks of interpretation. Along with language, mental rehearsal brings these patterns inside the mind and makes them explicit objects of representation and manipulation. This is what this essay endeavors to demonstrate. The demonstration has a motivation worth making explicit, since it may run counter to prevailing views on the relation between mind and interpretation.

2 Motivation

In an earlier work I developed an evolutionary account of interpretation as a practically motivated adaptation (Bogdan 1997). That work left me with (at least) one puzzle that this essay tries to solve. The puzzle grew out of a familiar but troubling observation, which is that figuring out and explaining what people think and do is what interpretation does well and cognitive science doesn't, at least not yet. Hence the oft-heard proposal that cognitive science should tap the folk wisdom of interpretation for a better understanding of the mind. If the assumption behind this proposal is that interpreters have a tacit, naive but largely true knowledge of mental architectures (programs and functional mechanisms) that cognitive science lacks, then the strategy of tapping folk wisdom is a nonstarter. I argued elsewhere that the naive knowledge interpreters have of minds seems indifferent to and silent about mental architectures (Bogdan 1985, 1991b, 1993, 1994), for good evolutionary reasons (Bogdan 1997). Yet there is something else to tap in interpretation to get a scientific grip on human mentation. It is the decisive role that interpretation played in the evolution of primate minds. It is a historical fact (documented below) that interpretation coevolved with primate mentation, and there is a growing body of theory and evidence indicating that interpretation may have been heavily implicated in the design of many faculties of the primate mind. A study of that coevolution could then guide and enrich the understanding of primate minds. This essay pursues that promissory note in the narrow but crucial area of reflexive thinking. And it does so as follows.

3 Lines of Argument

The demonstration will run along three converging lines. The convergence is crucial because no single line could carry the whole weight of the thesis. One line is *conceptual.* It explores the structural similarity, and at times isomorphism, between the tasks of interpretation and those of metamentation. To illuminate this conceptual parallel, I distinguish several key metamental tasks and analyze them in terms of categories and schemes required to handle the tasks. These categories and schemes turn out to represent objects of interpretation at different evolutionary stages. Hence the second, *evolutionary* line of argument. Its thrust is that interpretation is the chief model or blueprint for the categories and schemes of reflexive thinking. To make the idea plausible and biologically ground it, I begin with the background hypothesis, enjoying growing though not unchallenged influence, that primate social life was more apt—and more likely than foraging, tool use or other mechanical activities, directed at the physical world—to have fueled and molded the evolution of primate minds. Since primate social life selected for interpretation, more than for anything else, interpretation emerged as the mental activity most effective in the evolution of primate mentation. The phylogenetic and ontogenetic record favors this diagnosis, since it identifies the pressures for interpretive know-how as the strongest during primate childhood and suggests that metamental skills correlate consistently with skills for interpretation.

This brings in the third, *psychological* line of argument. Although drawing on some interspecies comparisons, the psychological story told below is mostly human, mostly developmental, and focused on checking when, how, and why advances in child interpretation precede, link up with, and facilitate, if not cause advances in, metamentation. Besides joining independent sources of evidence, the link between evolution and psychology has a further significance in this essay. The evolutionary debate over the primacy of physical work versus social life in driving primate mentation has a psychological echo in the developmental debate over the primacy of mechanical action (Piaget) versus social interaction (Vygotsky) in the formation of the child's mind. I think the echo is not fortuitous, not because phylogeny would recapitulate ontogeny, but because of a significant correlation (explored in chapter 3) between the unusually long and adult-dependent human childhood and the unique mind that results. This mental uniqueness seems to owe a good deal to the equally unique texture of the social and cultural surround in which human kids grow up and mature their mental faculties.

4   Level of Analysis

These converging lines of analysis will be pitched mostly at the level of the *tasks* executed (what is done) in interpretation and metamentation, and will remain silent about programs and brain mechanisms (how it is done). I often talk of programs or skills but think of them in terms of their tasks, not in terms of the nuts and bolts of their operation. The focal thesis—that metamentation evolved out of the interpretation at work in mental rehearsal—should therefore be understood and judged in terms of tasks: it is the tasks of metamentation, however executed, that emulated those of interpretation. Pitching an evolutionary analysis at the level of tasks may look controversial and risky in the light of the widely shared belief that evolution selects for programs or mechanisms. This is true of the targets of selection but not of the *reasons* for selection. Selection is for *what* programs or mechanisms *do* that results in reproductive fitness, and what they do can be aptly and fruitfully analyzed in terms of tasks. I find a task analysis apt because evolutionary biology is a science of functions, in particular of functions that become adaptations, and adaptations can be fruitfully described in terms of tasks. I also find a task analysis apt because cognitive scientists often discern tasks before figuring out the underlying programs and mechanisms (as happened, for example, in the cases of grammar and vision). I think that the current understanding of interpretation and metamentation is at such a stage.

Another methodological choice needs to be noted. The demonstration attempted by bringing together data and arguments from evolution, development, and conceptual analysis is going to be inductive or rather detective, as it looks for a variety of clues that reveal patterns of interpretive tasks that metamorphosed into forms of metamentation. Although interdisciplinary in scope and indebted to empirical data, the demonstration is largely theoretical and often speculative. Scientists also speculate, often boldly, particularly in fields such as those covered in this book, but their speculations tend to be narrow, constrained leaps from domain-specific data, accepted theories, and other authoritative sources. (So they cite a lot.) My sort of speculation is less domain-specific, more global and integrative, more philosophical, as it looks for patterns and connections often lacking firm and narrow empirical moorings. (So I cite less. Often whole pages may go by without a citation. Sorry about that.) Yet this sort of speculation is worth pursuing and may yield benefits because the current understanding of the reflexive mind, still limited and fragmented, is unlikely to emerge from any single, compartmentalized precinct of cognitive science. The reflexive mind is a hard puzzle, one of the hardest, precisely because it may be the outcome of independent developments somehow strung together by interpretation. The story of this outcome will unfold as follows.

5   Plan

The essay is divided in two parts. The first sketches the evolutionary background of interpretation as stimulus and shaper of metamentation, the second charts key moments of this coevolutionary saga in terms of a comparative task analysis. Chapter 1 argues that the phylogenetic and ontogenetic routes to metamentation begin in primate social life and the minds adapted to it. Among sundry kinds of socialized minds, only the human mind has the potential to turn reflexive. Why? Because of *how* it socializes. It is mind socialization through internalization of interpersonal relations during childhood. This hypothesis, first proposed by Lev Vygotsky, goes in the right direction but not far enough. This diagnosis sets the stage for chapter 2, where interpretation is found to be the missing link in the Vygotsky's story. Interpretation has solid and far-reaching evolutionary credentials among primates and is systematically implicated in the evolution of primate mentation in general and of thinking in particular. This later implication serves as a launching pad for metamentation, roughly as follows.

Social primates interact by generating and exploiting causal relations among themselves. So they must represent social causation under appropriate categories and schemes. Since interactions among primates are handled by interpretation, primate causal knowledge is represented under interpretive categories and schemes of subject-world relations. Mental rehearsal of social action involves manipulation of causal representations of subject-world relations. These representations are projected imaginatively and often calculated off-line. At some point late in human childhood, when the process is applied to one-self, conditions become ripe for developing categories and schemes for coding and mixing other-world and self-world relations as mental representings. Metamentation is just around the ontogenetic corner.

These developments occur only in the minds of human children and are responsible for the uniqueness of the resulting adult minds. Why? Chapter 3 argues that the answer should be sought in development itself. The human mind is unique because so is its development. Primate development is special in being very slow and adult-dependent, but its human version also involves a unique biophysiological regulation between infant and mother that grounds a give-and-take form of sentimental bonding and communication of emotions and experiences. Such sentimental bonding forms the basis for a truly novel ability, topical predication, which interpretation uses to design communication by shared meaning, language acquisition, and eventually metamentation. Thus concludes the first part of the essay.

The next four chapters chart the developmental progression from sentimental bonding to metamentation in conceptual, evolutionary, and psychological terms. Chapter 4 sets the stage by providing a conceptual profile of metamentation in terms that reveal its evolutionary complicity with interpretation. Metamentation operates through a battery of routines or sequences of tasks. The routines are decomposed into categories and schemes of representation that are objects of interpretation at different stages in the evolution of primate minds. To simplify, but not by too much, this is to say that the abilities to represent metathoughts, as units of metamentation, evolved out of the abilities to represent triangular mind-world-mind relations, as units of interpretation. The stages of this evolution are surveyed in the subsequent chapters.

Chapter 5 is about situated interpretation and its earliest contributions to the edifice of metamentation. Situated interpretation is perceptually immersed in the here and now and has an interactive version in apes and an intersubjective one in human children. At this stage, the interpretational contributors to metamentation are the grasp of intentionality (or a good portion of it), apparently a primate-wide ability, and sentimental minding by sharing and communicating about emotions and experiences, a unique human specialty. Chapter 6 turns to unsituated interpretation and its contributions to metamentation: the category of propositional attitudes emulated by that of explicit metathought (the atom of metamentation) and the turn to self-interpretation, which discloses one's own attitudes as mind-world relations, on a par with those of others. Chapter 7 examines the ability to hold many minds in mind, by iterating attitude attributions and embedding some in others, and also the abilities to format attitudes in common terms and integrate across domains the information represented in the contents of attitudes. The result is a unified mind that can traffic in explicit representations about whatever interests it—an accomplishment that is new and surprising from an evolutionary standpoint.

Chapter 8 wraps things up. It construes autism as providing overall empirical confirmation for the main thesis: autistic people fail at metamentation because, and possibly to the extent that, they fail at interpretation; even those who master most of the skills of language, formal reasoning, and public representations fail to extend this mastery to the mental representations of others and themselves, and thus fail to become reflexive thinkers. After a look-back review of the argument for that conjecture, the essay concludes with a forward look at a few outstanding questions.

Since these chapters tell a constructive and gradually built story and give relatively little space to critical exegesis of and comparisons with other views, I thought it would help to indicate from the outset how the reader could relate this story to other major positions on the relation of interpretation to metamentation.

6 Polemical Side

Besides its constructive role, the tripartite basis of my story—evolutionary, psychological, and conceptual—also has polemical import. I take my readership to fall into three groups: opponents, fellow travelers, and undecided. I do not expect any group to accept the thesis of this essay as is or be persuaded

by a single line of argument. Since the undecided are likely to decide relative
to how opponents are argued out of their positions and how fellow travelers
are persuaded to see it my way, it's going to be between the latter two groups.

The opponents must be shown that in primate evolution and particularly
child development, alternative routes do not add up to reflexivity either
empirically or conceptually. Several such routes can be envisioned. Those
steeped in the rationalist tradition may assume that mental reflexivity is an
innate gift, perhaps built into the brain architecture and maturing on its own.
Even though some basic skills of interpretation seem innate in primates, the
late development of metamentation in human childhood, mostly under the
impact of language and culture, speaks against this innatist assumption.
Followers of Jean Piaget may argue that metamentation develops out of formal
abilities for logical and mathematical reasoning, these in turn developing out
of sensorimotor schemes for physical action. Here the conceptual line is as
effective as the empirical: there is nothing in those formal abilities or the more
basic action schemes to serve as models for metamentation.

Language may also look sufficient to afford metamentation: thoughts are
encoded linguistically and thus are frozen and stable enough to be subject to
mental scrutiny, often by means of further thoughts linguistically encoded.
This gambit, necessary to making thoughts explicit (in the ways required by
metamentation) and linked to other thoughts, is far from sufficient. As this
essay will endeavor to show, thoughts link up reflexively with other thoughts
in ways and for reasons that are independent of language and are not exhausted
by its rules and constraints, whether semantic or syntactic; topical predication
is one such prominent example. Autistic people may handle well large fragments of language yet fail to predicate topically and to metamentate. Also
telling is the fact that young children master language years before they
metamentate. Finally, it may be thought that metamentation draws solely on
abilities to plan or solve problems, but again higher primates and young
children may be capable of such exploits without metamentating. Even mental
rehearsal with linguistic expressions is not going to be enough; autistic people
with reasonable language abilities might be able to mentally rehearse, but
again they fail to metamentate normally. The missing link in all these theoretical schemes is intersubjective interpretation.

Ironically, it is the fellow travelers (perhaps the largest group) that may
pose a greater challenge. For many of them may think (in a 'What's the big
deal?' manner) that the evolution of metamentation out of interpretation is no
surprise and no mystery, since, after all, interpreters naively theorize about
perceptions, desires or, indeed, thoughts. That is what makes them interpreters.
On some accounts, interpreters think about their mental states even before

thinking of those of others. Interpreters, then, would be reflexive thinkers by definition. Yet, there are good reasons to think that interpreters as such are not reflexive thinkers and certainly not by definition. Metamentation is the *joint* product of several developments (interpretation, topical predication, mental rehearsal), so metamentation can't be just interpretation or be derived solely from interpretation. Although interpretation provides the key tasks emulated by metamentation, the emulation is possible only because of these other contributions. It takes a probing look at evolution and development, not a definition or even a theory of interpretation, to prove this point and to show that the journey from interpretation to metamentation is no foregone conclusion. Apes may be credited with some interpretation, but they do not metamentate. Metamentation emerges late in human childhood, even though children have been interpreters, topical predicators, and mental rehearsers for several years.

Even the conceptual story is not as simple and straightforward as it may seem. The fact that interpretation is in general about mind-world relations and, in its intersubjective version, about mind-world-mind relations does not entail that thinkers think about their thoughts in the same ways or that they inherit metamentation from interpretation. The conceptual entailment is surely not visible to those philosophers and psychologists who envision a reflexive access to one's thoughts that is based on internal experiences (introspectionists) or practical-reasoning abilities (simulationists) and does not emulate the interpretation of others. Also important is the historical fact, again revealed only by evolution and development, that initially interpretation was not about *mind*-world, let alone mind-world-mind, relations. Apes and young human children represent only observable *subject*-world relations—such as gazing, seeing or being angry at something—whose mental component is meager and implicit. The mental component grows and becomes more explicit in later childhood when propositional attitudes are mastered, but even the categories of propositional attitudes are far from representing mental states in general, far from representing them reflexively, and far from originating in self-ascription. The turn to self-interpretation is a late development in childhood, and its explanation does not follow from just having the ability to interpret propositional attitudes, as many fellow travellers (and most philosophers) believe. When interpretation turns to self, it opens the way to, and provides a model for, metamentation. Yet even that process is not as obvious, simple, and predetermined as it may seem. There are still many variables needed to bring it to fruition. All in all, then, the fellow traveler may have at least as many reasons as the opponent or the undecided to read on. All are welcome.

PART I

Socializing the Mind

Chapter 1

Tales of Many Minds

This chapter plants the evolutionary seeds. It argues that the roots of mental reflexivity stem from primate social life as evolutionary surround and from the intersubjective rapport among humans as a proximate developmental basis. It turns out that interpretation evolves along the same lines. This coincidence suggests a collusion but not yet a direct or systematic link. Showing that link will be the task of later chapters. The reader already convinced of these truths may prefer to proceed to the next chapter, but he would risk missing some historical premises of later analyses and (of course) the fun that goes with historical speculations. In particular, that reader may miss a tactic of my argument about social versus mechanical agency and also a guess about how interpretation, in cahoots with mental rehearsal, begat mental reflexivity. So, while still holding his attention, I'd better sketch a brief preview before serious skipping gets under way.

My argument consists of three moves. The first, made in section 1, distinguishes between mechanical agency on physical objects and social agency on conspecifics, whence the contrast between the mind of a mechanical doer or physical worker and that of a socializer. These distinctions allow that a good deal of primate mentation serves mechanical agency and has nonsocial reasons and roots in planning, problem solving, and simulation of physical action, in spatial representation, mechanical imitation, and tool use. Yet what one hand giveth, the other taketh. For my second move is to argue that among primates, social agency may have evolved *first* and remained the most prominent and effective stimulus for the conative development of planning and control and the cognitive development of imagining and problem solving. My third move is to insist that social agency and the pressures on it account better than mechanical agency and its pressures for the escalating evolution of primate mentation. Reflexive thinking, an outcome of this escalation, shows signs of having evolved under social pressures on interpretation and mental rehearsal. If this argument is on the mark, it makes sense to focus on socialized minds as precursors of reflexive minds.

There are several sorts of socialized minds and in particular two interestingly different sorts among primates, as section 2 explains. Only one, uniquely human, is apt eventually to go reflexive because of how it socializes. It is an intersubjective socialization based on a mutual traffic of experiences and emotions, in addition to the behavioral coordination on external situations typical of the interactive socialization of other primate species. Such intersubjective exchanges with adults are internalized by infants, according to Vygotsky, and this internalization shapes the infant mind. But Vygotsky does not tell us much about how the internalization works. Interpretation, a most plausible internalizer, is missing from his account. Such is the argument of section 3. It becomes even clearer that interpretation is the driving force and enabler of internalization and mind socialization when, in section 4, we look at the process through the child's eyes and interests.

1 Workers versus Socializers

It is an old evolutionary conundrum: Was it physical work or social life that stimulated and even selected for the primate mind? In psychological terms, was it mechanical or social action that shaped primate thinking? There is a vast literature, ranging over several disciplines, which grapples with these tough and still elusive questions. Far from me to intend to survey or evaluate these debates.[1] But I have both constructive and polemical reasons to take up a few issues. Constructively, I want to show that metamentation evolved from social cognition via interpretation. Polemically, I want to show that metamentation could not have evolved from the form of cognition servicing physical work. In later chapters I argue for these claims by isolating and dissecting the patterns of relations involved in metamentation and by showing that these patterns arise only in the domain of interpretation (a conceptual claim) and that developments in interpretation correlate consistently with developments in metamentation (a psychological claim). This being a foundational inquiry, I want to ground these claims in evolution. The grounding is done chiefly in this chapter and the next two.

Let me begin with a query. Why would mechanical work—mostly of the technological sort, in the form of tool making and tool use—and social interactions among conspecifics be so widely thought to have shaped the primate mind and in particular to have selected for higher mental faculties? Why these domains of cognition and not others (e.g., physical, spatial or biological)? Why would technological cognition serving mechanical work and social cognition serving conspecific interactions be such potent launching pads for mental evolution? Because, I want to suggest, these forms of cognition alone have some unique properties: (a) they are dedicated to *instrumental intervention* in their domains, in the sense of using an object or conspecific as instrument to reach one's goals; (b) the instrumental intervention is of the *cause-causation* sort, in the sense of causing the instrument to cause further effects that attain one's goals; and (c) the instrumental intervention of the cause-causation sort is more successful and efficacious, and thus selected for, when the ways and means of intervention are mentally anticipated, controlled, manipulated—in short, *rehearsed*—before an action is initiated. As a result, the cognitive categories and schemes guiding instrumental intervention end up represented in some form and therefore become *targets* of mental activity.

Thus emerges a powerful mind-design formula whose evolutionary impact will be sampled in the pages that follow. This formula will be further examined in the next chapter (section 2). At this point, it is important to note that mechanical work (of the technological sort) and social interactions (of the primate sort) satisfy the conditions just outlined, which is why their forms of cognition come under the incidence of the mind-design formula. The question is which of these two domains and forms of cognition are more stimulative for mental evolution in general and lead to metamentation in particular. The rest of this chapter makes the general case for the social domain and its form of cognition.

The conjecture that mechanical work cannot be the sole force driving the evolution of human mentation and certainly cannot be the force behind metamentation is based on the nature of the tasks present in metamentation but absent in technological cognition. It is also based on a comparison between the evolutionary potential of mechanical work and that of socialization to stimulate and guide primate minds toward reflexivity. Both evidence and argument favor social agency and social interaction in primate phylogeny and human ontogeny as the driving forces behind the evolution of the primate mind, which is not to deny the mighty contributions of mechanical work. The following is a synopsis of the reasons for this understanding.

Not by Physical Work Alone
Although individualism and hard work (plus a stiff dose of northern Protestantism) may have created capitalism, as Max Weber speculated, they alone could not have created the human mind, certainly not its reflexive powers.[2] The case against physical work as designer of reflexive minds can be made in two steps. The first minimizes the evolutionary role of physical work in general, while the second establishes that the mental skills required for physical work fall short of what is needed for reflexive mentation. To simplify the terminology, let me stipulate that from now on the notion of work means

mechanical action on physical objects within well-structured activities, such as foraging, tool use, home building, and the like.

I begin with a sample of field observations that favor social life over physical work.[3] "A monkey that may require lengthy pre-training and adaptation to an apparatus as well as 20 to 100 trials to solve one two-choice object-discrimination problem will, in a matter of seconds or at most minutes, become thoroughly adapted to a particular dominance status when introduced for the first time to a social situation with three or four cage-mates" (Zimmerman and Torrey, quoted by Jolly 1988, 28). Also, "the problem with chimpanzees is that they do remarkably little most of the time. They move slowly, eat grass, sleep for a long while, groom one another. On the other hand, when the chimpanzees do wake up and cause some social ripples, there is no way an observer can record with pencil and paper all that is going on" (de Waal 1989, 36). "The same is arguably true for natural man. Studies of contemporary Bushmen suggest that the life of hunting and gathering, typical of early man, was probably a remarkably easy one. . . . [He] seems to have established a *modus vivendi* in which, for a period of perhaps 10 million years, he could afford to be not only physically but intellectually lazy" (Humphrey 1988, 17). "Although ecological factors have undoubtedly contributed to the evolution of primate intelligence, nonhuman primates do not appear to manipulate objects in their physical environment to solve ecological problems with as much sophistication as they manipulate each other to solve social problems" (Cheney and Seyfarth 1990, 294). I could cite other sources but I trust the message is clear: physical work, as a deliberate pattern of mechanical actions on objects, is not as important as social life in the pressure for a thinking mind.[4]

The balance is further tipped toward social life when we factor in the social parameters of physical work. The most spectacular form of work among primates is tool use. Its surround is social; the lone tool user is a rarity. This is why individual work cannot be a sufficient evolutionary stimulus. When physical work is viewed socially, it becomes hard to separate its action on the mind from that of its social fabric. Cheney and Seyfarth note, "The challenge of exploiting widely dispersed and ephemeral food sources may therefore have led to increased intelligence not simply because food collection itself became more difficult, but also because ecological complexity placed increased selection pressure on *social* skills, including the ability to defend resources, to detect nonreciprocating cheaters, and to communicate about resources that are displaced in time and space" (1990, 294). The same is true of tool use. Apes cooperate symmetrically by doing the same thing at the same time in order to facilitate a common goal; humans do it by division of labor, face-to-face coordination, and role complementarity (Reynolds 1993, 412; Tomasello and Call 1997, chapter 3). This difference in styles of physical work is more likely to originate in their social environments than in the intrinsic demands of the work itself.

Add to this list two impressive empirical correlations. Brain size, or more exactly the neocortex ratio (neocortex volume divided by the volume of the rest of the brain), covaries with average group size among primates, an index of social complexity, but not with any other factor. "This makes sense, because as group size increases, not only do individuals have to remember more details about their dyadic interactions, but there is an exponential increase in the strategic possibilities within polyadic interactions" (Barton and Dunbar 1997, 246). This correlation hints at the possibility that polyadic interactions may have selected for thinking skills in planning, imagining, and problem solving—a possibility explored in chapter 2, section 4 below. The other correlation is with evolutionary arms races. Neither food gathering nor home building nor tool use nor other forms of physical work are likely to stimulate and sustain arms races that would push primate thinking to higher sophistication. Yet there seems to be an arms-race escalation in the evolution of primate thinking. Food and tools do not retaliate, nor do they mutate innovations in response, but conspecifics do. Social life has the potential of generating new and increasingly complex mental challenges that foraging and tool use cannot match on account of their structure and repetitiveness (on which more anon) and their relative infrequency (noted earlier). The contrast is plain: the most challenging mental problems facing primates are other primates, not stones or sticks or even other species. Recent research also suggests that the primate abilities for foraging and tool use are not that unique and may be more widely shared throughout the animal world than previously thought (Tomasello 1998). So if there is something unique about the primate mind, it must come from elsewhere.

Let me throw in another brainstormer to tip the balance even further toward its social end. It is about dolphins and reveals an interesting contrast with primates. Primates may physically work with tools and also socialize intensely, whence the difficulty in assigning a clear and unique role to one factor rather than another in fueling their mental evolution. Dolphins do not work with physical objects. Yet their minds are quite developed. Reiss, McCowan, and Marino report, "Encephalization quotient data suggest a level of intelligence or cognitive processing in the large-brained dolphin that is closer to the human range than are our nearest primate relatives. . . . Laboratory studies have also provided suggestive, yet inconclusive, evidence of mirror self-recognition in the dolphin, an ability previously thought to be exclusive to

humans and apes." What could be the explanation? The same authors continue, "Field studies indicate a fission-fusion type of social structure, showing
social complexity rivaling that found in chimpanzee societies" (1997, 140).
This means that stable relations alternate with temporary and tactical alliances
(politics) and frequent migrations from one group to another. Such alliances
and migrations require plenty of sociopolitical wits. Interestingly, the same is
true of chimpanzees, perhaps the most mindful among nonhuman primates,
but apparently not of other primate species (Cheney and Seyfarth 1990;
Dennett 1987, 275–276).

There is still another important fact to consider. The physical work of
primates normally takes place in *social arrangements.* Chimpanzees are credited with some planning and foresight in using tools (Cheney and Seyfarth
1990, 297; Tomasello and Call 1997, chapter 3). True, but they acquire their
tool-use expertise in social contexts of learning, mediated by interpretation
(Tomasello, Kruger, and Ratner 1993). Moreover, the targets of their tool use
are socially shared and most frequently form the focus of social interactions
(Vauclair 1984). These observations, true of human children as well, suggest
that tool use is socially and interpretationally constrained and configured from
the outset. Even more important is the fact that primate infants *first* face many
more social rather than physical challenges, and because of their helplessness
and dependence, those fewer physical challenges are almost always socially
structured and constrained in interactions with others (more on this in chapter
3). To prosper, develop, and get what they need, including food and tools,
primate infants need first to evolve the interpersonal skills that help them
engage adults, and those skills are bound to include planning and problem
solving of a *social* sort. Human infants also need adults for the regulation of
their bodily parameters and for food and protection. Socialization is thus
imperative from the outset and thus becomes a first and potent stimulus to
their mental life (Bowlby 1982, Dunn 1988, Trevarthen 1993). The social
cognition of the primate young is thus likely to predate in importance and
development any other form and domain of cognition.

Yet the case for physical work may not seem entirely lost. Work does
actually correlate with brain and mental evolution. Tool use is greater among
primates than nonprimates, and primates are deemed mentally more developed
than nonprimates. Among nonhuman primates, chimpanzees are more into
tool use than other species, and again, chimpanzees are deemed mentally more
developed, more planning, than other primate species. The same is truer of
humans in comparison with chimpanzees. Little doubt, then, that tool use
correlates with keener mental faculties (Byrne 1997; Cheney and Seyfarth
1990, chapter 9; Gibson 1993; Tomasello and Call 1997). Byrne (1997) goes

further and claims that, while the social life of all nonhuman primates is basically the same and poses the same cognitive challenges, the mindful chimpanzees are the only ones seriously into tool use. And that could make the critical mental difference. Not among humans, though. Human tools changed little from 1.5 million to 400,000 years ago, yet brain evolution went apace during that period. In contrast, from 300,000 years ago there is no marked increase in brain evolution but there are tremendous changes in technology. In short, there was little technological progress when brain evolution was explosive and explosive technological progress when brain evolution was stagnant. On the basis of this contrast, Wynn concludes, "Most of our technology developed after the evolution of modern brains and modern intelligence. Therefore, it seems an unlikely selective factor in and of itself" (1988, 281–282).

So much for the broad evolutionary picture. It gives a general sense of why socialized minds won over mechanical minds as nerve centers of primate thinking. But the argument of this essay needs a finer-grained sense of why social life is a winner when it comes to the abilities that evolved into reflexive thinking. Hence the point of the next distinctions concerning primate thinking.

The Thinking That Matters
Like all animal minds, those of the primates are likely to be functionally specialized and adapted to specific tasks in specific domains (not a universal but an influential view these days). Given a distributed functional adaptedness of primate minds, one expects physical work and mechanical object manipulation to leave their marks on distinct mental abilities, such as cognitive maps and spatial representations of the body and the environment, as well as formal programs operating over mental representations in virtue of their structure. When one thinks of human thinking, one so often thinks of logical, mathematical, and perhaps grammatical programs. According to the influential conception of Jean Piaget, thinking bootstraps itself out of the sensorimotor cognition servicing mechanical action in the physical domain. I take this conception to explain fragments of the naive physics of primates and, in the case of humans, the formal abilities to reason logically and mathematically (Piaget 1936, 1960) and perhaps even grammatically (Greenfield 1991). The evolution of primate physical and formal thinking may indeed owe little to their social life and may have actually followed the blueprint proposed by Piaget. But that is not the blueprint for mental reflexivity.

Another sense of thinking, equally important, underpins more directly the evolution of metamentation. It has to do with imagining, planning, and problem solving—that is, mental rehearsal. Physical work, particularly as tool use, is often credited to have been the evolutionary force behind primate planning and problem solving (Byrne 1997, Calvin 1993, Parker and Milbrath 1993). While not denying some contribution, I (with the humility of an outsider) propose to question the promise of this approach to explain the following facts:

• The earliest and hence primary domains of imagining, planning, and problem solving
• The arms-race escalation leading to such thinking abilities
• The evolution of metamentation

   Origin aside, we ought to give closer scrutiny to the idea that physical work may have *stimulated* and *fueled* the evolution of planning and problem solving and their transformation into reflexive thinking. On some accounts, the planning and problem solving involved in primate physical work are too simple to generate an arms race leading even to ground-floor, unreflexive thinking. Thomas Wynn (1993) notes that tool-use skills are learned in a primitive fashion, by serial memorization, with no clear idea of how each action relates to the other or how they combine to achieve a result. He also notes that such sequence construction, by chaining elements together in spatial or temporal contiguity, applies to any behavior requiring motor coordination, and quotes Piaget as saying, "Sensorimotor intelligence acts like a slow-motion film, in which all the pictures are seen in succession but without fusion, and so without the continuous vision for understanding the whole" (Wynn 1993, 395; Piaget 1960, 121). Problem solving in the domain of physical work may not fare better. If problem solving is viewed as an ability to improvise and adjust cognitive and behavioral routines to specific but often unexpected or new tasks and their contextual parameters, then tool-bound planning does not augur well because of its relative rigidity, lack of flexible hierarchy, and rote sequencing. Apes are known to solve new problems in the mechanical domain, at times showing great ingenuity. But, we are told, this happens rather rarely and mostly in captivity, under cultural pressures and stimuli unknown in the wild (Humphrey 1988, Tomasello and Call 1997). So understood, the issue is not whether apes are capable of some planning and problem solving (they are) but whether these abilities originate in evolutionary pressures accumulated in the work place in the physical domain (possible but not likely) and, even more important, whether these pressures can push the abilities toward human heights (unlikely).

   Not all primatologists buy this estimate of ape thinking. Richard Byrne (1995, 1997) argues that the planning and problem solving required by the mechanical work of apes is not only complex enough, in terms of hierarchical and combinatorial productivity, but has the potential to evolve into advanced thinking. Other critics find unconvincing the argument that the social domain of conspecific interaction has more complexity and calls for more sophisticated computational prowess than the physical domain of mechanical action (Byrne 1995, Gigerenzer 1997). It seems to me that this debate is about formal complexity and computational power and thus about the formal sense of thinking. My interest, however, is in the mental-rehearsal sense of thinking and its interplay with social interpretation. My strategy is to argue (a) that the pressures on and opportunities of planning and problem solving are much greater in the social than in the mechanical domain, (b) that the patterns found later in reflexive thinking bear more structural similarities to interpretive skills operating in the social domain rather than to simple physical skills operating in the mechanical domain, and (c) that metamention becomes possible only when the patterns tracked by interpretation in the social domain become objects of mental rehearsal.

I also think that the domain of social interpretation has a texture unmatched in the domain of mechanical action in that it displays *patterns of relations,* unique to the social domain, that call for distinct representational skills, those of interpretation, and also stimulate novel forms of imagination and mental rehearsal. The argument for this conjecture must wait until next chapter (section 4). Still, it is important to note here that my argument will be *not* about formal thinking or about complexity as such but rather about a certain relational texture of the social domain. Similarly, my argument that metamentation emulates interpretation relies *not* on considerations of formal complexity but on a unique *structural* parallel between the tasks of interpretation and those of metamentation.

To put things together, the argument of this essay endeavors to demonstrate, on the one hand, that the tasks of interpretation explain those of metamentation and, on the other hand, that a certain texture of relations in the social domain explains why primate mentation had to stretch beyond perception into imagination and mental rehearsal in order to track actual and possible relations among conspecifics. These are *distinct* developments whose interplay eventually led to metamentation. One development, interpretation, explains the design of the metamental tasks. The other development, mental rehearsal, explains why interpretation tasks and formats metamorphose into metathinking tasks and formats: it is because humans have to interpret off-line and unsituatedly by imagining mind-world relations stretching in time and space over complex patterns of social interactions. If these two developments conducive to metamentation, namely interpretation and mental rehearsal, come

together only in socialized minds, minds that mind other minds, the next
question to ask is, What sort of socialized minds would have the resources
and opportunities to graduate to reflexive thinking. This question calls for
further evolutionary probing.

2   Kinds of Socialized Minds

Think of a mind as a set of programs, run by appropriate mechanisms, whose
overall job is to align sensory inputs and internal states to goal-pursuing
behaviors. The programs execute specific tasks in specific domains defined by
the organism's goals. Evolution has a way of mixing and reshaping programs
for new uses and in the process builds new minds out of old ones. Seen
historically, the human mind is a potpourri of programs, some ancestral and
shared with many other species, others newer and shared with only a few
species (mostly primates), still others quite new and unshared (see Donald
1991, Lock and Peters 1996, and Mithen 1996 for recent surveys). It is during
this mind-building process that interpretation adds its contribution to the
design of the human mind, particularly to its metamental component. To see
how this contribution may have come about, it helps to take a brief and rough
measure of the broader evolutionary scene.

Primate Distinctions
Not all primate minds are created equal. Differences abound and are often
radical. Of interest here are those differences that locate mental reflexivity and
its pedigree in the larger phylogenetic and ontogenetic scheme of evolution
and disclose its complicity with interpretation. Since the territory is vast but
not unfamiliar, my survey is going to be as sketchy and brisk as befits the
needs of the demonstration. One distinction, between situated and unsituated
minds characterizes the degree of immersion in current motivation and perception. The other (perpendicular) distinction is between interactive minds (all
situated), which socialize and communicate solely in terms of visible goals
and behaviors on the utilitarian basis of immediate and urgent needs, and
intersubjective minds (some situated, some not), which socialize and communicate also by sharing and communicating emotions, experiences, attitudes,
and the information that goes with them, without an immediately practical
need.[5] I explain later, particularly in chapters 3 and 5, why intersubjective
socialization is uniquely human. Although its most remote antecedents are
situated and interactive, mental reflexivity inhabits only intersubjective *and*
unsituated minds. This is where this section takes us. Graphically, the territory
to be traveled can be diagrammed as in figure 1.1.

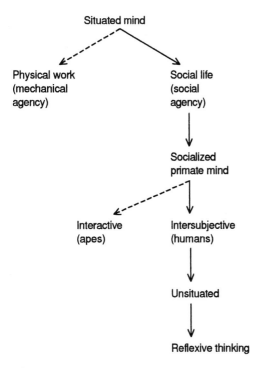

Figure 1.1

A few preliminary remarks are in order in order to get a sense of the choices made along this evolutionary journey and of the reasons for the choices. First, a note about the eligible candidates. Although all prehuman minds are situated, my focus is on primates alone because their intense socialization correlates significantly with a high degree of mental sophistication. So delimited, the first contrast sets older human children and adults, whose minds are unsituated, apart from other primates, including younger human children, whose minds are situated in various degrees. At the same time, humans alone socialize intersubjectively, situatedly in infancy, unsituatedly later. Next, a word about the travel plans. From the perspective of the primate traveler going down the diagram, the road taken in this chapter (the solid arrows in figure 1.1) goes left from situated minds to social life as the evolutionary stimulus for primate minds, then left again to intersubjective minds, and from there to unsituated minds and metamental thinking.[6] At each juncture the choices are determined by considerations about the identity and impact of three factors: (a) the most potent evolutionary pressures for metamentation, (b) the mental resources that at a given juncture are most apt to underpin the developments incrementally relevant to metamental thinking at the next juncture, and (c) the most likely sources of emulation for metamentation. The argument will be that the pertinent evolutionary pressures are those of social life, that the mental resources are those of the intersubjective mind, and that intersubjective inter-pretation is the source of emulation for metamental thinking.

Thus apprised of the travel plans, it is time to proceed. In this chapter I move rather breezily through choice destinations, staying at each just long enough to mark it for later reference. In the next chapters I return to each spot with more details as they become relevant to the ongoing analysis. The first destination is the situated mind.

Mental Situatedness

Socialized or not, a situated mind is tightly glued to its current goals and perceptions of the world. It is a sensorimotor mind that maps stimuli into behaviors. Most such minds are instinctive: their perceptions drive their behaviors in ways determined genetically or through rigid habituation. Their encoding and processing of data is analog and yields continuous alignment of behaviors to perceived states of the world. Their sensorimotor schemes select which aspects of the perceived world go with which behaviors. These features render the operation of a situated mind thoroughly procedural in a sense captured by conditional input-output instructions of the sort "*If* the world is such and so, *then* do this and that." Procedural situatedness has important implications for our discussion. The explicit knowledge it makes available is to be found in the outputs of current perception or memory recall. That knowledge is episodic, particular, and needs current activation. The durable knowledge of a situated mind is domain-implicit and domain-dependent.[7] The knowledge is built into instructions, as opposed to being represented explicitly under concepts in flexible and expandable lists of properties. Such knowledge is domain-implicit. Knowledge can also be contained as much in the instruc-tions as in the domain itself. This is to say that the instructions engage specific features of the domain and kick off when the input signals those features. If those features are not there or are altered beyond recognition, the instructions are impotent. Such knowledge is domain-dependent. Domain-implicitness and domain-dependence define the *situatedness* of a mind (Bogdan 1997, chap-ter 5, based on Cummins 1986, 119–120).

The point of these details is to indicate that a situated mind cannot *be* reflexive: its domain-implicitness rules out the possibility of explicitly repre-senting aspects that could eventually afford reflexivity, and its domain-depend-ence rules out the possibility that such explicit representations (were they available) could be abstracted from a currently perceived domain and re-

enacted mentally. Yet some situated minds evolve to transcend such limitations, turn unsituated, and *become* reflexive, if they meet some conditions.
The minimal conditions are those of minds socialized through interpretation.
These are conditions that only the primates seem to meet. The question is,
Socialized in what way? Set in evolutionary motion along the road mapped
in figure 1.1, the situated primate mind is now past the work-socialization
divide, on its way along the socialization route, and heading toward another
dramatic bifurcation.

Interactive versus Intersubjective

Within the exclusive club of socialized primates, the contrast is between
interactive and intersubjective minds. These sorts of minds can be understood
best in terms of what they do most of the time and most intensely, which is
to socialize in communal, epistemic, and political contexts that call for
interpretation. Distilled from the current literature and far from technical or
definitive, the notions proposed below provide a classification useful for my
analysis.

Interactive socialization takes place among agents whose goals are external
contingencies current or easily anticipated, whose actions are observable ways
of satisfying goals, and who exchange information by way of visible bodily
postures and behaviors. Interactive socialization is almost always utilitarian
in the sense that it reflects current needs and goals and aims at their satisfaction. It is a form of socialization that has been solidly documented in joint
foraging, grooming, play, cooperative hunting, communication, and various
political shenanigans (Byrne and Whiten 1988, 1991; Cheney and Seyfarth
1990; Gomez 1991; Povinelli and Eddy 1996; Quiatt and Reynolds 1993;
Tomasello and Call 1997; Whiten 1991, 1997; Whiten and Byrne 1997).
Interactive minds are those able to socialize interactively and selected for this
very reason.

Intersubjective socialization is uniquely human and involves agents who
engage each other by way of emotions, experiences, affects, and other stances
and attitudes, and exchange information about each other and the world they
attend to through such engagements (Bruner 1983, Hobson 1993b, Tomasello
1998). It is a form of socialization that need not always be utilitarian and
express current needs requiring immediate satisfaction. In its earliest phases,
intersubjectivity draws on innate resources for bilateral contact. The story of
intersubjectivity and its roots will occupy a good deal of chapters 3 and 5.
Now it suffices to say that *intersubjective minds* are those able to socialize
intersubjectively and selected for this reason. These are the minds that stand
an evolutionary chance to become reflexive. For, as the next chapters argue,

it is the forms of intersubjective engagement, managed by interpretation, that set up the foundation for developments leading to metamentation.

3 Society in Mind

The design of the intersubjective mind begins in its socialization. It is a process that was first and best explained by Vygotsky, as I show next. Then I argue that something of evolutionary import is missing from his work. It is interpretation. This section covers only the more familiar half of the story, which construes mind socialization as a one-way street from adult society to the young mind. The next section turns to the less familiar but equally crucial half of the story that tracks the process from the child's perspective.

Mind Socialization

What does it take to socialize a mind? For starters, think of the process as forming the means and finding the routes by which society gets into the young mind and leaves its imprint on it. To *socialize a mind* is to develop in it the skills that enable society—through its natural but unelected representatives, such as parents and educators—to engage and communicate with its youngsters in order to induct them in its ways. This picture is rather unilateral, but I will worry about that after getting its general contours right. Mind socialization is dictated by natural selection and largely enshrined in the genes of both sides, socializing minds and minds socialized. The result is innate skills for socialization. Primates' maturation is lengthy and laborious, which allows for the intrusion of culture. In captivity that intrusion can affect apes as well, as in the case of Kanzi, the enculturated ape who learned to communicate through arbitrary symbols (Savage-Rumbaugh and Lewin 1994). Kanzi, however, also indicates the limits to how much linguistic competence and enculturation can be built on such mind-socializing skills. So the question arises as to what it is about mind socialization in humans that could explain the difference. This is where Vygotsky comes in.

Mostly Vygotsky

The American philosopher George Mead (1934) and the Russian psychologist Lev Vygotsky (1981a, 1986, but writing in the 1920s and 1930s) are widely credited with the most coherent and sustained early attempts to explain the human mind in terms of its socialization.[8] They saw the process and its psychological explanation as going from society to mind. They also realized that the human mind is socialized by having to respond and adjust itself to what others do and say. They viewed linguistic communication as the main avenue from society to mind and saw gestural and later linguistic signs as the key mediators between social interaction and mental activity. Since Vygotsky's analysis goes deeper and is more comprehensive, and since its intellectual influence is greater than that of Mead's, I focus on it and in particular on its concepts of internalization and mediation.[9]

Internalization is not a Vygotskyan invention. The concept has been entertained by many theorists concerned with how mental processes reflect, and even reenact in their formative stages, external constraints such as sensorimotor coordination, imitation, social interaction, and enculturation. Janet, Piaget, and others worked with the notion of internalization, and Mead himself had interesting things to say about it.[10] Yet Vygotsky again went further than all others in exploring how *social* interactions are mentally internalized. The guiding principle of his exploration was formulated as the (now famous) "general genetic law of cultural development," which says, "Any function in the child's cultural development appears twice, or on two planes. First it appears on the social plane, and then on the psychological plane. First it appears between people as an interpsychological category, and then within the child as an intrapsychological category. This is equally true with regard to voluntary attention, logical memory, the formation of concepts, and the development of volition" (Vygotsky 1981a, 163). He adds, two pages later, "The very mechanism underlying higher mental functions is a copy from social interaction; all higher mental functions are internalized social relationships."

How is internalization realized? Through *mediation*. For Vygotsky *semiotic* mediation is the chief internalizer. Although public language is most favored, Vygotsky is aware that some other semiotic mediators must already be in place to ground language acquisition. His analysis is specific enough to give an intuitive feel for the fine-grained structure of internalization based on semiotic mediation and is also representative enough to generalize to more complex cases. So I quote him at some length:

As an example, let us consider the history of the development of the indicatory gesture. . . . It plays an extremely important role in the development of the child's speech and in general is largely the historic basis of all higher forms of behavior. . . . At first the indicatory gesture is simply an unsuccessful grasping movement at an object and designating a forthcoming action. The child tries to grasp an object that is too far away. His/her hands, reaching toward the object, stop and hover in midair. The fingers make grasping movements. This is the initial situation for all further development; it is the first point where we see movements we have a right to call indicatory gestures. . . . When the mother comes to the aid of the child and comprehends his/her movement as an indicator, the situation changes in an essential way. The indicatory gesture becomes a gesture for others. In response to the child's unsuccessful grasping movement, a response emerges not on the part of the object, but on the part of another human. Thus, other people introduce the primary sense into this unsuccessful grasping movement. And only afterward, owing to the fact that they have already connected the unsuccessful grasping movement with the whole objective situation, do children themselves begin to use the movement as an indication. The functions of the movement itself have undergone a change here: from a movement directed toward an object it has become a movement directed toward another human being. The grasping is converted into an indication. Thanks to this, the movement is reduced and abbreviated, and the form of the indicatory gesture is elaborated. We can now say that it is a gesture for oneself . . . after first being an . . . indication and gesture for others. Thus the child is the last to become conscious of his/her gesture. Its significance and functions first are created by the objective situation and then by the people surrounding the child. (Vygotsky 1981a, 161)

This is a good example and a lucid analysis of how mind socialization hijacks an instinctive form of mechanical agency (reaching toward and grasping an object), converts it into a semiotic pattern with social import (an indicatory gesture), and internalizes it as a mental function (referring). The example illustrates the spirit of Vygotsky's approach, even if the actual details of reference acquisition may turn out to be different. Vygotsky also considers more advanced internalization games in which, for example, public speech becomes inner speech, attention becomes specific and voluntary under adult verbal direction, adult supervision metamorphoses into self-regulation, and so on (1981a, 1981b). The metamorphosis of interpretation into metamentation can also be regarded as a form of internalization by task emulation (as I call it in chapter 4, section 3).

How do children and adults manage to play internalization games with such remarkable outcomes? What sort of representational capacity is available to children and adults to allow the former to internalize what the latter do or say? Vygotsky takes it to be a semiotic capacity that internalizes public gestures, other signs, and speech into mental representations.[11] But this can't be enough. Being told that external signs take mental form and come under voluntary control is not yet being told *what it takes* to carry out the process. I do not mean programs or mechanisms, let alone neural details. I mean *cognitive tasks* that would handle the semiotic or other forms of internalization. Vygotsky may have thought that "the very mechanism underlying higher mental functions is a copy from social interaction," but this cannot be taken literally. For, as he acknowledges, "internalization transforms the process itself and changes its structure and functions" (1981a, 163). Some other explanation is needed.

Internalization works only if children and adults do things that enable them to engage each other and bring the social and cultural messages conveyed by adults inside the child's mind. What I do not find in Vygotsky's account is how mother and child manage to focus on the same object from their different perspectives and how the child comes to take the mother's reaction as something to be emulated and translated into action. There is here a give-and-take of mental stances and information that makes semiotic transfer possible *in the first place*. It is this *prior* process that awaits elucidation. Vygotsky's semiotic mediation, which secures the internalization of overt functions, must *itself* be mentally grounded and thus explained. In short, a question still unanswered is the nature of the bridge between society and the child's mind or, to abuse another metaphor, the nature of the virus that infects the child's mind with social and cultural pathogens. To make this diagnosis intelligible and persuasive, I consider briefly the limits of Vygotsky's program, which could explain the incompleteness of its account of internalization.

Society versus Culture

Far from being random or arbitrary, the adult contribution to child development seems well patterned and uniformly so. Mothers tend to do pretty much what other mothers do, and probably always did, when talking to children in motherese or responding to their cries or communicative gestures (Fernald 1992, Trevarthen 1993). The uniformity may be innate or partly due to cultural pressures (selection?) for uniform practices of socializing the infant mind and guiding it into the ways of adult societies. Implied in this formulation, although not always easy to draw out, is a distinction between those adult practices and infant responses that merely socialize the infant mind and those that also enculturate it.[12]

There are several reasons for separating mind socialization from mind enculturation and placing the former ontogenetically ahead of the latter. First of all, society is not culture. Society means interactions among individuals and groups in patterns transmitted genetically and affecting directly the viability and fertility of individuals. Culture means deliberate instruction into practices that are not transmitted genetically yet allow functional integration into the group, with variable impact on viability and fertility. There are many social species but very few cultural ones. To cite just a few, bees, dolphins, elephants, and lower primates socialize a lot but lack culture. Among higher primates the distinction gets trickier. Perhaps only the tool-minded apes rate as having culture, to the extent to which each young generation learns from the older one how to use tools. In any event, the social skills, but not the cultural skills, are fixed genetically, as naturally selected adaptations. Not surprisingly, then, the socialization of mental skills is going to be different from and prior to their enculturation (see Ingold 1996 for a survey of the issues).

Second, it follows that mind socialization is a prelude to and a condition for mind enculturation. An adult must engage an infant mind by building bridges to it—emotional, gestural, behavioral, and communicational bridges—before carrying cultural materiel across the bridge. Mind socialization is that first bridge-building and engagement stage. As Tomasello, Kruger, and Ratner note, "The form of cultural learning that children are capable of engaging in depends on the form of social cognition they are capable of engaging in, quite simply because when children are learning through another person, how they conceive of that person is an integral component of the basic learning process" (1993, 502).[13] A third reason for the distinction is that mind-socialization practices, such as intersubjective sharing of emotions or shared attention, are universal among humans, whereas many (though not all) mind-enculturation practices, such as scripting actions according to accepted patterns or rituals, or instructing children in forms of symbolization like drawing or writing, are less widespread and may vary from culture to culture. Finally, a fourth reason is that interpretation, which underpins mind socialization and enculturation, operates differently in these two zones and, as a result, engenders different mental skills (Bogdan 1997). I begin with the evolutionary role of interpretation in mind socialization, whence my critical take on Vygotsky.

Beyond Vygotsky

For the present discussion, perhaps the most severe limit of Vygotsky's approach is its underestimating the presemiotic and precultural yet *intermental* patterns of interaction among infants and adults. This may sound like an odd, if not unfair, thing to say about the founder of the psychology of mind socialization, so I am ready to look at other diagnoses. Such an exegetical exercise allows a sharper view of Vygotsky's conception and its relation to what is argued in this essay.

One diagnosis, that of Wertsch (1985a, 41–46), notes Vygotsky's exclusive opposition between natural (organic, biological) development and cultural development and his exclusive focus on "cultural development" at the expense of "natural" or "organic development." There are many indications of Vygotsky's intense preoccupation with culture. Aside from primary gestures, his semiotics is mostly explicit and verbal. The higher mental functions he was interested in are cultural products. He thought that self-regulation was possible only through semiotic and cultural mediation, and believed that the natural forces of development cease to be active in early childhood, after which the cultural forces take over. Vygotsky also held that during early development the natural and cultural forces operate independently (a position later retracted by followers such as Luria and Leontiev). He was interested only in how culture changes the biological endowment and remained oblivious of the constraints that the latter may place on the former. Although unclear about the range of natural development, Vygotsky seemed to think mostly of the "structural and functional development of the central nervous system" (Vygotsky 1981b, 193). Primitive or lower mental functions he usually associated with neural processes, although occasionally simple activities, gestures, and emotional expressions also show up on the natural menu.

This is *the* problem. The contrast need not be between biology and culture, with nothing in between. Culture cannot be grafted directly on unsensitized neural functions. Left out are mental functions, however simple. The problem is not that such simple functions are neural; of course they are, in an implementational sense. The problem is that mental functions cannot be reduced to biological or neural functions, insofar as the former (but not the latter) have psychological or mind-world value. That psychological value concerns the relation between organism and world, both physical and social, and the impact of that relation on behavior. This is how psychology (but not biology or neuroscience) looks at organisms.

I can think of another diagnosis. Vygotsky may have seen the mind-formative interaction between child and adult as suffused with culture *from the outset*. Vygotsky saw culture not only as a domain of application for mental abilities but first as a developmental stimulus and designer of such abilities. So construed, the developmental psychology of the mind is cultural through and through. This is why Vygotsky may have conceived of mental skills as encultured from the outset and of mind socialization as identical with mind enculturation. The mind-formative interaction between child and adult *is* cultural indoctrination, always.

Yet even this diagnosis cannot get rid of the problem raised earlier. Still unanswered is the internalization question of how cultural indoctrination engages and takes over the child's mind. There must be *mental* internalizers (not just neural implementers) that secure the engagement and takeover. I find neither a recognition nor an account of them in Vygotsky's writings or those of his followers and commentators.[14] By positing a sharp contrast between nature and culture and by giving nature full and exclusive control over mental development during infancy and culture full and exclusive control afterwards (Wertsch's diagnosis), or else by making culture the initial and sole designer of mental abilities (my diagnosis), Vygotsky made the mind-design achievement of culture difficult to explain. On the first diagnosis, that achievement is hard to explain because culture is brought into the picture too late to account for design features that must already be in place when the young mind faces the assault of culture. On the second, the mind-design achievement is hard to explain because, even when viewed as an initial and sufficient mind designer, culture still needs prior mental props to engage the mind, and those props would pose constraints that culture must accommodate in order to exploit.

On either diagnosis, then, unregistered on Vygotsky's radar is a mental machinery that precedes and prepares the ground for the work of culture. This machinery is interpretation, the chief mind socializer and culturalizer. Once interpretation is factored in, Vygotsky's cultural insights need not be fundamentally altered. Altered, however, are their ontogenetic premises, the initial hook-ups through which culture engages the young mind and works on it. Provided by interpretation, these hook-ups design parts of the infant mind before culture gets the chance to barge in.[15] As important is the fact that interpretation stimulates and shapes a causally active form of imagination or mental rehearsal and thus further explains Vygotskian internalization and its role in the development of metamentation—a topic taken up in the next chapter and later.

4 Mind in Society

Mind socialization was portrayed so far as a one-way street, from adult society to the child's mind. Actually, it is a two-way street whose opposite direction is just as important. This is true of all primates but particularly of humans, as will be seen in chapter 3. The child's mind needs to socialize with and interpret other minds, on its terms, if it is to do well. To understand this basic fact is to abandon an old and widespread finalistic view of mental development as a passive and predetermined progress toward encultured maturity under adult supervision.[16] This is a biased and not very enlightening view. For enculturation builds on earlier and independent developments that are best understood as mind socialization and interpretation from *the child's* precultural perspective. Looking at development in this way vindicates the primacy of interpretation-assisted mind socialization, now viewed from the opposite direction, child to society.

The point should not be that controversial. Much as society is intent on invading the young mind and pouring cultural forms and contents into it, the child has her own evolutionary interests, which need not coincide with those of her society or culture. The two sets of interests must be negotiated and reconciled, a laborious process that needs a long time and much brain power. Mental reflexivity may be its incidental outcome. To understand the process and its consequences, we must also look at mental development from the child's evolutionary point of view. This I do in some detail in chapter 3. Right now I need only to note that the child has as much interest in mind socialization and interpretation as the adult, although from a different angle and for different reasons, and that this interest is as vital to her mental development as is the adult's intervention. The argument can be summed up as follows.

Not being born an autonomous survivor, the infant is bound to be a *social schemer*. That means using others to achieve her goals. The infant thus has, from the outset, evolutionary reasons to be a socializer and an interpreter of others. Evolutionary reasons from the outset imply specialized and innate skills. This is how I will look at the initial forms of intersubjective interpretation. These forms show that it is in the child's interest to be *mentally* active in socializing (and later in becoming cultural) in order to pursue *her* aims and solve *her* problems with the help of adults, and therefore in structuring *her* engagement of adults according to *her* agenda.[17] This means that when infants begin to socialize with adults, they are *already* equipped with mental skills enabling them to engage adults *on their terms*. It also means in general that the structure of the early encounters is formatted as much by the child's mental skills for intersubjective contact as it is by the adult's. Such contact and its initial formats are *precultural*, and so are their evolutionary rationale. Such precultural socialization will be shown (in the next chapter) to be the work of interpretation. In short, mind enculturation rests on mind socialization, which in turn rests on interpretation. These dependencies are evolutionarily motivated in both directions: from the standpoint of the adult society and culture and from that of the developing child.

Seen from the child's perspective, interpreting adults in order to socialize and play cultural games with them is only half of the developmental story of internalization and of the resulting metamorphosis of social relations into mental functions. The child also socializes adults in her own ways and according to her agenda by having them do what she wants. To this end, the child uses her interpretations of adults to *cause* them to *do* what she desires. It is in this active causal role, I will argue, that the child's interpretive categories and schemes become internalized. The reason is that the strategy of causing others to do things by using one's interpretive gear benefits from mentally rehearsing and imagining in advance the consequences of one's initiatives and the likely responses of the others. In this way one's interpretive categories and schemes become mentally re-represented (imagined, rehearsed manipulated) and reutilized in novel ways, including metamental ways.

To put this sketch of an analysis in an illustrative perspective, let us briefly return to Vygotsky's account (sampled in section 2 above) of how the physical movement (reaching toward and grasping an object) acquires semiotic function (becomes an indicatory gesture) and ends up internalized as a new mental skill (referring). My analysis of this example suggests two phases and components of internalization:

1. From physical movement toward an object to indicatory gesture (to an adult) with semiotic function. This development is achieved through bidirectional interpretation used to cause the adult to do things for the child.
2. From indicatory gesture with semiotic function to the new mental skill of referring. This development is achieved through mental reenactment and rehearsal of the interpretive categories and schemes that structure the indicatory gesture.

In the first phase the key role is that of interpretation. Its job is to assimilate a physical movement to a gesture directed at another person by coordinating the movement with several interpretable relations, such as gaze, bodily posture, exchange of emotions, and the like. In the second phase the key role is that of mental rehearsal or imagination, whereby the movement-interpreted-as-gesture is recast as reference. In chapter 4, section 3, I construe the outcome of this second phase as task emulation. On this proposed analysis, internalization amounts to interpretation (first phase) and task emulation through mental rehearsal (second phase). Both phases of internalization are stimulated and motivated during development by the child's propensity to intervene actively in the affairs of others to cause them to do things that further the child's goals. Metamentation is one by-product of this process.

The differences between Vygotsky's notion of internalization and the one adopted here bear on both pillars of internalization: interpretation is needed to map social relations onto the child's mind, and mental rehearsal is needed to reenact and mentally manipulate such mappings in anticipation of causal intervention in the social domain. To turn to the topic of this essay, metamentation will be shown to emulate interpretation *only because* subject-world and mind-world-mind relations are mentally reenacted and imaginatively rehearsed in order to be causally acted upon or influenced. Although Vygotsky insisted on social activity as the source and model of mental categories and skills (just as Piaget insisted on mechanical activity as a similar source and model), it is not clear the he envisaged (1) a causally active format of social intervention on the part of the child or (2) its reenactment in mental rehearsal. I think that these two conditions are crucial for internalization in general and for the one envisioned in this essay in particular.

To recapitulate, in addition to diagnosing the importance and limits of Vygotsky's pioneering analysis of mind socialization and internalization, this chapter has covered a lot of further territory. It began by arguing that social life (rather than physical work) and social agency directed at conspecifics (rather than mechanical agency directed at the physical world) were the driving forces behind the evolution of primate mentation. Socialized minds were said to be of several sorts, reflecting different forms and means of socialization. The key difference is between interactive and intersubjective socialization. Also different are the modalities of cognitively engaging the social world, whence the distinction between situated and unsituated minds. Only an intersubjective and unsituated mind has the evolutionary opportunities and cognitive means to develop reflexive thinking. In human childhood, interpretation is the main agent of that development. So our story turns next to interpretation, the key historical source and shaper of metamentation, as of so much else in the human mind.

Chapter 2

Minding Others

My discussion now moves from why to how primate minds are socialized through interpretation. This process holds the key to the distant impact of interpretation on metamentation, as this chapter begins to show. Section 1 looks at interpretation as mind designer by charting its close ties to primate mentation. Section 2 argues that it is *as* causal knowledge of the social domain that interpretation evolves categories and schemes later emulated by metamentation. Mindful that metamentation evolved out of the interplay between mental rehearsal and interpretation, section 3 reviews the evolutionary roots of mental rehearsal, which are independent of social life and predate interpretation, but conjectures that mental rehearsal may have had social origins and reasons. This conjecture is amplified and explored in section 4.

1 Interpretation as Mind Designer

Interpretation designed not only metamentation (in partnership with mental rehearsal) but also many other mental skills of primates and particularly humans, some of which contributed to the development of reflexivity. This widespread, persistent, and deep-reaching mind-design work of interpretation warrants the hypothesis that almost every major step in the evolution of primate mentation is closely linked to a major step in the evolution of interpretation. So argues this section. But it begins with a few words about the central notion of interpretation.

The Very Notion

Already familiar as the leading character of the plot, the notion of interpretation needs only a few further comments told briskly yet leisurely enough to make things intelligible and plausible; the longer story is told elsewhere (Bogdan 1997) and further details emerge in later chapters, as needed.

The background was outlined a chapter ago. Intensely social, primates mind each other constantly and vigorously in cooperation, education, family life, competition, and politics. Interpretation is the competence that enables them to socialize along these lines. Despite immense variations later on, primate interpretation seems to begin as a battery of specialized programs with a rather well documented, though not uncontested, evolutionary pedigree (Baron-Cohen 1995, Byrne and Whiten 1988, Cheyney and Seyfarth 1990, Tomasello and Call 1997, Whiten 1991, Whiten and Byrne 1997, to cite only a few important monographs and anthologies, but see Heyes 1998 for a recent dissent). This pedigree responds to a unique mix of features of primate social life. In an earlier work (Bogdan 1997, chapter 2) I divided primate interactions into three main types: communal, epistemic, and political. Communal activities range from collective foraging and tool use to cooperative hunting. Politics emerges in competition, tactical alliances, manipulation of information or behavior, and deception. Epistemic relations involve gathering and exchanging information in education, communication, cooperation, division of labor and knowledge, and self-regulation through social information. Many nonprimate species interact in communal, epistemic, and political contexts, but none seem to mix them so frequently as to require *specialized* skills that distill and manage what is *common* to these types of contexts. These skills are those of interpretation.

Bees commune and share information but do not engage in politics. Birds and other species do the same and may also perform simple deceptions, but the targets are usually predators of other species, not conspecifics. This is why such deception does not count as political. It is *conspecific* politics that makes a mighty difference, particularly in mental rehearsal, and this sort of politics seems to be a primate specialty. Socializing along epistemic, communal, and political lines is a constant, full-time, and very demanding job. Equally distinct and potent for mental evolution are the particulars of primate socialization. Members of most other species interact two at a time and often form coalitions and alliances and engage in cooperative ventures. Lions, wolves, and hyenas are such examples. What seem special about primates are that the selection of partners is based on (what may be called) local appropriateness, measured in terms of the particular contexts and individuals involved, and that the interactions with partners and others are often triadic or polyadic, with the third or fourth or nth party impacting on what happens between the first two and this impact being apparently calculated or measured by those affected (Tomasello 1998; Tomasello and Call 1997, chapter 7). As will be shown in section 4 below, such multilateral interactions force a unique structure on the primate social calculations, unmatched in other domains of animal cognition.

So do forms of multiple reciprocity as well as tactical and long-term alliances, which are typical of primate relations among kin and nonkin. Nonprimates support one another in conflicts but usually only when kin-related. Primate alliances reach beyond kin and operate in a variety of political situations, not just conflictual—a fact that hints at flexible social calculations (Byrne 1995, Harcourt 1988, Tomasello and Call 1997).

This, very roughly, is the evolutionary surround in which interpretation emerged as a specialized competence to handle the common denominators found in multilateral communal, epistemic, and political interactions among primates. As for a brief characterization of the competence itself, let me say that to *interpret* someone (a subject) is to make sense of his goals and other mental and behavioral relations to the world. I call them *subject-world relations* when they are observable in bodily or behavioral features and linked to aspects of the environment. Gazing, seeing, showing emotion at something are instances of subject-world relations, apparently interpretable by most primate species. In human interpretation such relations can become fairly complex and take the form of propositional attitudes, such as belief, intention, or hope. They are better characterized as *mind-world* relations. Chapter 5 explains why the simpler categories of subject-world relations underpin the more complex categories of mind-world relations, while chapter 6 explains why only the latter can turn metamental. Yet, according to the next chapter, the evolution of mind-world interpretation out of subject-world interpretation transits through a critical and (it appears) uniquely human phase: that of mental sharing or *mind-world-mind* interpretation. This latter form of inter-subjective or intermind interpretation affords the development of categories of shared attention and later propositional attitudes, which in turn will under-pin the development of metamentation.

After we have a serviceable notion of interpretation to work with, the next step is to show that the evolutionary complicity between interpretation and metamentation is grounded in a wider complicity between interpretation and primate mentation in general.

Close Ties
Here is the hypothesis, stated baldly and boldly:

Interpretation and mentation   There seem to be relatively few major changes in primate mentation that are not closely linked to, if not more often directly caused by, major changes in primate interpretation.

This is an exaggeration meant to catch and focus the reader's attention and is clearly in need of caveats and modulations. As noted a chapter ago, there are plenty of sources and forces in the evolution of primate mentation other than those of interpretation. Spatial maps, bodily representations, mental imagery, logical and mathematical reasoning, are among the candidates. The thesis I root for concerns strategic location, not ubiquity. The thesis is that key junctures in the phylogeny and ontogeny of the primate mind are contemporary with and nonaccidentally, if not causally, related to dramatic upheavals in interpretation. This is why it is worth looking for an active role of interpretation as mind designer. There are good reasons to do so, from general to specific.

The most general reason follows conceptually from the social-mind hypothesis outlined a chapter ago. If social life stimulates and shapes mental evolution earlier and more effectively than other factors, it can do so only if socialized minds have the ability to figure each other out. That ability is interpretation. So if there are systematic connections between pressures and changes in the social life of primates and their mental evolution, as argued in chapter 1, then interpretation is likely to be involved as the leading connector.[1] A more specific reason for tying interpretation to primate mentation concerns the dynamics of their coevolution. Recall (from figure 1.1 in chapter 1, section 2) the key turns in the phylogeny of socialized minds: (a) from situated animal minds to intensely socialized, still situated, and interactive primate minds, then (b) from the latter to situated but intersubjective infant minds, and finally (c) from infant minds to the unsituated minds of older children and adults. The last is also a turn to a reflexive mind. Each of these turns in mind design is not only contemporary, but often interlocked, with critical turns in interpretation. Here is, briefly, a sample of what I mean. The description of some of the items on this list will be expanded in the chapters to come.

The first interactive turn marks the onset of interpretation. As just noted, primates are the only species that appear to socialize intensely in epistemic, political, and communal forms that select for interpretation. They are also credited with some practical thinking in the form of simple planning and problem solving. Their practical thinking, first and most frequently manifested in social contexts, is animated by interpretation because it involves calculating what others are up to and how the result would affect the interpreter (more on this in section 4 below). In a word, the onset of practical thinking seems not only tied to interpretation but operative in contexts and according to rules set by it (Byrne and Whiten 1988, Cheyney and Seyfarth 1990, Humphrey 1988, Tomasello and Call 1997). One can say, then, that the primates get minded to some degree (i.e., acquire practical thinking) because they mind (i.e., socialize with and interpret) each other in interpretation-saturated patterns of social interaction. Add to this the fact that the prehuman primates suspected of a higher degree of practical intelligence, the chimpanzees, are the ones whose epistemic, communal, and particularly political encounters seem the most intricate and intense, and (not surprisingly) whose interpretive skills also seem the most accomplished. Thanks to such skills, the chimpanzees appear more receptive to human enculturation than other primates (Savage-Rumbaugh and Lewin 1994, Tomasello and Call 1997).

The next evolutionary turn, from the interactive minds of apes to the intersubjective but still situated minds of the youngest humans, is defined by a revolution in mental engagement, and hence in mind socialization, brought about by a new interpretive gadgetry that enables the participants to link up in triangular or mind-world-mind relations by recognizing, sharing, and communicating experiences and attitudes and the information these convey (Bruner 1983; Hobson 1993a, 1993b; Tomasello 1998; Trevarthen 1993). I call this *mental sharing*. The claim (developed in chapters 3 and 5) is not that nonhuman primates do not have experiences or attitudes (of course they do) or that they don't communicate them in some fashion (they do) or that they don't bond through such means (they do that too). The claim will be that nonhuman primates do not seem to *recognize* such mental conditions in others (Cheney and Seyfarth 1990, 235–240) and, crucially, do not seem to *use* such recognitions to exchange information about the world (Tomasello and Call 1997, but see Gomez 1994, 1996a, for a dissident view). The rudiments of mental sharing, shown in chapter 3 to operate since infancy as precultural and prelinguistic forms of interpretation, build the earliest bridges between infant and adult minds, affording the beginnings of a mind socialized at the intersubjective level. Thanks to such bridges, the infant mind develops into a mind quite different from that of prehuman primates. This is how an interpretational difference makes a mental difference in a revolutionary way. Here are a few instances of this difference.

Consider communication. Mental sharing enables communication to take a novel protodeclarative form in which experiential and attitudinal comments can be exchanged about topics of mutual interest. This innovation spills over into language learning by enabling the acquisition of word reference (L. Bloom 1993, Bruner 1983, Hobson 1993b, Tomasello 1996) and later develops into a formatting strategy for metathinking as well. And consider these other facts. The earliest attempts to transcend one's perception of the world (by taking the perspective of another or pretending) occur typically in social contexts of interpretation. This process starts in infancy but takes off dramatically around age four when children begin to display an increased ability to think and communicate more abstractly, beyond current spatiotemporal confines. They understand better their past involvements in various situations and become better at contemplating involvements in alternative or future situations.

These are signs of an escape from situatedness (Perner 1991, Wellman 1990). Abstraction and freedom of thinking are on the mental horizon. This is when interpretation turns to metarepresenting propositional attitudes. There are reasons to think that the two developments may be linked, with interpretation as a stimulus if not a cause of unsituated mentation, as chapters 6 and 7 will argue. Indeed, the pressures for mental unsituatedness appear to be the strongest in the social domain. Among all the capacities developing at this age, metarepresentational interpretation seems to be the first to respond to these pressures (Perner 1991, chapters 8 and 11; see also Bogdan 1997, chapter 6). Such interpretation recognizes that others differ in their desires, beliefs, and intentions, and that such attitudes can misrepresent or change over time or be projected to the future or the past, and so on. With the recognition that minds represent things differently, the world can now be seen through the eyes and minds of others; the world is no longer fixed by one's current perception and motivation. Through the tasks it handles, metarepresentation is best poised to separate mind from world and isolate and represent mind-world relations across situations that vary in space, time, and possibility. As the next chapters argue, this and further developments in interpretation become effective in the design of mental reflexivity.

Having made a preliminary and general case for the evolutionary complicity between primate interpretation and mentation, I turn next to how I think interpretation actually plants the seeds of metamentation. It does so through two distinct but eventually converging contributions. One results from how interpretation represents the social domain (the topic of the next section), the other from how this representation operates in and reconfigures thinking as mental rehearsal (the topic of section 3).

2 Cause to Cause

Interpretation designs metamentation by virtue of being practical, and hence causal, knowledge of the social domain. The basis of this important argument is set up in this section. I begin with a few words about the practical character of interpretation, as conducive to its evolution as causal knowledge of the social domain, and about its categories and schemes that eventually metamorphose into metamental counterparts.

Practical Knowledge

The evolutionary journey from interpretation to metamentation owes a good deal to the fact that interpretation is a *practical* enterprise in nature and aims.

Interpretation operates as a practice in that it categorizes subject-world relations in terms of effective strategies of involvement in the subject's affairs, and it has practical aims because it represents those aspects of subject-world relations that afford such effective strategies. The practicality of interpretation explains why it was selected in the first place and why it evolved among primates as it did. Having dedicated an earlier book to this hypothesis (Bogdan 1997), I use it here as a premise to show that, to be practically effective, interpretation operates as *causal* knowledge of the social domain and that, in this practical-cum-causal capacity, it had a formative impact on metamentation. Specifically, the hypothesis I propose to explore below is that the resources that interpretation contributes to the infrastructure of metamentation originate in how it represents social causality. In other words, it is as *causal knowledge employed in mental rehearsal* that interpretation designs the infrastructure of metamentation.

The causal knowledge of interpretation is embodied in its categories and representation schemes. I propose to think of *categories* as having the practical function of aligning what an organism can discriminate in the world to how it can act on the world. In most animal minds such categories are *behavioral,* in the sense that they feed their discriminations directly into behavior, while in humans they are also mental or *conceptual,* in the sense that they link up their discriminations with those provided by other categories to form conceptual structures (Bogdan 1989b; 1994, chapter 5). Whether behavioral or conceptual, categories generally join forces in capturing regular or significant patterns in their domain of application. The result is a *representation scheme.* Think of it as a rule or construction that coordinates several categories relative to a domain, action-relevant patterns of events in the domain, and types of mental calculations over such patterns. The interpretive category of intentionality, for example, coordinates three subordinate categories: a type of subject-world relation, its direction, and target. The domain of this category is social, and the patterns it represents are of conspecific interactions relative to a shared world. The mental calculations employing the category of intentionality and its subordinate categories focus on select aspects of the social patterns, such as direction of gaze or its target.

One last preliminary point, and then we are on to the argument itself. To discipline the terminology of the argument, I call knowledge of causality 'causal knowledge' and use 'causation' for the causal process itself and 'causality' for the cause-effect relation distilled out of a causal process. So critical for the entire essay is the argument to the effect that it is as causal knowledge employed in mental rehearsal that interpretation designs the infrastructure of metamentation, that I would like to begin with a preview of its main steps.

Preview of the Argument
Below are the main steps of the argument that interpretation as causal knowledge used in mental rehearsal provides the framework of metamentation.

1. *Piagetian insight* Causal knowledge is called for when an organism causes *further* causal relations. In evolutionary terms, being able to cause causal relations (with beneficial effects) explains why causal knowledge is selected for.

2. *General and separate* Causal knowledge is general in that it represents causal dispositions in a variety of ways and contexts and separate in that it represents causal dispositions separately from the particular actions that activate the dispositions.

3. *Social primacy* Primates have causal knowledge because they cause causal relations, and they appear to possess this sort of causal knowledge *first* in the social domain, where they cause conspecifics (as social tools) to cause desired effects.

4. *Interpretational form* Interpretation is practical knowledge of the social domain. To cause conspecific subjects to cause desired effects, interpreters represent causally manipulable aspects of subjects, which are *subject-world* and later *mind-world relations*. These relations emerge as causal leverage in socialization and call for interpretive categories and schemes that embody causal knowledge.

5. *Use in thinking* Plugged into mental rehearsals about social interactions, the causal categories and schemes of interpretation become targets of mental representation and calculation, that is, are explicitly thought about, and, in that capacity and form, plant the seeds of reflexive thinking.

Practical Reasons for Causal Knowledge
To be possible and effective, an organism's knowledge must recognize systematic relations between events in the world. There are plenty of relations to recognize. The chief candidates are regular correlation and causation. Causation includes a systematic or necessary connection, absent from mere correlation. Hume (1756) saw that perception fails to tell the difference between mere correlation and systematic connection, which is why the category of causality cannot be learned from observing the world. Hume, Kant, and others entrusted the mind with a propensity to supply the systematic connection in the representation of causality. What sort of propensity? There are several psychological accounts of causal knowledge. The major choice seems to be between representations that capture regularities in the interactions among objects and representations of sequences in which one event generates another in some active fashion like exercising force—what one may call expected

causality versus generative causality (Baillargeon, Kotovsky, Needham 1995; Leslie 1995). Expected causality may be too weak a category to be sharply distinguishable from the Humean expectation of mere correlations and hence too weak, I think, for the work it has to do in the social domain. That leaves *generative causality* as a candidate for understanding interpretation as causal knowledge of that domain.

A good guess as to why our knowledge of causality is generative is that the propensity to represent causality generatively is an evolutionary response to how an organism *engages* its world and to the benefits of such a mode of representation. The chief reason for, and also clearest symptom of, causal knowledge of the generative sort is *active intervention* in the world. Passive perception or merely anticipatory reactions to events constantly linked to other events will not do. Only instrumental actions that generate and control causal processes call for causal knowledge. This is Piaget's insight (Piaget 1967, 1974). To know a causal relation is to initiate, control, and manipulate one. This, I think, is the right evolutionary insight to start from. The question is, What sort of instrumental action, and hence what sort of knowledge, did evolution select for? The answers are critical to this inquiry. For it turns out that there are two distinct modes of causally engaging the world through instrumental action but only one that is cognitively apt and evolutionarily likely to select for causal knowledge. In the social domain, that is the mode that holds the promise of metamentation. Hence the importance of the next distinction.

Acting Causally versus Acting to Cause Causations

What is an instrumental action? I take the careful and insightful analysis of Anthony Dickinson and David Shanks (1995) as a representative target, relative to which I want to locate and sharpen my position. They mean by instrumental action one that is guided by beliefs in a causal relation between the action and the desired effect (Dickinson and Shanks 1995, 6, 13). It cannot be any action-outcome relation, for in that case *any* goal-pursuing action (such as avoiding boring meetings or eating paté) would be instrumental and hence require causal knowledge. The plausible candidate is an action with an instrument or implement. The difference, then, is between two causal scripts (where '→' stands for 'causes'):

(a) Agent acts → outcome

(b) Agents acts with implement → outcome

Rats can be trained to engage in instrumental action of the (b) sort by acquiring the causal belief that if they press the lever, they get the food. Do such actions call for causal knowledge, as Dickinson and Shanks assume? I think not, for two reasons. One is that such patterns of instrumental action can be learned through frequent exposure. But if causality is not transparent to perception or procedural habituation (learning to do things), causal knowledge cannot be acquired through learning from experience. It is tempting to think that if one learns to do *x* in order to get *y*, and one's doing *x* causes *y*, it follows that one has the *knowledge that x* causes *y*. But it doesn't follow, as I argue below. Dickinson and Shanks (1995) talk of correlations of frequencies between actions and outcomes to explain the performance of the rats. Correct, but it is hard to see why the mastery of such correlations would require more than habituation. Mechanical tool use is a cultural and hence learned acquisition. So if a pattern of instrumental action to outcome of the sort (b) can be trained, it is unlikely to require causal knowledge. If causal knowledge is a distant premise of mental reflexivity, as I suspect, then we see once again that mechanical action in the physical domain, even of the instrumental sort, is unlikely to select for causal knowledge and hence for the mental forms that underpin reflexivity.

The other reason is as decisive. Knowledge of action-outcome patterns need not be of causal relations. It may simply be knowledge of how to act to get results. Actions always cause effects. This is different from *recognizing that* actions cause effects, let alone recognizing that actions cause effects that cause still further effects. This is why causal script (a) need not imply recognition of causality. Appearances notwithstanding, the same lack of recognition of causality may apply to script (b), where an action is exercised on some implement to get a desired effect. The rat need not recognize that its action causally relates to an object (the lever) that causally relates to still another object (the food). The rat simply acquires a new instrumental-action pattern that causes culinary satisfaction. An instrumental action is more complex than a simple action, yet it remains tightly attached to its implement, as an extension of it. It is the rat's action with an implement causing an outcome that is trained by the experiment, not the rat's *recognition that* an implement acted upon causes something else. There is a parallel story in communication. When animals learn new ways to communicate displeasure, hunger, or readiness to act, they enrich their communication repertoires as action-outcome patterns. They need not *recognize,* as a new communication relation, that a new sound or behavioral pattern means something.

The point I am belaboring is that, with or without an implement, an action-outcome pattern, causal as it may be, need not entail *recognizing* causality. Most species do not recognize action-outcome relations *as* causal. They simply act, outcomes follow causally, and the successful pattern is learned or naturally selected and wired in. Their actions or the implements acted on to get desired effects are not perspicuous to them *as* causes, so represented and categorized. To be recognized, causality need not be registered by way of explicit representations (such as images or sentential structures) of cause, effect, and the relation in-between. Procedural recognition is possible and likely in most animal cognition. My point concerns not the manner in which causality is grasped but what it takes to have a grasp of it as a distinct relation. It takes active intervention of an instrumental sort.

Echoing Piaget, Dickinson and Shanks (1995) rightly insist that instrumental action, to be effective in intervention and control, calls for causal knowledge. But it has to be the *right* sort of instrumental action: action whose success depends on representing causality as a *distinct* relation. This can happen when an action is deliberately used *to cause a further causation,* not simply when an action causes something. One represents a causal relation when one can cause a causal relation or use it in causing something else. Only minds that cause causation recognize causality (at least in the generative sense). This insight of Piaget's (1967, 1974) can be parsed as follows:

(c) agent acts on $\rightarrow$ [object $\rightarrow$ desired outcome]

$\qquad$ cause$_1$ $\rightarrow$ causation$_2$

and read as 'Agent acts so as to cause [object to cause outcome]'. Cause$_1$ is causation produced by acting, cause$_2$ is the causation caused by the action in question. The square brackets are meant to indicate that the action is deliberately intended to operate on and hence cause a *distinct causation* whereby an object causes an outcome. Only (c) requires causal knowledge, because it requires the agent to represent distinctly the causation that her action causes. Most organisms are causal agents, simply because they act, but not causal knowers. What they do causally fits either (a) or (b) but not (c).

The conceptual distinction between the causal scripts examined so far is fairly clear and well expressed in their logical form. But what would distinguish them *psychologically?* The tough cases, of course, are scripts (b) and (c). Their patterns, actions on objects causing outcomes, look similar. What would tell them apart? What should observation and experiment look for to allow the right script attribution? My suggestion is to look for signs of two properties of causal knowledge: separability and generality. The questions to ask are these: Is the knowledge about a causal relation produced by action *separate* from the knowledge of the action and its causal powers? And is the knowledge in question *general* enough to apply to a variety of contexts and actions that generate causations and bring about desired outcomes? These are

psychological questions. They introduce thesis (2) of the argument previewed
in the beginning of this section. There is also an evolutionary question about
when and why knowledge satisfying these conditions is likely to be selected
for. My discussion of it, later, will bring in theses (3) and (4). I begin with
the psychological questions.

Generality and Separability

A rat learning to press the lever to get food acquires a new action pattern
causing a desirable outcome. A person who flips the switch to turn on the
light enlists an action (hand movement) to generate a causal relation between
a change in the position of the switch and a desired outcome (light). The
person knows that in general changes of switch positions cause bulbs to light
up. This is knowledge, however vague, of some *intrinsic* causal disposition of
the electrical setup. Knowledge of an implement's causal dispositions tends
to be *general* and treats the dispositions as *separate* from the particular actions
that activate them. The causality knower understands that the implement acted
upon has its *own* separate and possibly versatile causal powers, irrespective
of the action that activates them and the context of use. In the electrical-setup
example the knowledge is general because it applies to all sorts of devices
and all sorts of contexts of their use. The knowledge is also separate from the
specific action utilized (e.g., which hand or finger is used) or particular type
of action undertaken (say hand versus nose movement, if the hand is not
available). The key notions, then, are separability and generality.

To return to the paradigmatic causality ignoramus, the rat does not have
general and separate knowledge of the relation between an implement and a
desired effect. The rat does not know in general that pressing levers through
various types of actions causes food to materialize; it knows only that by (or
rather, after) pressing the lever through specific and well-conditioned actions,
it gets food. The lab-educated rat is not alone. Many other species, from birds
and mammals, use implements in more natural ways. Nonhuman primates also
use implements, such as sticks or stones, to get desired effects, such as picking
fruits, fishing termites, or breaking nuts. In captivity they do more complicated
things, including some primitive tool manufacture, such as fitting two sticks
together to reach something at a distance. These are surely instances of (b),
but they do not seem to go much beyond the other implement-using species
(Tomasello and Call 1997, chapter 3; Vauclair 1996, chapter 4). Neither the
generality condition nor the separability condition seems to be met, at least
not in any obvious way. The action-implement-outcome patterns seem limited,
standard, and repetitive. For a while human infants too do not seem to fare
better. Piaget notes that their sense of (generative) causality is first egocentric

and based on the accidentality of an action and its effects: grabbing a rope hanging from the top of his cradle, the infant discovers that all the toys there fall down. Some generality is involved because after that, the infant may use this same scheme to act at a distance on other things (Piaget 1964, 22). This too looks like (b). This may be trial and error, but it may be something else of greater importance here, namely some mental rehearsal.

Some primates anticipate their causal use of a physical tool. They show foresight as a form of mental rehearsal (Tomasello and Call 1997, 88–96). This is important, because mental rehearsal suggests that a representation of causality may be available to their imagination. In imagination one can envisage causal relations beyond the initial contexts of learning or imitating, thus *generalizing* their understanding. The generality condition is critical to causal knowledge and is met if there is mental rehearsal. And indeed, the primates suspected of some mental rehearsal seem also able to generalize their use of implements. Chimpanzees have been reported to use a fallen tree instead of a flat stone as an anvil for cracking nuts and to use sticks to open human-made boxes, without any overt trial and error (Tomasello and Call 1997, 78). This could be generalization by foresight, but not by learning through imitation or trial and error. Older children seem to follow the same path. Children 18-months-old may grab a stick to draw a distant object closer. Piaget finds this to be "an act of intelligence . . . because some means, here a genuine instrument, are coordinated with a goal fixed in advance; the relation between stick and objective must be understood in advance in order to discover this instrument" (1964, 18). The generality condition thus seems to be met, at least to some extent.

What about the separability condition? Here is where a leitmotif of this essay rears its head again. The satisfaction of the separability condition may be problematic in the domain of mechanical action. Foresighted as they may be, apes and young children probably fail to understand the intrinsic causal powers that stones or sticks have *separately* from being grabbed and pushed in some specific way as *part of* some action pattern. And that may be the problem with sticks, levers, stones, and other implements used mechanically as physical *extensions* of bodily actions (Tomasello and Call 1997, 388). Their use need not require causal knowledge. The causal dispositions of the implements need not be represented *as separate* from the actions that enlist them to produce desired effects. When an implement is a mechanical extension of an action, the action does most of the causing. It is the action-implement pattern, and not the implement as such, that generates the desired outcomes. Although mental rehearsal may afford some generalized use of the action-implement patterns in different contexts, what it anticipates and generalizes is still a tightly packaged action-implement pattern, not an independent and separate representation of the causal powers of the implement. Phrased in evolutionary terms, the point is that if an implement works as a mechanical extension of an action, then the action-implement pattern would be unlikely to select for causal knowledge and more likely to select for motor imagery, for example. Primates may even use motor imagery to rehearse new applications of their mechanical knowledge.

Social Tool Use

The explanation for the evolution of causal knowledge that I root for is that the separability condition on causal knowledge is first and conclusively met in the social domain by interpretation, for good evolutionary reasons. And that fact may make all the difference insofar as the onset of primate causal knowledge is concerned. We are thus closing in on theses (3) and (4) of the main argument. To harmonize terminology and analysis, I propose to distinguish between implements and tools as follows. *Implements* are instrumental extensions of bodily actions. Although often generalizable, knowledge of implements fails to meet the separability condition and therefore is not causal. *Tools* are implements knowledge of which also meets the separability condition and hence is causal. This distinction makes sense in the social domain.[2]

A primate conspecific is rarely a mere extension of one's action. Using him as shield could be a rare example. The frequent challenge in primate social life is to deal with others on their terms. A conspecific has, literally, a life of its own. Many organisms know this about others and also know that others are goal-directed, and hence self-caused agents. Yet few species, among them primates, factor this information into their causal knowledge; most species merely factor it into their action patterns. But then again, most species are not social tool users, although they may use physical or social implements as extensions of bodily actions. One cannot be a social tool user if one cannot represent the other as a separate autonomous originator of causations. It matters to the evolution of primate social knowledge that a conspecific is not only separately and autonomously causal but complicatedly and smartly so, having many causal dispositions that interface in various ways. Such complex, smart, separate, and autonomous causal dispositions pose to primate minds a mighty challenge with arms-race potential.

A tool user causes a tool to cause some desired effect by harnessing the causal dispositions of the tool and, through them, the systematic relations between action on the tool (initial cause) and the result of what the tool does (final outcome). Acting on the causal dispositions of a tool to bring about a desired effect is an *effective strategy* of reaching one's goals. As Nancy Cartwright notes, "There is a natural connection between causes and strategies; if one wants to obtain a goal, it is a *good . . . strategy* to *introduce* a cause for that goal" (1983, 36; my emphases).[3] Tools are such intervening causes. In primate social life, conspecifics are quite often the tools that cause desired goals. As a competence dedicated to handle causal interactions among conspecifics, interpretation evolved effective strategies to cause conspecifics to cause desired goals. These strategies take the form of categories and representation schemes. Strategies of situated interpretation are likely to work as fixed, reflex, wired-in sequences of instructions appropriate for definite types of sensory inputs, contexts, and action patterns; strategies of unsituated interpretation work as explicitly represented and often consciously accessible rules (Bogdan 1997, chapter 5).

The causal dispositions of physical tools are mechanical, whereas those of conspecifics are shot through with conative, emotive, and cognitive properties. It is the latter sorts of dispositions that the interpreter represents in order to exploit causally to generate desired outcomes. This claim must be parsed carefully. (The full defense of this analysis is offered in Bogdan 1997.) The interpreter's causal knowledge is not of an agent as such or of his mind (whatever that means) but of his *relatedness to the world*—first of all, his agency, sensibility or ability to sense, and intentionality. This is to say that the interpreter represents the subject's causal dispositions *implicitly,* in the forms in which they are *reflected* in his ways of being related to the world. It is these forms of relatedness to the world, implicitly expressing the subject's causal dispositions, which are caused to cause outcomes desired by the interpreter. This is a crucial point. (Rereading this entire paragraph before moving on is encouraged, particularly at night, while eating, or in a noisy surround.) To bring about such outcomes, the interpreter needs causal knowledge of agency, sensibility, intentionality, and other subject-world relations, *as separate and general relations with their own causal powers* yielding effects intended by the interpreter. This is what the categories and schemes of interpretation represent as effective strategies of causal intervention in the social domain.[4]

Review by Example
Time to catch up and illustrate. Two distinctions were made: between actions that cause desired effects and actions that cause further causal relations as effects; and, consequently, between minds that represent action-outcome patterns, with or without implements, and minds that separately represent causal relations as effects of actions. Only the latter minds represent causality and

thus possess causal knowledge. This causal knowledge enables agents to cause causations according to script (c):

(c) agent acts on → [object → desired outcome]

In the social domain the interpreter targets subject-world relations, such as agency or intentionality, in order to cause social causations with desired effects. Interpretation as causal knowledge of the social domain operates according to the following version of (c):

(d) interpreter acts on → [subject-world relations → desired outcome]

Script (d) should be read as 'Interpreter as agent acts in such a way as to cause [subject-world relations to cause desired outcome]'. The square brackets signify a whole package as target of causation and hence separate representation. Script (d) works only if the interpreter evolves categories and schemes that represent the target of her actions, which are subject-world relations and their effects:

(e) interpreter mentally represents subject-world relations caused$_1$ to cause$_2$ a desired outcome

It is through such categories and schemes that interpretation manages its effective strategies of causal intervention. The scripts outlined so far pick out different sorts of effective strategies to achieve a socially assisted goal through mere action, as in (a), through an action-implement package, as in (b), or through an action on some tool, as in (c). These choices are illustrated in an elegant and insightful study by Juan Carlos Gomez (1990b, 1991). The examples are of social tool use in its paradigmatic form, that of communication (Parker and Gibson 1979). Nonhuman primates use communication in an imperative form, whereby a conspecific is requested, pressured or ordered by another to do something (Bard 1990; Tomasello and Call 1997, chapter 8). This is worth stressing because imperative communication often treats information almost as a physical implement, as mechanical action does. I help myself to an analysis undertaken elsewhere (Bogdan 1997, 128–131) and expand on the points needed here.

Gomez' study involves a young gorilla who over time switches from physical use of an implement to social tool manipulation through communication to achieve the same end, which is opening a door by reaching a latch that is high up. She tries three solutions. One is to bring a box on which to climb, the second to get a human to open the latch by pushing him to do so, the third to get the human to do the same through imperative communication by visual means, such as looking at the latch, then at the human, then again at the latch, and so on. I focus on the last two solutions because they provide a parallel useful to this discussion. The gorilla manipulates causal relations in settings that display procedural similarity between physical and interpretational solutions to the same problem. The solutions differ with respect to how the subject is treated (object versus agent), which of his properties are causally engaged (physical versus intentional), and how they are engaged (mechanically versus informationally). The similarities point to tool-like causal manipulation, the differences to what is manipulated and how.

Similarities first. Both solutions have the form 'cause human to produce action that causes desired effect', and both share (distinct) sequences of actions deployed to realize the required causal structure. I stress this procedural similarity because I read Gomez's study in an evolutionary light. Imagine that, way back, selective forces pressured apes to treat conspecifics as tools in contexts of vital interaction. Imagine also that the first move was to treat others physically, much like the first solution in Gomez's account. Nonhuman primates and other species are known to use conspecifics physically to achieve some goal (Vauclair 1996, 93–94). This may look like implement use—treating someone as shield or pushing him to get something. The mechanical handling of the human agent in Gomez's study may be of this sort. On this reading, favored by Gomez (1990b, 344), the gorilla uses a version of script (b): gorilla wants and acts to move the human subject to act and bring about the goal.

Consider another reading. The gorilla cannot fail to know that another primate is a self-caused agent, who can resist or fight back or cooperate. In this case, the gorilla may count on the cooperation of the human agent (an interpretive insight) but, cognizant of his physical properties, tries a mechanical gambit first. As here, so in the past: the mechanical gambit did not work, or not always, or not efficiently. Some apes chanced upon skills that worked with information instead of physical impact. The rest (we know, we know) is history. Projected back into the evolution of interpretation, the problem may appear to be one of substitution: How to treat conspecifics causally as social tools and use them effectively to serve one's goals by informational rather than mechanical means? It was a problem of action at a distance rather than by direct contact. Action at a distance by way of information suited social life better than immediate contact, and was vastly more versatile and efficient. But it required a new take on the subject as social tool. Whence a critical difference.

In the mechanical scenario, the gorilla alone knows her goal and, to bring it about, acts physically on the (presumably ignorant) agent, as implement.

By contrast, in the communicational set-up, the gorilla publicly identifies a state of affairs (latch opening the door) as her goal and communicates imperatively about it by engaging various subject-goal, interpreter-subject, and interpreter-subject-goal relations, such as gazing, bodily posture, and so on, in different combinations. By pulling the subject into this mutually recognized teleological envelope of agents having their goals and aware of dealing with other agents with their goals, the gorilla can effectively choreograph a mutually intelligible, albeit imperative, exchange of information through which she causally influences the subject's goal and cognitive access and coordinates them with hers. In real history, it is the recognition of a subject's goals and access to the world and its inclusion in a teleological envelope defined by the interpreter's own goals that starts the evolutionary ball rolling.

Human infants also operate as causal knowers in the social domain. They, too, begin with social interaction and communication (Gopnik and Meltzoff 1997, chapter 5). They base their causal knowledge on representations of animacy and agency, on which knowledge of intentionality is later built (Poulin-Dubois and Shultz 1988). One-year-olds treat their parents as independent agents who can be caused to bring about the goals desired (Golinkoff 1986). As Henry Wellman puts it, "To understand someone as an agent is to understand that the person is independent of oneself and that the person's acts are self-caused. In brief, agents are autonomous causers" (1990, 233).[5] This point about infancy dots an important *i*. Young primates deal with conspecifics causally even *before* having, and being able, to deal causally with physical objects. The point is not that infants do not relate to physical objects causally (obviously they do) but rather that they do not cause such objects to cause further causal relations, as they do, earlier, with people. This is why it is possible that primate infants may have first evolved causal knowledge of the generative sort in the social rather than physical domain. The fact that all primate youngsters have such knowledge, very early on, suggests some innate basis with a history of natural selection. Interestingly, physical-implement use among primates is a cultural acquisition, apparently based more on imitation and instruction rather than on domain-specific and innate causal knowledge (Cheney and Seyfarth 1990, Kummer 1995, McGrew 1993, Tomasello and Call 1997). This fact may explains why so few primate species are physical-implement users and why so many are social-tool users. There is less vital urgency for primates to engage physical implements than conspecifics.

Representing Social Causality

How does all this bear on the evolution of metamentation? Recall the leitmotif of this work, now embodied in the fifth and last thesis to be argued in this section. Plugged into mental rehearsals about social events, the causal categories and schemes of interpretation become themselves *targets* of mental representation and calculation, thus paving the ground for metamentation. This is to say that, once (re)represented in mental rehearsal, the categories and schemes of interpretation make available *new objects of thought* whose format anticipates that of thoughts about thoughts. What are these new objects of thought? This section suggests that the answer resides in how interpreters represent social causality.

The analysis of interpretation as causal knowledge has been conveniently ecumenical so far. It is time to get more realistic and specific, and mark the contrasts. Not all primate minds are created equal and the differences are reflected in who gets to evolve mental reflexivity. There are many differences along the evolutionary way, as anticipated a chapter ago (in section 2, figure 1.1), but the one that matters now is about how social causation and its fulcrum, the subject-world relations, are mentally represented. The difference is between situated and unsituated interpretation. Very roughly, it amounts to the following. Situated interpretation represents subject-world relations inexplicitly in terms of *situations* currently perceived. A situated interpreter does not have categories of perception or belief *as such.* Instead she represents those features of situations, such as gaze, facial expression or bodily posture, which reveal relevant subject-world relations (Bogdan 1997, chapter 5; Perner 1991, 217–218, 225). Mental situatedness was said (in chapter 1, section 2) to be domain-implicit and domain-dependent, and hence not conducive to explicit representation. Since not explicitly represented (just built into programs that generate specific interpretations), the situated knowledge of subject-world relations cannot be mentally highlighted, revised, or reasoned about. Only the latter abilities, based on explicit representation, afford reflexivity.

The difference can be analyzed as follows. When the situated interpreter acts to achieve desired outcomes, she directs her mind and actions at those features of social situations which reveal relevant subject-world relations (relative to assumptions and procedures built into her implicit knowledge). For example, an ape interpreter who wants to distract the attention of a subject may manipulate causally those aspects of the subject-in-situation, such as direction of gaze or objects in the vicinity, which link up with his attention. What the ape interpreter cannot directly manipulate, by failing to represent as such, is the attention relation itself. Procedural knowledge may also be at work in the young child's interpretation. In short, situated interpretation affords strategies of causally influencing subject-relevant aspects of a situation *without* explicitly representing and manipulating subject-world relations as such.

That changes radically when interpretation turns unsituated and metarepresentational and when subject-world relations become explicitly represented
and targeted for causal manipulation (Perner 1991, 225). It does not mean that
desires or beliefs are imaged or symbolized in some explicit form but rather
that their categories and schemes can now invariantly identify types of mind-
world relations out of a variety of clues about situations, actions, utterances,
expressions of emotions, cultural norms, and so on (Bogdan 1997, chapters 6
and 8). Human interpreters represent desires and beliefs as mental relations
to propositions, aka propositional attitudes. These are relations that can
change, be misaimed or false, be influenced by other mental relations, depend
on evidence, and the like. Although this is a composite and incomplete profile
of an attitude, it is nevertheless explicit and systematic in what it picks out
reliably and univocally. The mentally situated ape and very young child do
not know any such things about subject-world relations—independently, that
is, of their manifest and perceived display in current situations or even
imagined situations.

All of this is important because of what interpretation feeds into thinking
as objects of mental rehearsal. What it feeds are representations of social
causality and in particular of subject-world relations as targets of causal
manipulation in social situations. The differences in how these relations are
represented and hence mentally rehearsed will affect the evolution of
metamentation. The difference between situated and unsituated interpretation
is a difference between representations of actual or hypothetical social *situations,* implicitly revealing (causally manipulable) aspects of subject-world
relations, and *explicit* representations of actual or hypothetical *mental relations to propositions* (equally manipulable causally). Only unsituated thinking
about explicitly represented relations to propositions would develop into
metamentation. It is now time to explore this evolutionary option from the
standpoint of thinking itself, the other major evolutionary partner in that
development. It turns out that the thinking that will turn reflexive is itself
socially stimulated and possibly socially scaffolded. So I argue below.

3 Thoughtful Partnership

Partnership means separate participants. And indeed, it appears that mental
rehearsal originated in a distinct ability whose roots and modes of operation
are independent of and prior to those of interpretation. Partnership also means
interplay. And indeed, it appears that mental rehearsal does create the premises
for mental reflexivity by coopting and operating on the causal knowledge
embodied in interpretation. So suggests the present section. It begins with a
few words about the evolutionary roots and format of mental rehearsal, then

explores the reasons why mental rehearsal was considerably stimulated and possibly scaffolded in the social domain of primate cognition, in tandem with interpretation, and concludes by distinguishing among several forms of mental rehearsal the one animated by interpretation as causal knowledge. Given the argument of the previous section, that is the form to watch as the most potent and likely evolutionary partner in the metamentation deal.

Goal Scripting by Mental Rehearsal

To eat, reproduce and do other vital things, organisms evolve cognitive resources that guide them to their goals. The guidance is secured by internal models of a goal situation, which can be called *goal scripts* (Bogdan 1994). Goal scripts can be wired-in, procedural and reflex, as in most animal minds, or involve complex and multiply branching instructions, as in ape minds and those of young human children, or use concepts, explicit representations and reflexive access, as in mature human minds. Only the primate versions count as thinking minds because they alone appear to do mental rehearsal. Goal scripting is phylogenetically older than mental rehearsal or interpretation. The latter are recent strategies of goal scripting, perhaps as recent as the primates.

Think now of *thinking* as a version of goal scripting which shows up late in evolution in the form of mental rehearsal; and think of *mental rehearsal* as the ability to form representations of how the world could or will be or could have been, usually (though not always) relative to some action-to-goal pattern. Early forms of mental rehearsal are imagining, planning, problem solving, and later (only in humans) reasoning, theorizing, and so on. All organisms are goal scripters but few, perhaps only primates, manage in different degrees to free themselves from the tyranny of current perception and represent *nonactual* situations. Thinkers, then, are only imaginers, planners, and problem solvers. Yet neither thinking, so construed, nor freedom from current perception would entail unsituatedness: the thinking of nonhuman primates and young children is glued to and structured by current motivation and perception, while at the same time imagining, on-line and linearly, limited modifications to currently perceived situations. Unsituatedness is thinking about situations and facts not displayed in or linked to current perception. Thinking can thus be situated, on-line, and linear (apes, possibly very young children) or unsituated, off-line, and reflexive (mature humans) or somewhere in-between, largely unsituated but not yet fully reflexive (older children). To keep track of these distinctions, I take the first and last sort to constitute *ground-level* thinking, and the one in-between *higher-level* or *reflexive* thinking.

Situated thinking operates at ground level. When a situated thinker projects a (partly) nonactual situation, she represents a linear or horizontal alternative (as it were) to a currently perceived situation. Such is a mental image of a scene that differs in some limited respects from the current perception of the same scene. This is different from thinking of completely nonactual situations (e.g., thinking of possible scenarios) and also from higher-level or vertical representations, which go up one or more levels and form (meta)representations that loop back on and aim at lower-level representations. The horizontal thinking is *on-line* if it is determined by and continuous with ongoing perception. A *ground-level* thought, then, is a mental representation that operates on-line in ground-level thinking. Thinking is *off-line* if it represents nonactual situations, entirely divorced from current perception. Higher-level or metarepresentational thinking is also *off-line* if it brackets out a current perception and represents some lower-level thought. The heart of thinking, whether on-line or off-line, is imagination.

Imaginations

Any form of mental rehearsal—anticipating a movement, planning an action, or attempting to solve a problem—relies on *imagination* as a core ability to envisage alternative, nonactual situations, whatever the manner of the envisaging—motor or mental images, symbolic representations, whatnot. I assume that in its early phylogenetic and ontogenetic stages situated imagination is imagistic and probably inimical to metamentation. Encoding aside, the question is what form of imagination and hence mental rehearsal is apt and likely to join interpretation in shaping metamentation.

On paper at least, there are several versions of imagination. The simplest would envisage situations that resemble a currently perceived one but differ through some permutation, omission, or addition of some elements. Let *simple imagination* be its name. It is a horizontal, ground-level, and on-line form of mental rehearsal. An ape may anticipate, for example, that if the big alpha male (she now perceives) would turn around and see her ready to groom his main competitor, trouble might follow; so she looks upwards, seemingly concerned about the weather. This would be simple imagination in the service of script (a) of the last section: agent acts → outcome. Simple imagination also operates in the physical domain and may actually have started there, for example, as anticipatory motor images of movements to be initiated in a mechanical goal script.

An ape may also imagine using another as physical implement (e.g., hiding behind him to avoid being seen by the big alpha), according to script (b): agent acts on implement and outcome follows. Here the imaginer injects in her mental projection of a possible situation a representation of an object or organism embedded as implement in an action pattern intended to reach some goal. I call this *instrumental imagination*. Finally, a third type of imagination rehearses ways of causing a causal difference between a current and a possible situation. That would be *causal imagination.* If the means contemplated to produce a causal difference are psychological, as in communication or inter-pretation, it could be called *psychocausal* imagination. Suppose, for example, that in Gomez's story of the last section, after failing to get the trainer to open the latch by physical means (script b), the gorilla next imagines how to communicate with him, by gaze and gestures, to cause him to do it. That would be psychocausal imagination envisaging things according to script (c): agent acts on → [causal dispositions of subject → outcome]. For this gambit to work, the imagining gorilla must represent acting on the *subject-world relations* that express the subject's mental dispositions, such as having a goal, gazing in some direction, recognizing the gazing of another, and so on. It is such disposition-expressing relations that the gorilla's communication is di-rected at, according to script (d): agent acts on → [subject-world relations → outcome]. As a foresighted interpreter, the ape represents such subject-world relations in imagination, as script (e) requires: interpreter represents causing subject-world relations to cause desired outcome.

Rehearsed in psychocausal imagination, script (e) is (I conjecture) the one that will lead eventually to metamentation, but only with the right interpretive resources and other contributing developments. The interpretive resources represent parameters of subject-world relations reenacted in imagination. According to chapters 4 and 5, monkeys represent and therefore might imag-ine only the agency relation (having goals); apes may also grasp and imagine the direction of agency (e.g., following gaze); only young children categorize and imagine full intentionality by systematically tracking its target; and only older children master metarepresentation and later reconstruction, which ex-plicitly represent mind-world-mind relations. Only the categories and schemes of these latter two forms of interpretation, reenacted in psychocausal imagi-nation, stand a chance to be emulated in reflexive thinking.

4   Thinking of Others

Although goal scripting and interpretation originated in distinct lines of evolution, thinking as the *mental-rehearsal form* of goal scripting may owe a good deal to social life and interpretation. This possibility builds up on the hypothesis, entertained a chapter ago, that social life and interpretation may have first and most insistently called for planning and problem solving as versions of mental rehearsal. The defense of the hypothesis was based then on broad evolutionary correlations between what primates do most of the time, most intensely, and the sophistication of their mental gear. What I want to suggest now is that imagination, as a core ability for mental rehearsal and hence a premise of mental reflexivity, is motivated and largely shaped socially. A useful way to develop this suggestion is to ask what would explain the evolution of imagination from simple to instrumental to causal. This question invites a closer look at the patterns of primate socialization which call for mental rehearsal and reward its interplay with interpretation. A chapter ago I noted that these patterns display a unique texture that may have fueled an escalation in the powers of primate imagination. The nature of that texture is discussed next.

Multilateral Relations

Vital for primate social life are bilateral, trilateral, and plurilateral relations among individuals. I call them *multilateral* relations. Broadly speaking, one represents multilateral relations when one maps and factors into one's thinking and behavioral strategies durable types of conspecific relations among several individuals (Kummer 1988, Tomasello and Call 1997). These are mostly relations of kinship, friendship, alliance, dominance, and so on (Cheney and Seyfarth 1990, chapters 3 and 6; Harcourt 1988; Tomasello and Call 1997, chapter 12). Three facts in particular may generate strong pressures for social imagination: first, multilateral relations spread over many individuals related in intricate patterns; second, these patterns can range widely over space and time; and third, variations and novelties in primate interactions along multilateral relations are rather frequent and sometimes go beyond past experience. These facts explain why it is not enough to store knowledge of individuals, their durable dispositions, and the typical situations where these dispositions are manifested. The facts also explain why the representation of and calculations over such patterns of multilateral relations force the primate brain to reach beyond the information perceptually given and become imaginative. This is a critical difference.

Equally critical is another fact. In many social encounters, the actions and reactions of the primates reflect not only their knowledge of who is who, who outranks whom, who can be trusted on the basis of past alliances and reciprocity, but also an ability to respond to current challenges with an eye to *possible* or *future* consequences. The responses require some advance calculation of multilateral relations and of their implications, more like in a game of chess. Think of a case (idealized but not by too much) where ape A confronts the bigger ape D in the presence of ape C. A figures that if B is allied with C, and B is also A's friend, then A might count on C were he to challenge D. A must anticipate this multilateral pattern, and even allow for possible variations in it, before deciding whether to challenge D, hide behind

C, or walk away (drawing on Kummer 1988, Whiten and Byrne 1988b). This is where mental rehearsal by way of imagination can help. In many encounters the relevant portions of the networks of multilateral relations must be retrieved and factored into possible strategies for action. The fast-changing and forward-looking dynamics of primate political life is such that those portions often include individuals and relations *absent* from a current situation. This is why interpretation, as causal knowledge of the social domain, is pressured to spread far and wide across space, time, and possibilities, in order to be effective (Humphrey 1988; Whiten and Byrne 1988b). This is also why its causal strategies must often foresee those nonactual multilateral relations that may affect a desired outcome.[6]

In short, mental rehearsal may have been an adaptive response to the pressures of representing multilateral relations in advance and beyond the information perceptually given. Conversely, if the data reveal that some primate species do rehearse mentally, and do so by means of causal (not just simple or instrumental) imagination, it would be hard to see what pressures other than those of interpreting and causally managing multilateral relations could have selected *initially* for such a novel and expensive cognitive gear. Tool use and other complex mechanical behaviors could always benefit from imaginative anticipations but, as noted already, these activities do not spawn sufficient pressures for mental rehearsal or causal knowledge.

This was the general half of the story, about how multilateral relations in primate socialization call for mental rehearsal. It was not a story about the complexity of such relations but rather about the pressures to think ahead, beyond the perceptually given. Complexity and hence computational agility would come into the picture when the formal texture of the multilaterality of the conspecific interactions is factored in (Whiten and Byrne 1988b). That is an empirical matter that is beyond the brief of my inquiry, although a few tentative remarks in this direction are made in the next subsection. My main interest is in the *sorts* of multilateral relations amongst nonhuman and human primates and the commensurate differences in their mental rehearsal. This is the second and more specific half of the story, where differences in interpretation are shown to generate differences in mental rehearsal via differences in multilateral socialization. An insightful way to capture this chain of differences and anticipate its evolutionary sources is to take the perspective of some abstract but thought-provoking models of primate mentation.

Machiavelli versus Hume

It is widely thought that nonhuman primates make clever politicians, whence the catchy characterization of their minds as 'Machiavellian' (Byrne and

Whiten 1988, Whiten and Byrne 1997), but are less active than humans in educating their young or engaging in sustained and well-coordinated group activities. The idea is not that nonhuman primates do not cooperate, play, enjoy each other, or learn from each other. They do all these things, with intensity and gusto (Cheney and Seyfarth 1990, Tomasello and Call 1997, de Waal 1989), although not in the human way, and that will make a mighty difference. The speculation, rather, is that it is their politics, more than other social activities, which spawned strong pressures for interpretive skills. Suppose this is so. How would this fact illuminate their socialization patterns and hence their cast of mind? Recent models schematize the texture of primate politics and the thinking behind it in terms relevant to this inquiry. The models, coming from conflict and game theory, suggest that the zero-sum nature of the rough politics practiced by nonhuman primates (I win, you lose, and vice versa) raises representation and computation problems that are different from and simpler than those faced in the non-zero-sum forms of epistemic and communal coordination, which are uniquely human.[7] The idea is that nonhuman primates do not appear to evolve *specialized* interpretive skills dedicated to non-zero-sum epistemic and communal activities (such as learning or cooperation) whereas humans do evolve such skills.[8] This is the mighty difference anticipated earlier, because it is such skills of non-zero-sum coordination which matter most in driving the evolutionary complicity between interpretation and mental rehearsal toward metamentation.

In zero-sum encounters the action-reaction sequences can be represented as trees of alternatives which spread out from a *fixed* point and whose relative utilities can be calculated *in advance* because the preferences are known in advance. The social imaginings and plans contemplated by apes would be linear, forward-looking, limited, and probably coarse-grained permutations from current situations. Admittedly simplified, this picture squares with what is known (and noted earlier) about the interpretive skills of apes and the texture of their sociopolitical life (Humphrey 1988, Whiten and Byrne 1988b). The ape mind is situated, reflex, confined to present perception and motivation (the fixed point), yet able to imagine on-line forward-looking but partial alternatives to current states of affairs. The imagining is probably cued by genetic priming as well as past experiences and expectations about standard multilateral arrangements of the zero-sum sort (kinship, reciprocation, alliances, dominance). Such arrangements may have been the earliest and strongest forces to select for mental rehearsal. This matters because mental-rehearsal representations and calculations in the social domain range over subject-world relations and such representations and calculations constitute the raw material out of which evolves metamentation. The ape's situated, inexplicit, coarse-grained, linear, and on-line format of interpretive representation is not open to this evolution, however. Metamentation builds on formats of interpretation and imagination which are unsituated, explicit, fine-grained, off-line, meta-ascending, and back-looping. Human minds gradually develop such formats, thanks to their intersubjective interpretation and its role in mental rehearsal.

This apparently unique development (documented in later chapters) allows human minds to engage each other in *open-ended* and non-zero-sum or contractual forms of *coordination* in which what an agent would plan or choose to do, and do, depends on what other agents would plan or choose to do, and do. In this sort of coordination, agents succeed if and only if each does what others expect each to do. This is to say that the gambit works only if each agent *shares* with others the *recognition* of such expectations and of the contexts in which they work. Sharing recognitions is an absolute novelty in primate mentation. It is an ability that totally redesigns the human mind. Suppose that these patterns of mutual engagement, based on such mental sharing, displays regularities that the participants recognize and conform to, and recognize that the others recognize and conform to them, and also recognize that such mutual recognition and conformity ensures the success of their collaborative actions. The conformity in question is to rules and norms, mostly cultural, of which social and linguistic conventions are a distinguished subclass.

The sort of coordination that fits this account can be called 'Humean' because, as David Lewis (1969, 3–4) notes and quotes, it was Hume who first realized that such coordination emerges from "a general sense of common interest; which sense all the members of the society express to one another, and which induces them to regulate their conduct by certain rules. . . . When this common sense of interest is mutually expressed and is known to both, it produces a suitable resolution and behavior. And this may properly enough be called a convention or agreement betwixt us, though without the interposition of a promise; since the actions of each of us have a reference to those of the other, and are performed upon the supposition that something is to be performed on the other part" (Hume 1756, III.ii.2). Following this line, Levinson calls *Humean* the cast of mind capable of securing such coordination through implicit contract (1995, 227).

Far from transparent, the workings of the Humean mind are not easily deciphered. I do not mean neural mechanisms or cognitive programs but their tasks. I do not think that the Humean tasks of social coordination are transparent without a look at their evolution, which is true of the tasks of interpretation in general (Bogdan 1997). An evolutionary look at social-coordination problems and the Humean minds evolved as responses to them can illuminate the tasks approximated by the rational models sampled earlier. I see no other way because I see the construction of the Humean mind as a complex evolutionary process in which bits and pieces come together, mostly during child development, from unexpected directions and for a variety of reasons. The rest of this essay attempts to track this process, as it careened toward mental reflexivity. The tracking begins in the next chapter by asking about the origins of the Humean minds.

It is time to sum up. This chapter has proposed several partners in the evolutionary deal that eventually yields mental reflexivity:

• *Causal knowledge,* of the generative or cause-causation sort, involved in tool use, because it alone calls for categories and representation schemes of causal relations that are targeted for manipulation, represented as separate from the initiating actions, and general in their manifestations.
• *Interpretation* in general, because it alone targets subject-world relations for causal manipulation. These relations provide the distant models for the objects of reflexive thinking.
• *Intersubjective* interpretation in particular, typical of Humean minds, because it alone secures the mental sharing and mutual recognition of expectations and attitudes that afford the social coordination and communication through which language and culture penetrate the young mind and allow it to unsituate itself and mentally reenact representing relations as forerunners of metamentation.
• *Mental rehearsal,* because it alone (meta)represents representations of subject-world relations as objects of mental scrutiny and manipulation and eventually of reflexive thinking.

The evolutionary deal works as follows. Causal knowledge of the generative sort is limited, nonarbitrary, and generalizable because it concerns highly specific classes of properties intrinsic to the objects or relations causally manipulated; it ranges over such objects and relations often widely separated in space and time; and it is independent of the actions that causally manipulate. For these reasons, causal knowledge is likely to require specialized and possibly innate resources, something which would explain its alleged rarity (Kummer 1995). This diagnosis squares with the specialization, innateness, and rarity of interpretation itself. In the social domain causal knowledge does take the form of interpretation. To manage effective strategies of social intervention, interpretation engages highly specific relational properties of subjects, such as agency, intentionality or attitudes, and tracks their causal impact across the wide space-time expanses of multilateral relations. The tracking is done by mental rehearsal. The fast-changing sequences of multi-lateral relations and the need to foresee their possible implications call for the mental rehearsal of the strategies and actions to pursue. Such is the cognitive ambiance in which interpretation plants the seeds of reflexivity into the fertile territory of mental rehearsal.

Why is mental rehearsal so crucial for the evolution of metamentation? Because, alone among cognitive capacities, mental rehearsal has the function of deliberately imagining nonactual situations. The thoughts one thinks about are also deliberately formed and quite often about nonactual situations. Yet not any form of mental rehearsal will do. Thinking about thoughts requires a form of mental rehearsal which is off-line and meta-ascending. Suppose the thoughts one thinks about are representations of manipulable causal relations, according to the script (c) of causal knowledge examined in section 2. Then these would be thoughts about causal representations. Suppose also that those causal representations are about subject-world relations, according to scripts (d) and (e). Then, in principle, the way is open to thinking about repre-sentations of agency and intentionality. And suppose, finally, that the non-zero-sum or Humean skills afford the novel interpretation of mind-world-mind relations, eventually leading up to shared attention and the metarepresentation of propositional attitudes. The novelties in turn open the way to metamenta-tion. Such is the thrust of the argument of the next chapters.

Chapter 3
Unique Development, Unique Mind

The previous two chapters noted a dramatic difference between ape and human minds. Chapter 1 phrased it as a difference between interactive and intersubjective minds, reflecting a difference in socialization. Spelling out the latter difference, chapter 2 restated its mental impact in terms of Machiavellian versus Humean minds. The question now is where Humean minds come from. The answer, instrumental in explaining the origins and evolution of metamentation, is mental development. The human mind is unique because so is its development. So argues this chapter. It begins with an evolutionary backgrounder about the singularity of primate childhood. It then turns, in section 2, to the uniquely human intersubjectivity which bonds infants and mothers and is rooted in a biophysiological pattern of mutual regulation. This pattern, promising a Humean socialization, affords a prelinguistic protoconversation in terms of mutually exchanged emotions and experiences. According to section 3, this ability joins interpretation in building up topical predication in a comment-topic format. It is within this format that interpretation designs developmentally the abilities for learning word reference, communicating by shared meaning, understanding propositional attitudes, and on this cumulative basis, becoming metamental.

1 Primate Development

The K-story
The reproductive strategies of species are of two sorts. The *r-sort* consists in rapid and massive reproduction, on the principle that the more, the better for survival.[1] The alternative *K-sort* strategy ensures reproduction at replacement levels, on the principle that the fewer and better the offspring, the more efficient the exploitation of scarce resources. K-selection operates on species whose intraspecific competition is intense. Thanks to their sociopolitical life, the primates are on the top of the K-pile. Importantly, K-selection achieves

adaptability through selection for *prolonged* development. K-selection encourages fewer offspring but those few are protected, cared for, and educated in ways that increase their chances of survival.[2] This form of development tends to boost adaptability because individuals have more time and opportunities to "learn about their highly competitive and complex environments before they lay their reproductive value on the line" (Chisholm 1988, 82).

There is a solid neural story behind this evolutionary estimate (Changeux 1985, particularly chapter 7; Chisholm 1988). By retarding the rate of somatic development, neural structures have more time to grow and differentiate and thus more time and opportunities to be affected by and adjust to new experiences. Phenotypic variability is inherent in neural development, as the latter generates redundant and variable synaptic forms, thus allowing a sort of neural selection to favor the preservation of those synapses with functional value in one's environment.[3] The functional values define what is adaptive in that environment. The fact that the genotype allows alternative strategies, whose selection is made by the environment, should *not* be construed as pointing to individual learning afforded by totally plastic dispositions. Turning worker rather than queen, because of dietary stimuli, is not something that individual bees learn from their experience; it is rather an adaptive flexibility afforded by the bee genome itself, not unlike the adaptive phonetic or grammatical flexibility afforded by the genetic predispositions for language when the infant's luck is to grow in one linguistic environment rather than another. This is worth noting because neither the extended duration nor the multiple opportunities for exposure to social experience nor the multiply influenced patterns of growth should be construed (as they might) as signs of individual learning. The whole process through which children reach mental maturity—its tight schedule, its eventual neural specialization, its universality—would be unintelligible if regarded as an unconstrained learning experience.

Adaptive and subtly constrained as it may be, the K-strategy of delayed development is rather surprising from an evolutionary standpoint. It is not in the usual style of natural selection. As George Williams notes, "natural selection will always, *ceteris paribus,* favor rapid development; the sooner an organism matures the less likely it is to die before maturing and reproducing. Selection can never directly favor a lengthening of the juvenile period. The development of longer juvenile phases in a phyletic line must always be considered a price paid for some more important development" (1966, 87–88). What could that "more important development" be? I think the answer should be sought in development itself, construed *as* a form of evolution. In human development, interpretation holds the key to that answer.

Development as Evolution

It is customary to view development as adulthood writ small and partial—a series of interim stages toward adult forms. This finalistic view is wrong for several reasons. It not only ignores the child's evolutionary interests and her developmental strategies, which operate as a survival kit at each stage, but also presumes that, being the goals of development, adult acquisitions act as distant pressures on and shapers of development. This view ignores the fact that development is a slice of evolution, as it were, with its *own* selective pressures and solutions. Thus Williams, once again: "Ontogeny is often intuitively regarded as having one terminal goal, the adult-stage phenotype, but the real goal of development is the same as that of all other adaptations, the continuance of the dependent germ plasm. The visible somatic life cycle is the indispensable machinery by which this goal may be met, and every stage is as rightfully a goal as any other. First, it must deal with the immediate problem of survival, a matter of ecological adjustment. Secondly, it must produce the next succeeding stage. The morphogenetic instructions must provide for both jobs" (1966, 44).

Each stage in development is an evolution game in itself: not the survival-and-reproduction game of accomplished organisms but the prior game of survival-and-making-it-to-the-next-stage. Each developmental stage is subject to local, dated, often unique pressures, to which equally local, dated, and often unique responses evolve as developmental adaptations. Neither the pressures nor the responses can be fathomed and explained finalistically, from the vantage point of adulthood. The only forward-looking goal of development is the "next succeeding stage," itself a stage of development, most of the time. For example, infants communicate with mothers by taking turns in expressing and acknowledging emotions and other experiences. These exchanges emerge as a developmental solution to a developmental problem, that of infant-mother bioregulation. Once mastered, this solution will later underpin the acquisition of word reference but without the pattern of exchanges that made it possible in the first place. (Most of us manage to refer to things without mother smiling helpfully.) The developmental ladder needed to get to word reference was long since abandoned and is no longer visible from the perspective of later accomplishments. Only a close look at development, with its unique pressures and responses, could discern the presence of the ladder and the constraints and formative opportunities it afforded. The same is true of so many other uniquely developmental conditions and problems encountered by interpretation, as it blazes ahead on its long and convoluted journey to mental reflexivity.

Human development is subject to natural selection and cultural indoctrination. Both have unique influences on development, for reasons that concern only development, with mighty implications for mind design. The role of natural selection in development varies and this variation matters to the present argument. The development of plants and most animal species is entirely under the grip of natural selection. That need not be true of mental development. Up to a point, the latter is governed by natural selection, as it responds to the demands of protection, biological regulation, and other vital needs. But that changes with time, and natural selection loosens its grip on mental development, as the ecology turns increasingly cultural. As a result, what happens in the next developmental stage may often be beyond the reach of natural selection. For example, it is rather unlikely that natural selection would dictate that adult-infant joint attention be used to build up a word-reference ability as a next stage in mental development or that word reference be later used to scaffold metarepresentation, and so on. I find it more reasonable to think that it was cultural evolution that universalized such practices of inserting new abilities in prior and naturally selected skills. (It is in this light that I read Bruner 1983; Gomez 1996b; Rogoff 1990; Tomasello 1996; Tomasello, Kruger, and Ratner 1993). Yet in so doing, culture does not seem to change the evolutionary rules of development. The process still responds to local, dated, and often unique coordinates (pressures, adaptive responses) of each developmental stage and designs mental abilities within these coordinates. This is why a good deal of the cultural design of the mind remains exclusively developmental.

Cultural Adaptation
From this angle on mental development, an answer to Williams' earlier question begins to take shape. The answer is made of two parts. The first says that the "more important development" calling for longer juvenile phases in the primate phyletic lines is likely to be the *socialization* of mental development through interpretation. Knowledge of social relations and its use in prediction or planning are vital for all primate kids at every stage in their development and therefore call for specialized skills. These skills take time to mature. Without them any primate is unadapted during development as well as maturity. But the forms of socialization and hence interpretation (mapped out in earlier chapters) are different among primate species and the difference is reflected in the length and laboriousness of mental development.

The brains of human infants are larger, relative to the body size, and grow much faster and for a longer period after birth, than those of the nonhuman primate infants (Low 1998). This difference may be explained better by social rather than physical challenges. Within the social sphere it may be explained by the contrast between interactivity and intersubjectivity. The reason why these differences matter is that the naive physics of one-year-olds is about the same in all primate kids, while their interpretation differs right from birth along interactive and intersubjective lines. Nonhuman primates reach interpretational (as well as physical and sexual) maturity faster, apparently under the exclusive watch of natural selection. They socialize and interpret (interactively) by making eye contact, following gaze, guessing behavior, and do it much earlier and more expertly than human newborns (Tomasello and Call 1997, 404–405). It does not take that long to mature these interpretive skills, at least not when compared with what it takes human children to mature those of intersubjective interpretation. The latter in turn creates opportunities for a further and mightier challenge to mental development, in the form of *enculturation.* Thus the second part of the answer to Williams' question.

Enculturation slows and complicates mental development still further. It is a process that feeds on itself. As it slows down mental development, it finds new and more reasons and opportunities to enrich the cultural ecology of the child with new tasks, thus producing further slowdown and complication. It is during this laboriously self-feeding and self-complicating process of enculturation that the child's mind acquires a Humean profile. To stay attached, protected, regulated interpersonally, and prosperous in this new cultural ambiance, and do so on her evolutionary terms, the child must go along and master the rules of the Humean games—from protoconversation to language learning, contractual coordination, and norm following. The cultural rules of the Humean games are much harder to master than the natural rules of Machiavellian games because, unlike the latter, the former are neither written in the genes nor easily discernible in gaze, bodily postures, behavior, and basic goals identified in the natural environment. Hard to master means long apprenticeship, which cannot but further prolong maturation and lead in turn to new opportunities for cultural indoctrination and thus Humeanization. So construed, then, the Humean environment of cultural adaptedness appears as eminently *developmental,* to an extent unmatched by its Machiavellian precursor. Humans become Humean because of how they develop mentally under cultural constraints.

This developmental pattern explains in part why K-minds, compared with r-minds, and within the K-group, human minds, compared with other primate minds, embody more complex and hierarchic organizations, take more time to organize themselves through slow instructional development, and are more open and flexible toward the natural and social environment. In the human case, complexity and hierarchy may well be the price paid for and the benefit derived from cultural adaptation during child development, with mental reflexivity as a distant by-product. This line of analysis might also make sense of the hypothesis, proposed by George Williams and shared by other theorists, that "the creative intellect of adult humans is an incidental effect of selection for high intellectual capacity in juvenile humans" (Alexander 1990a, 25; Gopnik and Meltzoff 1997, 18–19; Low 1998, 133–136; Rogoff 1990, 77–78). A version of this idea is that "science is a kind of spandrel, an epiphenomenon of childhood" (Gopnik 1996, 490).[4]

In sum, there are good reasons to take mental development seriously, on its evolutionary terms, and expect its pressures and constraints to translate into mind design. This is how I propose to understand the idea that "a developmental perspective is essential to the analysis of human cognition, because understanding the built-in architecture of the human mind, the constraints on learning, and how knowledge changes progressively over time can provide subtle clues to its final representational format in the adult mind" (Karmiloff-Smith 1992, 26).

Uniqueness Relocated

If the K-form of development is rare, the culturally driven K-form of mental development in human children is unique. It is this unique development that produces a unique mind. The uniqueness of the process explains the uniqueness of its outcome. This conclusion shifts the *locus* of uniqueness of the human mind in several respects. It relocates the causes of uniqueness in a *process,* not in a property or faculty. It has been long customary to think of the uniqueness of the human mind as God's gift or a sudden break in evolution or some weird brain mutation, resulting in a privileged faculty, typically cognitive, like speech, grammar, formal reasoning, or the like. The hypothesis I prefer expects the uniqueness of the human mind to result from a process of assembling its sundry faculties. Equally importantly, the hypothesis opts for a starting point of this process which is *not cognitive* and by itself has little if anything to do with the mental, let alone the cognitive. The next section explains why. Finally, the uniqueness of this developmental process, initiated noncognitively, is attributed not only to a lengthy accretion of naturally selected outcomes but also to cultural evolution.

2   Sentimental Bonding

The intersubjectivity of human interpretation begins in a physiological regulation between infant and mother, a phenomenon that appears to be exclusively human and exploited in singular ways during mental development.

Regulation through Sentimental Bonding

Developmental slowdown means the child's helplessness and dependence on parents. The dependence extends from feeding and defense to regulation of vital physiological and emotional parameters. Both parents and infants have an evolutionary interest in making this relation viable: parents in order to protect their reproductive investment, infants in order to survive and make it to the next stage. It has been long assumed that for the infant the name of the game in the earliest phases is attachment (Bowlby 1982; see also Bjorklund 1995, 330–337, and Bremner 1988, 171–191, for surveys). Attachment is found in many species whose little ones are born helpless and dependent. Yet only in humans it takes elaborate forms of exchanges of emotions and experiences through bodily and facial expressions, gestures, and vocalizations. I call the family of these exchanges *sentimental bonding*. The difference between animal and human attachment may be linked to their domains: animal attachment seems geared mostly to feeding and protection whereas its human version also handles the interpersonal regulation of biophysiological parameters. The difference is not that prehuman animals do not express stress or some emotion, such as distress or happiness, to secure attachment; they do, perhaps as intensely as human infants. The difference is that human infants also use expressions of emotions in the regulation of their internal states through interaction and communication with mothers, who respond in kind (Trevarthen 1993). *This* is the deeper phenomenon and the critical difference—initially a biophysiological one—that explains why and how intersubjective interpretation designs the young human mind.

Why interpersonal regulation and why through sentimental bonding? Inside the womb the fetus is part of the biological system of the mother. Outside the womb, the infant becomes self regulating in many but not all respects. If the infant is an incomplete system and in particular an incomplete regulatory self, it makes evolutionary sense to delegate part of the regulation to those genetically closest and hence most likely and interested to be around most of the time. Homeostatic regulation, involving immunological, metabolic, cardiovascular or endocrine parameters, is effected by mother. The infant also regulates some maternal functions, including, through feedback, those that are infant-directed. The initial infant-mother exchanges thus rest on mutual regulation that ensures a physiological permeability between the partners (Pipp 1993). Although incomplete self regulation may be true of other species (Hofer 1987), what seems to be true solely of humans is that key homeostatic parameters of the infant are expressed in *emotions* and can be regulated by adults through them. This is how sentimental bonding connects with the basic physiology of the infant. I find sentimental bonding through emotions and other vividly expressed experiences a critical basis for mental development. So let me elaborate.

The regulatory permeability between infant and mother extends beyond homeostasis. Colwyn Trevarthen (1993) talks of "motives" as mental functions that drive and direct actions toward goals and seek information that guide such actions. Motives seem close to desires but may be physiologically more basic and less cognitively penetrable; they also seem close to needs but less instinctive, more active and versatile. The point to stress here is that their "central energy and self-regulating quality are *expressed in emotions*" (Trevarthen 1993, 124; my emphasis). This means that mother can regulate an infant's motives, from attention and arousal to specific desires, by regulating the right emotions. Infancy involves a good deal of motive regulation through communication of emotions, not just for the current well being of the infant but also, forward-lookingly, in the interest of adaptive socialization and enculturation, as in learning words. Emotions and various expressions of inner experience thus emerge as regulatory tools whose initial and basic function is later redeployed, redirected, and used in ways that steer the infant's mental development toward novel acquisitions. This extraordinary process takes off when mutual regulation begins to operate as communication.

It is a clever ploy of evolution to secure intersubjectivity sentimentally. (I would do it this way, if asked.) Emotions and other expressions of motives and experiences are excellent interpersonal regulators—direct, honest, and reliable. Since infants can neither move much nor perform many actions nor speak, exchanges of emotions provide the best if not the only means for mutual regulation *at a distance,* when physiological regulation through bodily contact is beyond reach. Emotions, feelings, and bodily postures can be easily, effortlessly, and often unconsciously recognized in others, thus providing a secure basis for comparison and coordination. Given these qualities, they also provide solid foundations on which to build new functions and skills, as will happen in interpretation, communication, and other areas of mental life.[5]

The sentimental route to intersubjectivity fits the theme of this essay in another important respect. Mental reflexivity was said to be a joint evolutionary output of interpretation and mental rehearsal. The neuroscientific evidence shows that prefrontal brain areas do social regulation through processing of emotions. It turns out that the same brain areas also do mental rehearsal, such as planning and decision making (Damasio 1994, chapters 4 and 8; Perner and Lang 1999). This discovery backs the sentimental route and lends further and weighty support to the notion (explored a chapter ago) that mental rehearsal may have evolved most vigorously in the social domain, in constant and intimate commerce with interpretation and probably under its influence.

All these considerations add up to the estimate that minding others senti-mentally makes evolutionary sense as a strategy of interpretation, notably in the initial ontogenetic phases. If the child's mind was to be designed socially, by minding other minds, it seems natural to recruit *first* for this job resources that allow a direct and vivid window to that part of the adult's mind that is directly involved in the design, at least in its early but so decisive stages. This ploy seems feasible because those resources are already in place for other vital reasons, such as mutual regulation and attachment. I return in chapter 5 to sentimental minding as a strategy of interpretation and its emulation in the build-up of mental reflexivity. Right now my aim is to continue tracking the evolutionary roots of the strategy.

Protoconversation
Protoconversation is an affective, emotion-based but prelinguistic communi-cation between infants and mothers by way of facial expressions, bodily movements, gestures, and vocalizations in a give-and-take, address-and-reply manner. Much before language and for independent reasons, protoconversa-tion begins as a modulator and expression of intersubjective regulation (Bateson 1979, Bruner 1983, Fernald 1992, Hobson 1993b, Tomasello 1995, Trevarthen 1993). Its analysis reveals systematic patterns of exchanges, taking turns, making vocal, facial, and bodily comments and replies to comments, almost miming normal conversation but without language. Protoconversation starts soon after birth. Its key props are already in place: motherly vocaliza-tions are recognized even in the womb and facial expressions and the emotions they convey are recognized just after birth, and reacted to, in kind. There is robust evidence of the transcultural universality of protoconversation (Fernald 1992, Trevarthen 1993). All these facts suggest an innate and probably natu-rally selected programming of protoconversation *as* biophysiological regula-tion. Even when protoconversation becomes increasingly linguistic and geared to the child's learning of new words, it still continues to function for a while as a regulator of social interactions (Akhtar and Tomasello 1998). Culture is grafted on nature at joints with which the child is already familiar.

The regulatory origin and function of protoconversation explain something else that has momentous consequences for mental development in general, language learning and metamentation in particular. Since interpersonal bioregulation effects a coordinated and mutual adjustment of internal parame-ters, its object—a shared homeostasis, as it were—resides in this very balanc-ing act, and in nothing else. It does not have any *outside* import and hence no specific external correlate or target. As bioregulation through sentimental bonding, protoconversation inherits this targetless autarchy. It begins and develops for a while as a *topicless* exchange of emotional protocomments. It is this initial *freedom from specific topics,* indeed any topics at all, that I find momentous in its mental implications. Think of it as follows.

Animal communication of the nonhuman sort is thoroughly utilitarian not just because it is done through functional and specialized means (so is human communication) but because it is almost always geared to some behavior and its vital goals as specific targets. Nonhuman animals communicate because something specific happened or is about to happen, which is relevant to their behavior and vital goals. Even when based on eye-to-eye exchanges, animal communication is utilitarian in the sense of being outwardly oriented toward establishing aggression or reconciliation or the like. Human infants protoconverse with mothers as part of internal regulation (a utilitarian function), but they need not initially protoconverse about something specific that is tightly tied to their behaviors and vital goals. Given infant helplessness, the utility is just making and maintaining contact with others. Infants smile at a facial expression or gesture but not always with a specific goal in mind to be reached by a specific behavior. The surrounding world does not have much initial relevance to infant protoconversation. Infants protoconverse with adults before becoming aware of the rest of the surrounding world and before developing the abilities to recognize its denizens.

This initially topicless, behaviorally irrelevant, and world-indifferent proto-conversation has several major implications for mental development. First, it works almost as a rehearsal and fine tuning of the communication gear, particularly of exchanges of comments, before shared topics are introduced by the cognitive routes of interpretation, such as gaze following or joint attention. It may be that the roots of Humean coordination, first operating in infant-adult communication, are set up during this early phase of topicless protoconversation. By smiling and being smiled at, and repeating the cycle with variations that are in turn acknowledged, the infant not only engages in (topicless) mental sharing but also begins to recognize that the other recognizes and enjoys (or reacts in some other way to) the sharing itself. Expectations are thus formed about what the other expects from the partner and this reciprocation of expectations is itself recognized. The mutuality of acknowledged experiences and its recognition are finely adjusted and ready, when the time comes, to engage topics that the partners share. This is a mind-mind pattern awaiting the introduction of the tertium, the world, to complete the triangular mind-world-mind format. At that point, one would suppose, communication by shared meaning can take off.

Second, topicless protoconversation may keep the infant's mind free from behavior-to-goal concerns with the surrounding world, at least in the early stages of sentimental bonding, thus affording an evolutionarily unprecedented freedom of choice of communicable topics, often arbitrary from a biological or physical standpoint. This freedom of choice of topics paves the way for learning all sorts of concepts, some unintuitive and abstract, and plants the seeds of open-ended imagination, thinking, and creativity. Even when they appear to show mutual awareness, the closest primate counterparts to human children, the chimpanzees, cannot break from the outward-oriented and strictly imperative matrix of their communication.[6] One plausible explanation may be that infant chimpanzees do not engage their parents in a sentimental bonding sustained and bilateral enough to afford topicless protoconversation. The same may be true of autistic children: not sharing sentimental bonding and protoconversation, their communication remains utilitarian and imperative, tied to current goals and behaviors. Later in normal human infancy, protoconversation acquires shareable topics and the interpersonal relatedness moves beyond bilateral contacts into mutually shared and world-sensitive patterns. At that point, topical communication takes off, though still in prelinguistic terms. It does so in a format that will prove crucial in how interpretation eventually designs metamentation and, in-between, so many other abilities that run the human mind.

A third implication, acknowledged but not pursued in this work, is that a topicless and world-indifferent protoconversation allows culture to organize the child's cultural habits and expectations and her interactions with others and the world in patterns that later scaffold the semantics and pragmatics of her language and her modes of thinking (Bruner 1983, Lock 1980, Nelson 1996, Ninio and Snow 1996, Tomasello 1996). This does not happen in species or mentally handicapped individuals whose mentation and behavior are thoroughly utilitarian, hence functionally dedicated and world-directed from the outset. Culture apparently cannot build well upon a tightly programmed and thoroughly utilitarian frame of mind. Culture needs flexible points of entry into the infant mind and those are afforded by sentimental bonding through topicless protoconversation. In time, those points of entry acquire a generic format of their own, also uniquely human, on which most of the novel mental acquisitions rest, from understanding symbol and word reference to mental reflexivity. The basis of that indispensable and powerful format is outlined next.

3   Topical Predication

The Very Idea

One smiles at a gesture, finding it amusing, or gets excited recalling an event as surprising, or represents a thought as plausible or a landscape one sees as exhilarating. Such examples have this much in common: about some target of attention or mental focus (gesture, event, thought, scene), one represents it as being in some way (amusing, surprising, plausible, exhilarating). The target of attention is the *topic*, its representation as being some way or another is the *comment*. The resulting structure is a *topic-comment parsing* or segmentation and the mental routine that effects the parsing is *topical predication*, as I will call it.[7] More familiar examples of topical predication can be found in language. One can use intonational stress (on 'Pipa') or one can say 'It was Pipa who found the book', using the cleft construction ('It was Pipa'), to separate the topic, that someone found the book, from the comment, that that someone was Pipa.

Although topical predication has been studied most intensely in its linguistic embodiments, the latter emerge later in mental development and build upon prelinguistic antecedents. (I would not be surprised to hear that language development consists in part in adjusting the child's emerging grammatical competence to prior topical-predication formats.) Work in linguistics, psycholinguistics, and philosophy has shown that topical predication cannot be reduced to logical or grammatical predication (see Clark and Clark 1977 and Ninio and Snow 1996 for psycholinguistic surveys; see also Bogdan 1987 and Dretske 1972 about implications for propositional attitudes). This irreducibility can be grounded in the hypothesis that topical predication is prelinguistic and rests on mental sharing by sentimental bonding and physiological regulation. Also supportive is the fact that autistic people, whose minds are not socialized intersubjectively, can do logical and grammatical but not topical predication (chapter 8, section 1).

To account for these developmental truths and the reasons for them, it helps to start with the liberal notion that topical predication indicates a mental take (comment) on something of interest (topic). The topic can be whatever is a target of attention or interest—a thing, event, property, relation, scene, sentence, thought, image, picture, sign, or complex structures of such. The topic can be out there in the world or up here in the mind, whether one's own or somebody else's. The comment is some mental take on or mental relation to a topic, expressing an experience, emotion, stance or attitude. Depending on whether the topic is a worldly or mental item, the comment can be a representation of something out there in the world or a representation of a representation in the mind, respectively. There are many ways in which topics and comments can be represented—in perception, memory, thought, mental imagery, bodily posture, action, with or without language.

It may look as though topical predication is one of the simplest cognitive tasks, manageable by almost any species with decent categorization capabilities. That would be the wrong impression. Despite its apparent simplicity, topical predication is one of the hardest tasks imaginable and, from all the evidence available, human minds alone can handle it, with enormous consequences for their modus operandi. It is not conceptual or computational complexity that makes topical predication hard. It is its singular format that is hard to come by in evolution, for it appears to require an intersubjective socialization and interpretation, capable of sustaining triangular mind-world-mind relations, and all these are rare. An indirect way to measure the radical novelty of topical predication is to see why prehuman minds are unlikely to evolve it.

Mechanical Minds

Consider first a purely sensorimotor mind dedicated to mechanical actions in the physical domain. Call it a mechanical mind. Its discriminations feed into categories that classify things and events in formats conducive to goal-satisfying behaviors. Suppose those formats are of the sort 'flower-red-smelly' or 'running-fast-scared'. Although such a mind might engage in (what looks to us as) thing-property predication—for example, 'The flower is red'—this could be just the fusing of several perceptual discriminations—in this case, of shape, color, smell. Many species perceive by fusing multiple discriminations. There is nothing here to prefigure topical predication. Would an ability to attend to something perceptually fare better? Such an ability, also possessed by many species, may be necessary but is far from sufficient. What perceptual attention buys is a target for behavioral routines but not a sense of a mental take on or relation to (comment) something specific (topic).

What's missing? A mechanical mind registers the world in ways that guide behavior to its targets. Topical predication can carve up patterns that look *arbitrary* from the standpoint of behavior-guiding perception. The arbitrariness can be described (loosely) as 'About *x* (whatever topic), I think that *y* (whatever comment).' Or, more fully, 'About *whatever* is of *interest now,* given *whatever* else I know about it, I think or say or remember *this* rather than *that.*' The italicized words pick up slots whose contents vary with context, interest, available data, assumptions, form of representation, and alternatives ruled out. Thus works topical predication. Could a mechanical mind evolve it? Not likely. There is little room for arbitrary and complex variations of interest and hence of attention, background data, or alternatives in a mind that lives and operates solely in the sensory here-and-now, for the sake of mechanical action. How would such a mind handle these variations and complexities without a computational explosion for which it has no apparent solution? This is a question about *resources.* But what would be the *reasons* for the resources? Why would such resources be needed when the (naturally selected) job of mechanical minds is to convert stimuli into behaviors in ways that respond to a limited but recurrent number of basic goals?

It won't do to say that topical predication emerged as an answer to cognitive tasks faced by mechanical minds, for it is hard to see why and how such tasks in the domain of mechanical agency could have called for topical predication. What aspects of a physical or biological world, perceived and mechanically acted upon, would stand out as variable topics for even more variable comments? The question now is about the *domain* of cognition. Why would it be carved up topically rather than in a simpler sensorimotor fashion? Why, for example, would an organism judge a tasty nut as 'Lo, a nut. About it I now judge that it is tasty' and not simply as 'Nyam, nyam, tasty-nut-here-and-now'? Such paraphrases may sound equivalent but, as we shall see, the mental resources employed and the reasons for them are not. If equivalence it was, then evolution would have done better (as it did) to encourage the simpler ('nyam nyam') formula, congruent with the sensorimotricity of mechanical minds.

To figure out the reasons and opportunities for topical predication we need to look at other kinds of minds—those that do more than engage the world mechanically. These are social minds. But not any sort of social minds, only the interpreting sort. Why? To put it bluntly but not too misleadingly, because in the beginning it takes (at least) two to triangulate a target of mutual interest (topic) in terms of relations which each has to the target and which the other registers as such or interprets. It turns out that an interpreter *first* registers a relation to a target *as* a subject-world relation and later turns it around and tracks it in her own mind. From topical predication to the grasp of intentionality, word reference, and mental representation this seems to be a pattern consistently found in the evolution of interpretation. But social triangulation through interpretation is not enough for topical predication. It has to be the right style of interpretation. Whence the next question.

What about Interactive Minds?
Why didn't apes evolve the ability to predicate topically? They are social, they interpret each other, may show reciprocal awareness, often in contexts where they have mutual interests in a perceived target out there. So what's the problem? Here is a guess. Recall that the interactive socialization of apes is utilitarian (requests, threats, favors) and mostly mechanical in execution (hiding, gesturing, grabbing). As a result, their interpretation and communication have imperative aims only—pushing conspecifics and physical things around, as it were. These features reveal, and reinforce, a rather coarse-grained behavioral interaction among individuals with respect to vital goals and other

widely shared and visible targets, such as food, mates, enemies and danger situations, physical implements, and the like. The identification of the goals and targets of others is done in the here-and-now of current perception and motivation. As a result, an interactive interpreter is prone to triangulate external targets of social interest in terms of her *own* goals or things perceived (which she interprets others as relating to) or in terms of *vital* and *species-uniform* goals, perceived and acted upon in the same way by everybody. There would seem to be little pressure to evolve a nonegocentric and context-free method to identify variable shared targets that are *less* vital, obvious, or egocentric.[8] Topical predication is an excellent strategy precisely for representing and sharing information about variable, flexible, often arbitrary or culturally determined (hence less vital, obvious, species-uniform or purely egocentric) targets of mutual interest, and was probably selected for that very reason.

It may be for lack of topical predication that (as noted in chapter 5) the ape mastery of intentionality remains incomplete: it deploys specialized skills to grasp the relatedness and direction of intentionality but not its target. The target seems to be supplied either subjectively (my goal is his goal) or in species-wide terms (my goal is everybody's goal), not by a specialized skill. Such a skill, completing the representation of intentionality, may actually draw on topical predication (as noted in chapter 6). And topical predication, as the evidence abundantly suggests, is something that interactive minds do not do. They do not, according to the argument of this chapter, because they do not evolve sentimental bonding which translates interpretationally into sentimentally minding each other and protoconversing in triangular mind-world-mind relations.

A review is now in order. Topical predication is made of two halves evolving on distinct tracks: the recognition of comments as mental takes or stances and the recognition that comments are about topics (Bruner 1983; Hobson 1993b, 1994). The first recognition (on the comment track) originates in the sentimental bonding between infant and mother, which is grounded physiologically in their mutual regulation and takes the interpretational form of sentimental minding (recognizing the emotions and experiences of others). The second recognition (on the topic-aboutness track) originates in interpreting the others' relations to the world and, via sentimental minding, coordinates that relation with one's own in a mind-world-mind pattern.[9] The developmental meeting of these two tracks provides intersubjective interpretation with a potent format in which to design new mental skills throughout childhood, as it socializes and enculturates the young mind. Since metamentation builds upon such earlier skills, the survey of the evolutionary journey to reflexivity, undertaken in the next chapters, will occasionally acknowledge the emerging body of evidence and theory which recognizes and explains the central role of topical predication, in the hands of interpretation, in designing the child's mind.

Although the fulcrum of the human mind, topical predication did not emerge as a cognitive solution to a computational problem of complexity or to a categorization problem of classifying objects or properties in either the social or mechanical domain. The evolutionary oddity is that topical predication built on an initial response (neurophysiological processes turned into affective protoconversation) to selective pressures (for infant-mother regulation and attachment) that had nothing to do with cognition. Yet once coopted by other abilities, chiefly those of interpretation, mental rehearsal, and later language, topical predication develops to handle mighty computational complexities and very subtle and variable categorizations and, as a result, provides the format in which other mental abilities are shaped. One of them, metamentation, thus appears to have been assembled out of a variety of abilities and resources, many of which evolved initially for functions that had nothing to do with the final outcome.

It was the aim of this first part of the essay to sketch the broad evolutionary pedigree of this mosaic-like process that will eventually mix and scaffold the infrastructure of metamentation. Having done that, it is time to bring metamentation to center stage and analyze it in terms that allow a finer-grained demonstration of why and how it evolved out of sentimentally based intersubjective interpretation and mental rehearsal in the social domain.

PART II
Minding Itself

Chapter 4

The Reflexive Mind

This chapter provides a conceptual profile of mental reflexivity in terms that help identify those of its abilities suspected to have been brought about by developments in interpretation. Given its narrow focus, the profile is not meant to yield a detailed, let alone exhaustive account of reflexive or metarepresentational thinking. Nevertheless, the abilities handling the tasks surveyed below form the core of mental reflexivity. Left out of the discussion, but assumed throughout, are various other contributing abilities and props, from logical reasoning to language and mental imagery. These contributors and props, however, do not add up to metamentation: one can form sentences about sentences or images about images, and play with them mentally, without metamentating, as the case of autism suggests (chapter 8, section 1). It is this critical difference this chapter is after.

Section 1 looks at the abilities to think reflexively in terms of the tasks they carry out. Essential are those for metamental predication, metathinking, taking a metamental perspective, and imagination of mental contents. (The names of these abilities may look forbidding but their meanings should be familiar, as long as the meta-difference is factored in.) Section 2 dissects the tasks into several categories and schemes of representation—metaintentional, promental, metarepresentational, and so on. These categories and schemes are objects of interpretation at different evolutionary stages, whence the structural parallel on which rests the argument of this essay. It is not a coincidental parallel, because interpretation is about how minds relate to the world—intentionally, representingly, and so on—and reflexivity is the relation of thoughts to thoughts, whence the conceptual rationale for the conjecture that the tasks of metamentation emulated those of interpretation. Section 3 explains the notion of task emulation and its conceptual, evolutionary, and psychological grounds. Admittedly abstract and fast-paced, this chapter should be read as a skeletal frame to which later chapters will add empirical and illustrative flesh.

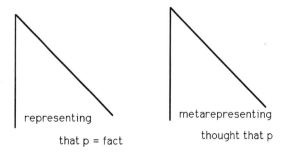

Figure 4.1
Representing a fact, metarepresenting a thought.

1 The Infrastructure

The tasks identified below play an infrastructural role in reflexive thinking. The role is *infrastructural* in the sense that the tasks operate within and across various forms of metamentation (such as thinking about plans, evaluating solutions to problems, engaging in moral deliberation, inner dialogue or scientific theorizing) and their execution lies beneath, and is not necessarily visible in, the logical and linguistic forms accessible to consciousness and public language. Since the tasks are often executed in standardized sequences or patterns, I treat them as *routines*. The ones I focus on need not be as distinct or exercised in isolation as my account may suggest, nor do they exhaust the metamental infrastructure of thinking. But they are basic, indispensable, ubiquitous. I offer no technical definition of metamentality: what counts as metamental is defined jointly and implicitly by the analyses of the tasks examined below. For our purposes, reflexive thinking simply consists in deployments of metamental routines. I begin with the central notion.

Metarepresentation
There are public representations, such as photographs, drawings, utterances, or written sentences; and mental representations, such as judgments or images. Both types represent and both can be represented. The latter relation is *metarepresentation*. To metarepresent is to form a higher-order representation about a lower-order representation. Thus, when one merely represents or thinks of a fact, one's thinking is at the ground level; when one represents or thinks of a thought, one ascends at a higher or meta level and therefore metathinks (figure 4.1).

Metarepresentation can pick out different aspects of a lower-order representation: it could be the logical, grammatical or pictorial *structure* of the

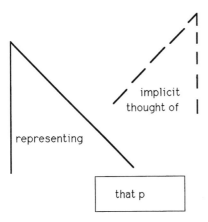

representing

implicit
thought of

that p

Figure 4.2
Implicit metathinking.

representation or some other properties of the structure or it could be the *relation* of the structure to what it represents. In the former sense, metarepresentation is nonrelational, in the latter relational. When one represents a judgment as logically valid, one metarepresents it nonrelationally; when one thinks that a judgment is true, one metarepresents it relationally (a judgment-to-world relation). Metarepresentation can be public (photograph of photograph) or mental. The latter can be of public representations (memory of photograph) or of mental representations (memory of thought). It may appear that these are different sides of the same coin. Not so. Distinct tasks and presumably skills are involved. Autistic children can metarepresent public but not mental representations.

The sense of metarepresenting needed in reflexivity is *mental and relational.* To metarepresent in this sense or *metathink* is to represent a thought as a mental relation to a content. The routines surveyed next are of this mental and relational sort. They range from simple to complex, in terms of the levels involved and the articulation of metathoughts at each level. The progression from simplicity to complexity may have some developmental significance but that will be of concern later.

Implicit Metathinking

When one metathinks, one represents a thought, not just a fact the thought may be about. There are different ways of thinking of a thought. If one specifies a thought in terms of its content *and* determines the content in terms of what it is about (its truth conditions), then one's metathinking is implicit and semantic. It is *implicit,* because the mental identity of the thought is acknowledged (one is marginally aware of it), but it is not focused on and spelled out structurally, is not represented explicitly; and it is *semantic,* because of how the content of the thought is specified, by appeal to how the world is (figure 4.2).

Thinking imagistically or daydreaming come close to metathinking implicitly. Suppose I image my way to a distant empty seat in a crowded concert hall. The sequence of mental images with which I rehearse the optimal route are specified semantically in terms of what they represent. The imaging itself is backgrounded and implicit in the minimal sense that its mental identity is acknowledged and not mistaken for (say) perception. This is not the only way to metathink, although it may be the simplest and developmentally the first. There is also explicit metathinking, of various sorts.

Explicit Metathinking

One metathinks explicitly and semantically when one represents a thought qua thought (focuses on that sort of mental relation) but specifies its content semantically. For example, when I think of my decision to play music to drown surrounding noises, I represent a mental relation (my thought of something) and specify its content semantically, in terms of a state of affairs in the world (playing music to drown noises). Likewise, when I think about what my friend said about that decision ('You still can't get used to *hoi polloi* and their simple ways', he said), I think about the thought he expressed yet specify its content semantically in terms of a fact he pointed to. But the explicit metathinking that matters most to metamentation and will be under scrutiny from now on is of the *thought-to-thought* sort, where both the identity and the content of the target thought (the thought thought about) are explicitly represented as thoughts. In this sense, one metathinks explicitly when one represents thoughts whose mental identity is fully represented as thoughts, as mental structures that represent, and their contents are specified in terms of other thoughts or are linked to other thoughts in various patterns. These alternative ways of specifying or linking thoughts generate distinct metamental routines, all versions of explicit metathinking. Without excluding other versions, I distinguish four, which I deem sufficient for my argument.

Reflective Metathinking

Instead of specifying a thought semantically, one may or need to specify it in terms of *other thoughts.* These other thoughts replace truth conditions as content specifiers. When a child thinks that what the teacher said is what she remembers her father saying, the child represents a thought (what the teacher said) in terms of (her memory of) another thought (what father said). When

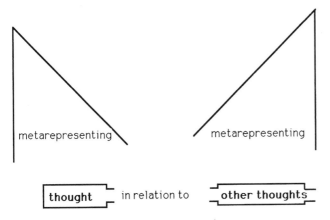

Figure 4.3
Reflective metathinking.

logicians think of modalities, such as necessity, in terms of the notion of possible worlds or when analytic geometers think of abstract properties of space in terms of algebraic concepts, they specify thoughts by thinking about or in terms of other thoughts. When one learns concepts from a dictionary, one metathinks about them in the same way. This is *reflective metathinking:* one categorizes a thought as thought (explicitly represents its mental identity) *and* specifies its content in terms of other thoughts (figure 4.3).

Quite often the reflective metathoughts have no intuitive or experiential grounding affording direct access to their truth conditions. In his perceptive analysis of this phenomenon, Dan Sperber (1997) notes that there are thoughts one can think with *only* by thinking about in terms of other thoughts. A good deal of thinking in science and philosophy is like that, rarely if ever touching ground with truth conditions. (This chapter may look like that at times. Even better, try Hegel, perhaps der most metametametareflektischen guy ever, for an almost-never-touching-semantic-base accomplishment.) Reflective metathinking operates in communication, education, indoctrination, scientific theorizing or argumentation, and often takes the form of sequential metamentation, whereby a metathinker deploys thoughts about other thoughts about still other thoughts. These deployments are run by generative routines. Perhaps the most prominent among them is the next.

Mimagination

What I mean by this mouthful is the following. We often rehearse mentally a decision, a plan of action, or a verbal exchange with somebody. We do it by contemplating possible situations (past, future, fictional) that fit, or even result from, what is mentally rehearsed. This is imagination. Often enough, the situations so imagined are populated with thoughts and other mental contents, ours or others'. In this latter case, we represent possible situations containing mental representings. This is metamental imagination, which I dub *mimagination* (for ease of processing). A case of mimagination would be my thinking now how I used to believe in adolescence that philosophers fantasize that they live their lives according to the precepts they preach and teach. (It is by exploiting such credulous romanticism that the profession still hooks up the young. I should know.) My current thinking thus imagines a situation populated by beliefs about other situations and facts, themselves populated by further thoughts.

This is different from *merely* imagining a quiet world in which dogs purr almost inaudibly instead of barking and suburbanites write poetry into the early morning instead of lawn-mowing at that time. In imagining such blessed but unattainable possibilities, I project situations that are different from a current one in respects that do *not* include further thinkings (which matinal lawn-mowers may not possess, not at that hour, anyway). Plans for action, such as transforming a current situation into another, are merely imaginative. Social plans and plots, which envisage changing situations in terms of what oneself or others would perceive or intend are mimaginative. Whereas the other routines reveal abilities to represent thoughts, mimagination fingers an ability to link up and iterate such representations of thoughts.

Metamental Predication

This routine builds directly on topical predication, said a chapter ago to operate a segmentation of information into an area of interest, the topic, subject to a mental take or attitude, the comment. Unlike topical predication, metamental predication goes one level up and produces thoughts as comments about other thoughts as topics. For example, when I think that it was the cat who licked the spilled wine (she likes heavy reds), someone having licked the spilled wine is the topic, and that someone being the cat is the comment. Or, put differently, I could have thought as follows: About someone having licked the wine (topic), I mentally comment that it was the (discerning) cat. This is topical, not metamental predication. But when I think that this illustration of the topic-comment structure may be less than apt (though I cannot resist red-wine-loving cats), I metathink thus: About this thought [that it was the cat who licked the spilled wine] intended as illustration (topic), I form the mental lament (a higher-level thought) that it may be less than apt (comment). This is topical predication at a reflexive level, hence *metamental* predication. Mere topical predication, as in the first example, is not metamental because its topic is a state of affairs—someone having licked the spilled wine. The comment fills an open slot (someone) in that state of affairs; it identifies someone as the cat. The second example is metamental because the mental comment, understood as a thought, is about another thought explicitly understood as a representation of a state of affairs.

As a piece of scientific analysis, the topic-comment distinction comes from linguistics, yet the pattern it points to and the mental ability that discerns the pattern (sentimental minding) were noted to precede language acquisition and may have been responsible for it (Bruner 1983, Hobson 1993b).

Metamental Perspective

Human thinkers can contemplate thoughts of actual and possible situations from different mental perspectives, often from the perspective of opposite thoughts. One can think how an event would look probable or a further thought would look plausible if thought of in some way, but less so or not at all if thought of in another way. Likewise, descriptions may be true or plans adequate, if represented one way rather than another. 'Look at it this way', we often say, proposing a change of mental stance. What is mentally represented often depends on how it is represented and hence on the mental perspective taken. This is mental but not yet metamental perspective-taking. The latter also requires (a) that one think explicitly of thoughts as mental representations (the sorts of structures that are about something), not merely in terms of what they represent, and (b) that such metathinking explicitly represent the thoughts in some fashion, under some mode of representation and not another.

The ability to adopt and shift metamental perspectives toward thoughts is exploited by lawyers or politicians discussing a line of defense or the selling of a legislative measure ('Let's see how this idea will fly if I represent it this rather than that way'), by detectives looking for a motive ('How would I look at the story if I were in his place? Does it look plausible?'), or by philosophers sensitive to how potential counterarguments shape the design and formulation of their arguments ('How would this argument look if objected to in this way? And how about that way?') Metamental perspective-taking is also familiar from daily experience, when people rehearse the pros and cons of a case to decide which strategy would work best, or to solve conflicts between preferences, or to judge rationalizations or justifications of actions, or to plan what to say, foresee what others would say, and think of further replies to that (Lehrer 1997). In so doing, metathinkers are not just taking and playing with mental perspectives but directing them at thoughts qua mental representations. This is metamental perspective-taking. It is what novelists, humorists, and many philosophers do for a living. They propose and formulate thoughts as explicit targets of mental attention, then play with other thoughts intended as distinct forms of representing them, and evaluate the force, pertinence or some other value of each of these forms.

2 Scheming to Metamind

The next move in the argument is to parse the metamental routines into simpler tasks that closely match those of interpretation. This match is best explained by the conjecture that the categories and schemes of metamentation emulated those of interpretation. It could even be that some metamental schemes evolved directly out of interpretation schemes. These are distinct claims. The one about matching is mostly conceptual, the one about emulation and evolution mostly empirical. The match between metamental and interpretive tasks becomes increasingly apparent as this section unfolds but is documented and defended with greater vigor and detail in chapters 5 through 7.

Preparing the Ground

To demonstrate the claims about matching and emulation, I will frame the analysis of metamental tasks and routines in terms of representation schemes linking up distinct categories. It is up to developmental psychology to determine whether interpretation is actually responsible for the categories and schemes of metamentation, and if so, to determine how the categories and schemes were implemented, in what psychological shape and order, and how these developments turned into metamentation. Not to prejudge that determination, my analysis stays minimal, abstract, and pitched at the level of tasks.

With an eye to the actual evolutionary and developmental dynamics sampled in the next few chapters, I single out those categories and schemes that highlight the main points of incidence of interpretation on metamentation. I also introduce the schemes in an order that highlights key historical moments of that incidence. So unfolded historically, the proposal is that there are several steps along the road to metamentation, each contributing something important to the final outcome. The schemes are meant conceptually to be necessary for metamentation, each building on earlier ones by adding new categories apt to handle new tasks. Only occasionally do I gesture toward actual acquisitions in the ontogenesis of metamentation. The reason is that until rather late in child development the parallel between interpretive and metamental tasks is an abstraction. In early childhood interpretation alone shows psychological reality and robust maturation. It would be unwise then to suppose that, by acquiring a new interpretive category or scheme, the child also acquires a bit of mental reflexivity—unless one countenances mere potentialities. It is only when several interpretive categories and schemes and other enabling conditions are in place, later in childhood, that reflexive thinking is likely to kick in as an *independent* mode of cognition. This is why it would be rather hard to document, at each ontogenetic step, the antecedents and components of metamental tasks. This is also why the reader is kindly invited to put up with the schematic story that follows and wait for details and illustrations in the next four chapters.

Why this exercise in abstraction? For both conceptual and psychological reasons. The conceptual reason is that I want to display as clearly as possible, step by step, what goes *analytically* into the tasks of metamentation and, in so doing, finger the domain of interpretation as the only one, among the domains of mental activity, which contains patterns of relations whose mental representation could serve as models for metamentation. One psychological reason is that I take interpretation to have evolved gradually among primates and in human childhood, and to have built just as gradually the opportunities and resources for metamentation. I want this *gradual build-up* to be obvious as a blueprint of the coevolutionary process. This is not to say that the process was neat and smooth. It rarely is in evolution or development. Instead, one can expect breaks and deviations in the phylogenesis and human ontogenesis of interpretation, with commensurate implications for mental reflexivity. Mental deficits, such as autism, are a case in point: as argued in chapter 8, autism fails at metamentation largely because it fails at interpretation. Mapping out step by step the links between interpretation and metamentation may help locating where the reflexivity of an autistic child was arrested and why.

Another psychological reason is that showing step by step what went into the make-up of metamentation allows occasional gesturing at other mental skills which interpretation designed or helped design along the way. Some of these skills—such as a sense of word reference or sharing meaning in communication—will be (briefly) acknowledged along the way. In addition, mental reflexivity has its own ontogenetic consequences, among which I count reflexive consciousness, reflexive selfhood, and reflexive morality. These developments are outside the brief of this essay and will be touched upon only lightly, yet their importance is obvious. I take such developments also to be distant by-products of the design work of interpretation in collaboration with mental rehearsal. Like metamentation, they do not come out of the blue, fully clothed, fully operational. Charting the gradual evolutionary road from interpretation to metamentation can help trace the routes along which these new acquisitions develop and identify which interruptions or deficits in interpretation, echoed in mental reflexivity, would explain abnormalities (if any) in reflexive consciousness, selfhood or morality.

Having thus prepared the ground, it is time to turn to the categories and schemes cumulatively built into the operation of a reflexive mind.

The Metaintentional Scheme

This scheme is the first, most basic, and most consequential in conceptual and evolutionary order. I distinguish three categories integrated by this scheme and describe them in terms general enough to accommodate competing accounts of their origin yet specific enough to capture what is unique about intentionality. The basic idea is this: a mental condition *a* is *represented as* being *about* another condition *b*, whether mental or worldly, only if (1) *a* is recognized to relate to *b* purposely or deliberately and (2) the relation itself is recognized as having a direction from *a* to *b* and (3) the relation is recognized as having *b* as target. Taken separately, the categories involved in this scheme are these:

• *Purposed relatedness* Mental conditions are recognized to relate to other conditions. Metamentally, one thought *a* is about another thought *b* only if *a* is related to *b* and a metathinker who forms the thought *a* recognizes its relation to *b*. The relatedness must be *purposed* in the sense that, whatever initiates or brings it about, it is its business or job to relate to something. A thought does not just happen to be about another thought or stumbles by accident into that relation. It is either so willed or intended or else achieves such relatedness in virtue of its formal and semantic properties.

• *Directedness* Mental conditions are recognized to have directedness. Metamentally, thoughts are recognized as being about other thoughts only if the former are recognized as being directed at something.

• *Target* Mental conditions are recognized as directed at targets. Metamentally, thoughts are recognized as being about other thoughts only if the former are recognized as directed at the latter as targets.

When a mental condition, such as a thought *a* is recognized to be purposely related to, directed at, and having another condition *b* as target, the relation of *a* to *b* is categorized as *intentional*. This categorization is encapsulated in the *metaintentional scheme:*

Metaintentional scheme A mental condition is categorized as *intentional* when it is purposely *related to* and *directed* at another condition as *target*.

Metamentation cannot work without the metaintentional scheme. One cannot metathink, semantically or reflectively, without representing a thought as purposely related to and directed at another thought as target. Nor can one comment on a mental topic or mimagine what one would think in a hypothetical situation unless the commenting thought were directed at the mental topic or the mimagination directed at the hypothetical situation. The metaintentional scheme is the distant core of metamentation, necessary but very far from sufficient. The subsequent schemes can be construed as variations on and additions to the metaintentional theme, some new and radical. To mark this pattern of development, I will emphasize (in italics) the novel categories in each subsequent scheme and leave unemphasized those inherited from previous schemes.

The Promental Scheme

The novelty of the promental scheme resides in the following category:

• *Promentality*   An intentional relation between a mental condition and a target is recognized as *promental* when the relation is understood to reflect other mental conditions or properties that affect dimensions of its intentionality, such as its direction or target.

Promentalized (so to speak), the metaintentional scheme becomes the following:

Promental scheme   A *promental* condition is categorized as relating directedly to target under the influence of other mental conditions.

Suppose I experience an emotion about an idea. (I am so excited about the idea that we metamentate because we interpret others that I am writing a whole book about it.) Suppose I also recognize that the emotion rests on *further* beliefs and desires, such that if the latter change, the emotion and its relation to the idea in question may also change. The recognition of promentality is the recognition of intentionality *modulated* by the recognition of intramental interactions that may affect it. One categorizes intentionality *as* promentality when one recognizes such intramental modulation.

Why *pro*mentality? Its justification is ontogenetic. The recognition of promentality by the very young child need not compute the *representing* properties of the intentional relations involved, which is what the metarepresentational scheme will do, later. (This is representing *as* conceptualized by an interpreter.) Mastery of the promental scheme affords in principle the recognition of a representation-free mentality. This possibility is needed to account for how a young child comes to realize that a mental condition, such as an emotion, is about something (is intentional) and how its aboutness may be affected by other mental conditions, without realizing that the emotion or other mental conditions represent and how they represent. The evolution of interpretation shows that recognizing the aboutness of a mental condition, as in seeing, is not yet recognizing that it represents, as in believing; apes and children younger than 3 recognize the former but not the latter. The realization that mental conditions represent is a crucial step toward mental reflexivity.

A representation-free recognition of promentality makes room for the possibility of an interim topical-predication scheme. Given the crucial role of topical predication in the build-up of mental reflexivity, I interpolate versions of topical predication, as they may interface in ontogeny with the schemes that build up metamentation. This interface is crucial in two interdependent respects: on the interpretation side, the interface is thought to explain the development of intersubjective interpretation and specifically of shared attention (Bruner 1983; Hobson 1993b, 1994); on the reflexivity side, the interface explains the possibility of the relational specification of the contents of metathoughts. So motivated, the *topical-predication* version of the promental scheme can be expected to yield a topic-comment recognition of promentality:

Topic-comment promental scheme   A promental condition is recognized as *commenting* on the target as *topic*.

In principle, this scheme operates when one (child but also adult) experiences a diffuse pleasure or emotion, as comment, about an image or experience, as topic, without computing the representational relations between comment and topic. Ontogenetically, this scheme is needed to capture the possibility that a young child might be able to join her recognition of promentality with that of topical predication prior to her mastery of the next scheme.

The Metarepresentational Scheme

The metarepresentation scheme embodies the understanding that mental conditions relate *representingly* to targets. This understanding factors in several new parameters of the representing relatedness. For economy, I group them under two headings:

• *Semantic value*   The metarepresenter understands that a mental condition (thought) can represent but also misrepresent its target (fact or another thought).

• *Variable representation*   The metarepresenter also understands that different mental conditions can relate to targets by interacting among themselves or by picking up different properties of targets, that mental conditions can represent targets in some ways but not others, that what counts as target may depend on what is represented and how.

The understanding that a mental condition represents packs together insights about semantic value and variable representation.

Metarepresentational scheme   A mental condition is understood to *represent* the target.

The ability embodied in the metarepresentational scheme enables a thinker to understand that a thought (including a thought about a thought) may be false or misdirected or that a thought can target a condition of the world (state of affairs) or of the mind (another thought) by interfacing with memories, beliefs, or imaginings. The same ability enables a thinker to realize that the same state of affairs can be represented differently or that the same thought can be thought about differently. Ontogenetically, it is when promental conditions are understood by the child to represent their targets that those conditions are thought of *as* mental representations. Just as the promental scheme enabled the child to see that mental conditions modulate intentionality, the metarepresentational scheme enables her to see that a different kind of mental conditions now modulate promentality itself. The categories of promentality and representationality thus reflect constraints and influences under which one recognizes intentionality. One can reasonably expect that, once in place, the metarepresentational scheme conspires with language to afford a *topical-predication* version as well:

Topic-comment metarepresentational scheme   A mental representation *comments* on target as *topic*.

Turned inwards, the mastery of the new scheme enables the reflexive thinker to represent flexibly and creatively thoughts in the topic and comment positions. Finally, there is a scheme that governs the dynamic deployments of metathoughts.

Generative scheme   A metathinker also recognizes and tracks *iterations, extended sequences,* and *multiple embeddings* of mental representations about other mental representations (about still other mental representations).

Iterative metathinking or escalating metamental predications or mimagination would be unthinkable without the generative scheme. How else could one form beliefs about one's beliefs or desires or evaluate sequences of conflicts of interest and preferences or the like? Here is one example to compute with this scheme: I am just thinking about what Plato would think if he were to learn (and thus form the thought) that, centuries later, many philosophers would think that he imagined the cleverest arguments for the innateness of knowledge of logic and mathematics. And what do you think Aristotle would have thought about that? While you compute these propositions, I have one

last category to introduce. And mighty crucial it is, since it lies at the heart
of metamentation.

Explicit Metathought

The tasks handled by the metarepresentational scheme and its successors
exploit a common category that can be regarded as the core unit of metamentation. I call it the category of *explicit metathought*. Metamentation works
solely with thoughts which it recognizes explicitly as mental representings,
that is, as mental structures that represent facts or other thoughts. Mental
representings related to other thoughts will be called *explicit metathoughts*.
With the exception of implicit metathinking (which represents facts and only
implicitly thoughts of them), the other metamental routines work with explicit
metathoughts. One cannot form reflexively a thought *a* about another thought
b, as one does in metamental predication, unless *a* is recognized as a representing structure directed at or linked to another representing structure, *b*. Nor
can one mimagine situations populated by the thoughts of other people or
one's own unless those thoughts are recognized as thoughts, that is, as mental
structures that represent. This is the explicit recognition of the *mental identity*
of thoughts qua thoughts. Equally crucial is the *relational specification* of the
contents of the thoughts metarepresented, whereby thoughts can be commented on, embedded in, or otherwise related to, further thoughts. It is for
these reasons that explicit metathoughts may be said to be the currency in
which metamentation does its business. Thus:

Explicit metathoughts   An *explicit metathought* is a thought represented
as a mental representation related to (in terms of, about, commenting on,
linked with) other mental representations.

So much for the key categories and schemes inhabiting the routines of
metamentation for the time being. Their story will be expanded and further
illustrated in the chapters that follow. The aim at this point was to identify
the metamental tasks conjectured to emulate those of interpretation. Time,
therefore, to say a few words about the very notion of emulation.

3   Task Emulation

It would be appropriate to introduce the notion of task emulation through
examples first examined by the psychologist who pioneered this direction of
analysis, Lev Vygotsky. Self-regulation was said a chapter ago to begin
socially as regulation by adults, first in a physiological form and sentimental
mode, later in more cognitive forms. Interpretation enables and structures this

regulation and, in the later and more cognitive stages, achieves it by shared attention and taking the perspective of another (Tomasello, Kruger, and Ratner 1993). During this process the child first echoes the vocalizations, words, and postures of the adult but later, when capable of mental rehearsal and imaginative dialogue with self, replaces them with self-directed verbalizations and thoughts. This replacement completes the internalization of regulation. The tasks, those of regulative interpretation, may initially remain the same but the means change. As task executors, the child's self-directed verbalizations and thoughts can be said to emulate the earlier adult instructions directed at the child. Later, such self-directed verbalizations and thoughts may do jobs other than regulatory—new tasks modeled on the old regulatory ones. Another example of Vygotsky's, cited in chapter 1 (sections 2 and 4), was that of the grasping movement turned indicatory gesture and then emulated as referring. The internalization process thus starts with interpretation converting a physical movement into a signifying gesture and concludes with the latter emulated as reference.

It is on this basis that I suggested at the end of chapter 1 that internalization operates in two phases: in the first phase, interpretation maps some behavioral or observable relation into a scheme correlating several interpretive categories; in the second phase, driven by pressures to rehearse it mentally in a cause-causation script, the interpretive scheme is reenacted, possibly generalized, and used in new tasks—in a word, it is emulated. The internalization process can thus be parsed as follows:

• Certain tasks (e.g., regulation of behavior, gesturing) are carried out in one domain (social) by certain means (those of child-adult interpretation).
• The tasks are later reenacted and executed in mental rehearsal, first in the same terms, later with some terms changed (e.g., self replaces the other in regulation).
• Still later other terms are changed (thoughts instead of interpretive attributions) and eventually the tasks are different (judging one's ideas or plans replaces regulation of behavior), and so is their domain (thinking about some topic, instead of interpreting in the social domain).
• Yet the new tasks still fit the same pattern and display a similar structure (task emulation): for example, one comes to metathink in formats similar to those in which one interprets others, just as in earlier stages one comes to regulate oneself in formats (e.g., dialogue with self) similar to those in which one was regulated by others (dialogue with others).

The last three steps in this process are about task emulation: they capture the conversion and reenactment of schemes of interpretive categories into new schemes performing new jobs in formats similar to the original ones. Further examples can help fortify this diagnosis. The visually friendly Venn diagrams were and still are widely used in the teaching of logic and thus came to shape the ways in which many people think of sets and their properties. Likewise, people with some background in logic tend to think of, even visualize, necessary and sufficient conditions in terms of logical implications represented by arrows or again in terms of Venn diagrams. Science is full of models from one domain imported to conceptualize items in another domain (hydraulic pump for heart, the billiard ball model of physical causation, the planetary model of the atom, and so on). Analogies and metaphors are also potent task importers (ways of thinking) from one domain to another.

Having clarified and illustrated the hypothesis of task emulation, let me outline the work it is expected to do in the next chapters. The work proceeds along three tracks. One is *conceptual* and aims to show that metamental categories and schemes of representation are similar and at times isomorphic to those of interpretation. Explicitly thinking about thoughts calls for identifying thoughts as *mental structures* that *represent something*. Such thought identification emulates tasks of interpretation. Each of the emphasized words refers to categories that initially belong to interpretation. Interpretation alone is in the business of categorizing and judging how other minds relate to the world. If one replaces 'other minds' with 'one's thoughts', one gets the conceptual side of the emulation thesis: reflexive thinking is in the business of categorizing and judging how one's thoughts relate to each other and their targets.

Another and farther-reaching track is *evolutionary* and aims to show that there are good reasons why metamention emulated interpretation. These reasons explain the wider internalization process, of which emulation was said to be the second phase. Among these reasons: self regulation; the self anticipating social evaluation by others of what self thinks, says, and does; instruction by imitation and perspective-taking; task-specific cooperation and social problem solving; and so on. Each of these social endeavors relies on interpretation. What they have in common is pressuring the child to rehearse mentally her interpretations of others and herself prior to engaging in the appropriate social action. In this way conditions and opportunities are created for reenacting and reutilizing those imagined interpretations for other purposes, such as thinking about one's own images or thoughts.

The task emulation must also be documented *psychologically,* whence the third track of my argument. The psychological evidence bears particularly on child development. The ontogenesis of child interpretation seems to march in step with that of metamention, as glimpsed from the children's mentalistic talk, social planning and problem solving, self regulation, forms of social and cultural learning, as well as from deficits in interpretation reflected in deficits in metamentation, as in the case of autism. Through the convergence of these three tracks of analysis, the notion of task emulation is intended to fortify the possibility that humans metamentate because, and often in the formats in which, they initially interpret others.

To sum up, first distinguished were several routines as sequences of tasks at work in metamentation. The conceptual analysis distilled these routines into several schemes made out of distinct categories. This analytic exercise was meant to lay bare the key joints of the infrastructure of metamentation in order to mount a systematic and historical inquiry into how the infrastructure came about and why. This inquiry revolves around the possibility of task emulation from one domain (interpretation) to another (metamentation). Such task emulation is carried out solely by minds that recognize, represent, and rehearse mind-world relations as a prelude to acting causally on such relations. These are minds that interpret other minds. It is in terms set up by interpretation that some of these minds, the intersubjective or Humean ones, end up reflexive, minding themselves. This is what the next chapters endeavor to show.

Chapter 5

Situated Minding

Section 1 introduces a distinction that needs to be clear if the emulation argument is to have any force: it is the distinction between the minds that relate to the world (all minds) and those that also recognize such relatedness (very few). Only the latter (interpreting) minds can become reflexive by emulating their interpretation of other minds. Section 2 begins the emulation story by arguing that the metaintentional scheme emulates the earliest interpretive categories of agency, gaze following, and joint gaze. Section 3 turns to the promental scheme. How did it enter the evolutionary process? It is a crucial question because the grasp of promentality seems to mark a decisive break between interactive and intersubjective interpretation and, as a result, between ape and human minds. The section outlines the earliest and fully intentional recognition of promentality, in shared attention, and asks how it came about. Following the argument of chapter 3, the answer, full of implications for metamentation, explores the noncognitive roots of intersubjective interpretation.

1 Minds That Do and Minds That Don't

The distinction may have been lurking behind much of what was said so far but, to be on the safe and clear side, I want to bring it to the fore as explicitly as possible, before the demonstration takes off. On the one hand, minds relate to the world. On the other hand, interpretation represents mind-world relations. These are two distinct truths, intertwined (very rarely) as follows. It is because minds relate to the world that some (apparently only primate) minds come to interpret such relations in a systematic fashion by means of dedicated, specialized skills. To interpret mind-world relations is to recognize and represent them in a manner appropriate to social action. Just *having* mind-world relations offers no grounds and no opportunities for their recognition and representation. Without representing mind-world relations, there are no grounds and no opportunities to develop reflexive thinking. Let me parse these truths more carefully.

Most animal minds are *goal-directed* and hence *intentional,* in the sense that their internal conditions are systematically linked to goals and other states of the world. I say 'hence' because I think, and argued elsewhere, that intentionality evolved to service goal-directedness (Bogdan 1988, 1994). This is to say that an organism's mental conditions are about conditions of the world because the latter either are or point to its goals. Primate minds alone seem to *recognize* intentionality and human minds alone also *recognize* its representational form. These are minds that interpret. But it does not follow that interpreting minds recognize and understand the *intrinsic* properties of agency or intentionality or other mind-world relations, as cognitive science would. Primate interpreters do not know how agency or perception work, or how visual images or memories are formed, or what makes these cognitive abilities and their outputs intentional; nor do they care. Interpreting minds recognize only those aspects of mind-world relations which bear practically on their goals and strategies (Bogdan 1997). This conjecture has the implication that it is the practical aspects of mind-world relations that interpreters care about which end up emulated in metamentation. A further implication is that metaminders would know as much or little about the intrinsic physiological or psychological *nature* of the thoughts they think about as they know about the nature of the propositional attitudes and other mind-world relations attributed to others. If metamentation leads to reflexive consciousness and reflexive selfhood, then the same should be true of the knowledge one has of these mental acquisitions as well. Intriguing as they are, these are implications left undeveloped in this essay.

So much for the view from outside. Now the view from inside. Animal minds represent their goals as states of the world they aim to bring about. Through sensations and other signals, some animal minds may be aware of having goals in the form of desires. This, however, is not the same as distinctly representing goal-directedness or desiring as *relations* to the world. Many animal minds can also recognize *what* they perceive or remember, and may even be aware of being in a perception or remembering mode, yet they fail to *recognize* perceivings and rememberings as *relations* to the world. Only interpretation affords the recognition of such relations. The same is true of sundry inner experiences, ranging from emotions and feelings to being conscious. Such experiences function as signals of *having* or *being* in some internal condition related to the world in some mode, such as desiring or remembering. Yet the experiences themselves, including conscious ones, need not reveal or represent those relations as such. It takes interpretation to deliver the recognition of such relations.

The distinctions noted so far are meant to counter the expectation that a mind may turn metaintentional or metarepresentational simply because it relates to the world in some way. There is no such linkage, as comparative analyses among species amply show. Nor (perhaps more surprisingly) does a mind turn reflexive simply because it monitors or introspects its internal conditions, as argued more vigorously in the next chapter. The missing link is interpretation, a very rare aptitude among the many sorts of animal minds that are intentional, representational, even self-monitoring. The minds possessing the intersubjective version of the aptitude also get to symbolize, use a natural language, and metamentate. They get to be Mims because they were Moms in the first place.

Meet Mom and Mim
To illustrate the journey from interpretation to metamentation and engage the reader's intuitions, two fictional characters will pop up at some key junctures. Meet Mom and Mim. They are generic representatives of the (primate) minds that can do all the things noted in earlier paragraphs, which is why they mark the road to reflexivity. Mom has a mind that minds other minds—the minder of minds or interpreter. Mim has a mind that minds its mind—the mind minder or metaminder and, eventually, the reflexive thinker. Both Mom and Mim are composite characters whose traits are culled from many sources, ranging from ordinary observation to the evolutionary, ethological, and psychological literature cited throughout this work. The story of the next three chapters is about Mom's gradual meta-morphosis into Mim. In the early, metaintentional stages of this process (next section) Mom is an ape, after which she turns into a human child. Although Mim grows out of Mom sometime in late childhood and becomes fully reflexive perhaps as late as early adolescence, the logic of my inquiry requires displaying, at each significant phylo- and ontogenetic step, bits and pieces (however virtual) of the future Mim as they take partial or potential shape in Mom's mind. The figures, where Mom and Mim display their evolving talents, will further explain the plot and chart the growth of reflexivity in Mom's interpretive mind.

2 Metaintentionality

Metaintentionality is the fulcrum of it all. The human mind would not be what it is without its ability to recognize intentionality. Among others, education, language learning, and metamentation depend on it. As with other evolved abilities, the recognition of intentionality is unlikely to come in one piece and suddenly. According to the last chapter, three parameters are essential to the metaintentional scheme because only their joint representation yields a necessary (though insufficient) basis for metamentation. So let us explore what the categories of these parameters could emulate in interpretation.

The candidates for the origin of these parameters, as emulation source, should meet some plausibility requirements. In the light of the debates (canvassed in chapters 1 and 2) about the domains best poised to spawn novelties in primate mentation and drive its evolution, favored should be the candidates that a primate is likely to encounter and recognize *first* and for the *best* of evolutionary reasons. The candidates should also pass a test of *fit,* so that they blend naturally with the remaining parameters of intentionality. Finally, the candidates should pass the *practical* test, distilled from chapters 1 and 2, according to which only categories and representation schemes, mentally acted upon in view of instrumental intervention of the cause-causation sort, can create a blueprint or model for the evolution of new mental abilities, such as the reflexive ones. This is to say that a metaintentional category emulates a prior category only if the object of the latter is the object of causal knowledge (of the cause-causation sort). This said, let us proceed.

Purposed Relatedness Emulates Agency

The first parameter is that of purposed relatedness among thoughts as a condition of thoughts being *about* thoughts. This aboutness relation *begins* (but does not end) with a thought being purposely related to another. So the question arises as to where a sense of such relatedness comes from. Given the requirements just stated, what would be the most plausible blueprint for the recognition of purposed relatedness? I submit that the answer is the category of *goal-directed agency.* It is a category that allows an interpreter to represent a subject as a self-caused agent who relates goal-directedly to the world. The relation is systematic, because agency is identified across various contexts and from various clues, and is obviously purposed. Importantly, agency can be recognized in isolation, without direction or goal: such recognition makes sense because it would tell an interpreter that a subject is alive, not dead or inert, or awake and not asleep. The recognition of agency is also uniquely qualified to fit the recognition of the direction of a relation and of its target, for agency is normally directed and targeted. The cognitive priority of the category of agency is also plain, for nothing is more vital to an organism than being able to distinguish between an inert thing and one that moves and has designs on the world and on other organisms. Finally, the link to the deliberate causation of a causal relation is also obvious. Having registered another's agency, nothing is more vital to an organism than doing something about it, such as manipulating it. Most species cannot do such things, for lack of generative causal knowledge, but some primate species can, at least in the social domain. Those species stand a good chance of forming a specialized category of agency, whose use in mental rehearsal would make it an object of mental manipulation and thus a distant but vital model of its metaintentional emulator, purposed relatedness. Thus:

First emulation   The category of purposed relatedness emulates the category of goal directed agency.

There could other models for the category of purposed relatedness. Causal knowledge is one. As argued in chapter 2, its expectation version is too weak and general, while the generative version may actually piggyback on knowledge of intentionality. Also, a causal relation is often indeterminate about what counts as cause and effect, which is not true of goal-directed agency. A much stronger candidate would be knowledge of *one's own* agency (Tomasello 1995). Like other categories that represent mind-world relations from inside, as self-world relations, it is not clear that they emerge before the other-directed categories. Most don't, as seen later. As important (in the light of the practical test) is the fact that self agency is not a target of generative causation and manipulation, certainly not before someone else's agency. This said, it should be admitted that knowledge of agency is widespread among animal species and by itself buys an interpreter relatively little. On balance, though, I opt for the category of agency as emulable model for the category of purposed relatedness because it fits the requirements for a plausible candidate and is also supported by some facts.

The category of agency is primate-wide and possibly brain localized (Baron-Cohen 1995, 32–38; Leslie 1994; Premack 1990). It affords a dynamical representation of others as self-propelled movers and also a relational view of them as agents linked to the world. It may predate the recognition of any other form of relatedness. The primate kids recognize the agency of others soon enough to survive. This recognition frames a subject-world relatedness without yet discerning its direction or target. This is why there is little interpretation in recognizing just agency. Many species recognize agency but use context and their goals and perceptions to determine its direction and target. Those species do not interpret. This is why Mom, the minder of other minds, is barely an interpreter at this stage and why her distant reflexive emulator Mim is not even a blip on the evolutionary radar (see figure 5.1).

It takes more than a sense of agency to get the expertise to interpret; and it takes more of that expertise to represent direction and target. Although the category of agency is the bedrock on which interpretation stands, it is the categories of direction and target which explain what is unique about primate

Explaining the Mom and Mim Figures

Some of the figures in this chapter and the next are meant to provide some timely illustrations of some main moments in the story of emulation. Each such figure is divided in two: the left side illustrates the interpretation relation between Mom (minder of other minds or interpreter) and Sub (the subject) in versions that may have had an impact on the evolution of metamentation; the right side portrays Mom's mental rehearsal with the interpretive ability acquired at a particular stage. It is an open question when mental rehearsal shows up in primate phylogeny and human ontogeny and when it begins to operate with interpretive categories and schemes. When it does, mental rehearsal becomes an incubator of metamentation and the interpreter becomes a potential or virtual reflexive thinker, a Mim. For long phylogenetic and ontogenetic segments, however, there is no real Mim. The suggestion, rather, is to contemplate a virtual Mim whose future metamental gear is assembled gradually with (almost) each significant novelty in interpretation. It is in late childhood (and also late in chapter 6) that the metarepresentational Mom, handling propositional attitudes, is on her way to become reflexive and metathink explicitly. Until then the fragments of interpretation pile up in ever closer yet still virtual approximations of metamentation. This is why the speculations about such approximations remain confined mostly to the relevant figures. When the real Mim shows up, her virtual shadow exits gracefully, as does the argument of this essay.

So much for the general idea. Now some details of illustration. The figures employ several symbols.

'——(' stands for the form of interpretation typical of some specified phylogenetic or ontogenetic stage: in the early figures, it will be situated and interactive interpretation (prehuman primates); in later figures, situated and intersubjective interpretation and then unsituated interpretation (human children).

'——' stands for a subject-world relation or fragment thereof, such as a relation without direction or with direction or with direction but no target.

'-----' stands for direct perception (by either interpreter or subject).

'oooooo' stands for representation in mental rehearsal (only on the left side).

Other symbols will be introduced as we go along.

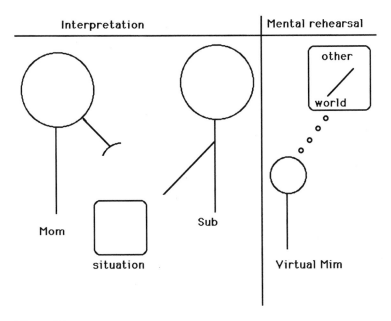

Figure 5.1

Interpreting relatedness. What Mom interprets at this stage is just the subject's agency, barely a soupçon of a relation to the world. Mom fills in the direction and target in terms of her own expectation and perception in a context. One would guess that when Mom (say a very young primate) mentally rehearses what to do about a subject's agency (assuming she can do that), she might mix a memorized representation of agency, produced by a specialized interpretive skill, with memories of the individuals concerned and the usual contexts of social interaction. The virtual Mim would thus categorize just the thrust of relatedness, as it were. It is important to note that relatedness as a minimal target of interpretation is domain-situated (in the sense of chapter 1, section 2) and therefore cannot be recognized outside a perceived situation. This has the implication that Mom would (if capable) mentally rehearse with memorized or projected representations of perceptual situations displaying a subject's relatedness as a distillation of agency. The same will be true of other novelties in situated interpretation until late in human childhood.

mentation and (later) human language and metamentation. Among the competencies apt to form such categories, interpretation alone stands a reasonable conceptual and evolutionary chance: conceptually, because it alone structures its domain in patterns that correspond to direction and target; evolutionarily, because it alone has reasons to structure its domain in such patterns and hence to select for the right categories; also because, in humans, interpretation alone experiences ontogenetic pressures to make such categories available to mental rehearsal, language use, and metamentation. True to form, the evolutionary process is laborious, baroque, piecemeal, and involving many developments outside interpretation. What follows is necessarily an impoverished sample of it but good enough for our purposes.

Direction Emulates Access, Orientation

Recognizing agency buys an interpreter useful information but not enough. Suppose the interpreter needs to ascertain the subject's awareness of a specific event and anticipate his action and its direction. New subject-world relations or rather new features of such relations must be discerned. Recognizing cognitive access, such as seeing, or its absence, is a good start. Sensitivity to bodily posture can do almost as much and also reveal the rough orientation of action. Recognizing gaze would pack these clues together and even predict what is about to happen and where. Thus, the next emulation step:

Second emulation   The category of direction emulates the category of gaze and bodily posture.

The sense of a subject's relatedness to the world is now constrained more tightly and is thus more informative. Like other species, primates recognize eyes but may be among the few or even the only ones that recognize gaze, follow its direction, and factor these exploits into their plans and actions (Baron-Cohen 1995, 38–43; Butterworth 1991, 1995; Byrne and Whiten 1991; Povinelli 1996; Povinelli and Eddy 1996; Tomasello and Call 1997, chapter 10). As a result, the relatedness revealed by agency has a sharper identity and a direction, though not yet a target. Before seeing how the target problem is solved, note that the category of direction passes the practical test of (generative) causal knowledge. An interpreter recognizes agency because she can exercise her causal powers on it to cause further causal relations. The same is true of direction: ape interpreters were observed to manipulate causally one's line of regard in order to prevent one from noticing something or to induce one to look in a direction in order to distract his attention from something else (Whiten and Byrne 1988a) (see figure 5.2).

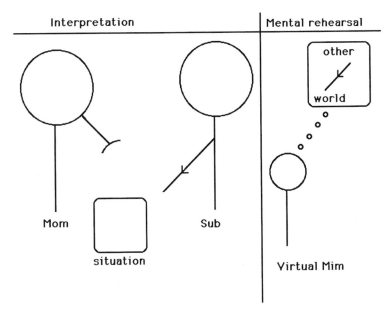

Figure 5.2
Interpreting direction. The direction of the subject's agency is now registered by Mom. It has an arrow in the middle, not at the end, because the target of agency is not yet recognized. As a Mom who mentally rehearses, the virtual Mim would now supposedly categorize and mentally manipulate the direction of relatedness.

Target Recognition Emulates Gaze Following, More or Less

Recognizing bodily orientation or direction of gaze need not specify what the subject aims at as goal. The interpreter must also *follow* gaze to a point that reveals the target of an action as its goal, say as the first object in the line of regard (Povinelli and Eddy 1996). Gaze following marks a definite advance in representing one's relatedness to specific items and thus provides a much sharper view of its possible aboutness. There is still plenty of indeterminacy—a problem long known to philosophers working on causal accounts of perception and reference. The ape interpreter may solve the indeterminacy *subjectively* and *contextually* by bringing in her perspective on the subject's goal and counting on a perceptually shared world and its clues and also on expectations about conspecific behavior and shared vital goals. I mark this interim stage as follows:

Third emulation   The category of target recognition emulates the category of gaze following. The recognition is still subjective, but somewhat less.

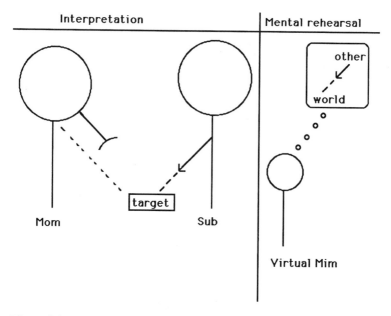

Figure 5.3
Interpreting target subjectively. The target of agency is now determinable but only through the interpreter's perception, not by a specialized interpretive category. Since interpretation metamorphoses only its specialized categories and schemes into metamentation, the virtual Mim is not much better off than before. At best, and of course virtually, she may find a way to coordinate the specialized representation of directed relatedness with some nonspecialized (perceptual or imagistic) determination of target.

Unlike agency and its direction, represented fairly invariantly, across clues and contexts, courtesy of *specialized* skills of interpretation, the recognition of a goal as target seems to remain subjective and unspecialized. Still, the last half-scheme is a step forward. Compared with gaze recognition, gaze following allows a finer-grained tracking along the line of regard and a sharper sense of direction which further reduces the number of possible targets (figure 5.3).

Gradual Desubjectivization
I pause briefly to signal a pattern in the emulation process. I interpolated the interim phase for two reasons. One is to get as fine-grained a conceptual match between metaintentional parameters and their interpretational sources as can be sensibly expected. The other is to track step-by-reasonable-step the phylogenetic unfolding of the match in order to map out a pattern of gradual *desubjectivization* of interpretation in the direction of *specialized* skills that

do their job *invariantly and objectively,* irrespective of the vagaries of context and of the interpreter's perceptual and behavioral coordinates. Only through such skills does interpretation become an independent mode of cognition and a launching pad for reflexivity. Reflexivity emulates interpretive categories that specialize in the invariant tracking of relevant aspects of subject-world relations. Those categories begin in a situated mode, which is where our story is right now. A warning, though: desubjectivization and specialization need not entail unsituatedness. Chimpanzees may have the specialized skills to follow gaze, irrespective of contextual variations, yet employ these skills only in current perception, relative to environmental clues. Reflexivity builds on unsituated interpretation, which prehuman primates lack.

With this clarification on board, let us move on with the emulation story. The grasp of the direction of agency got sharper and more objective when several types of clues (bodily posture, behaviors, visual access) were integrated. This is how the recognition of direction emerged as invariant *relative to* these types of clues. What would yield an invariant recognition of target and thus further de-subjectivize its identification? Evolution seems again to have favored a *social* solution to this problem.

Sharper Targeting Emulates Joint Gaze
The solution, quite revolutionary in its implications, involves a *joining* of gazes, achieved when several lines of regard converge on items of mutual interest. Joining gazes operates as a sort of equivalence relation that may tell interpreters and subjects what is the *same target* in a social context. When interpreter and subject gaze in the same direction and exchange gazes to ensure shared relatedness in the same direction, and follow this exchange by appropriate actions, a new and powerful formula emerges whereby a subject's goal or some other mutually acknowledged state of the world can be finely and objectively triangulated. It is an interpretive formula that leads to new opportunities for coordination of action, cooperative ventures, and causal manipulation—all seen in Gomez's study of the gorilla who gets the trainer to open the latch (chapter 2, section 3). Joint gazers recognize that a condition of the subject relates to a definite condition of the world as target of relatedness. Thus:

Fourth emulation   The category of target emulates the category of joint gaze.

It is unclear whether joint gaze secures an intentional target and grounds a sort of protoreference ability. Suppose it does. How objective and fine-grained would that be? Joint determination of target would buy as much objectivity and fine grain of reference as befits standard group activities. This is to say that a target could be nailed down by joint gaze *to the extent* that its identity is fixed by properties widely shared and recognized among conspecifics in standard contexts of sensorimotor interaction. For example, nuts can be represented as targets to which others are related *as* items-to-be-cracked-and-eaten or thrown-at-others; conspecifics can be recognized as targets that afford help, grooming, deceiving, and the like. This may be the best that joint-gaze interpretation can do for the ape mind (figure 5.4).

Yet prudence is in order. Evolution need not be that forthcoming and neatly fit interpretational parameters into a complete scheme of prereflexive mentation. It may take more interpretive knowledge than the apes possess to acquire the *entire* metaintentional scheme. My account, open to this possibility, is committed solely to the notion that the category of intentionality emerges out of the joint grasp of relatedness, its direction, and target. It is still unclear whether joint gaze is available to apes and, if so, to what extent. Gomez's studies (1991, 1994, 1996b) suggest that apes engage in joint gaze and can secure a somewhat precise focus on shared targets. But is the focus objective, invariant, or is it supplied by the interpreter's unspecialized perception and coordinated with the subject's? There are skeptics who prefer the second option. Tomasello and Call talk of agency and direction but not of full intentionality, construed as relation to a target (1997, 203; see also Povinelli 1996). What matters here is not the joint-gaze identification of a target but how subjective or self-centered it is. Mutual coordination of perception, securing public accessibility, is one thing; having the category of target is another. The situatedness and interactivity of ape interpretation hint at overwhelming subjectivity and lack of a specialized category of intentional target, in which case the ape mastery of the metaintentional scheme remains incomplete.

Thus Far

It takes the joint recognition of three parameters—relatedness, its direction, and target—to conceptualize intentionality. For conceptual and evolutionary reasons, interpretation looks as the most plausible supplier of the categories that add up to the representation of intentionality. Even though metamentation is far beyond the reach of the metaintentional scheme, it would be impossible without it. This makes evolutionary sense: many acquisitions stand on the shoulders of others to make still others possible, as seen next.

3   Getting in Touch

The possibility of metamentation depends on the recognition of promentality, according to chapter 4. It is the recognition that intentionality reflects the

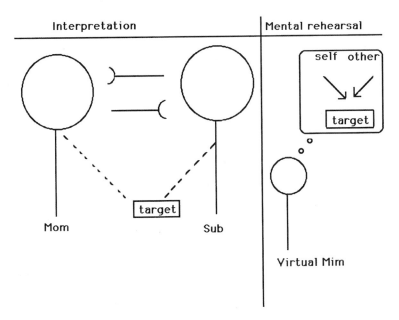

Figure 5.4
Interpretation by joint gaze. Interpretation now affords seeing a condition (of a subject) as being systematically directed at another condition (of the world) as specific target. Although the interpreter's and the subject's direct perception are also involved in zooming on a target, their work is integrated into a specialized joint-gaze scheme. A distant and minimal blueprint for the representation of a protoreference relation may be now in place. It is distant and minimal because intersubjectivity and topical predication may also be needed to bring about a full recognition of reference, and they are not yet in the phylogenetic picture. The recognition of visible (gestural) protoreference may be available to some apes (Rumbaugh and Savage-Rumbaugh 1996). This would be a novel, though not yet intramental, employment of an interpretive skill. Joint gaze is also the first interpretive category that coordinates self and other in determining the aboutness of a mental relation—a distant precursor of the mind-world-mind pattern of interpretation emulated in metamentation.

impact of various conditions inside another mind. This sense of promentality
is in turn part and parcel of mental sharing—the triangular mind-world-mind
pattern at the heart of intersubjective interpretation. I see *mental sharing* as
involving three distinct but interacting families of abilities: to recognize and
share experiences, emotions, stances, or attitudes about something; to recognize such sharing; and to use this shared recognition to convey or exchange
information about what is shared. There is an interpretive category that best
encapsulates the novelty and power of mental sharing. It is *shared attention,*
aka joint attention (see Moore and Dunham 1995 for a recent survey). I begin
with a profile of shared attention, briefly review several competing accounts
of its ontogenesis, and, as could be expected from chapter 3, settle for the
sentimental option.

Attention to Attention

As a visual version of mental sharing, shared attention may be described as
joint gaze plus intersubjectivity. It is a crude but useful description, with some
empirical support. Shared attention matures later than joint gaze. It begins as
joint gaze (Corkum and Moore 1995) but later draws not only on gaze or
pointing but also on awareness and emotional reactions as means to recognize
attention, its direction and target (Baron-Cohen 1991, 1995; Bruner 1983;
Hobson 1993a, 1993b, 1994). Whereas joint-gaze recognition (like other
categories of interactive interpretation) views others solely as "agents of
action," shared attention (like other intersubjective categories) construes them
as "agents of contemplation" (Harris 1996, 208–211; Mundi, Sigman, and
Kasari 1993, 188). In virtue of its intersubjectivity, shared attention has
declarative force, in that it shares information or experiences and signals a
stance or attitude toward them. On this account, the *cognitive* component of
shared attention overlaps considerably, if not entirely, with joint gaze. So the
question is where the novelty, the *intersubjectivity* of attention, comes from.
There are several answers in the literature. A brief look at them is useful
because it is the intersubjective novelty that explains the uniqueness of human
interpretation and, by implication, of metamentation.

Angles on Attention

There is a *modular* account of shared attention. Backed by some psychological
and neurological data, it posits an innate and specialized ability to detect and
share attention intersubjectively (Baron-Cohen 1995, Leslie 1994). Intersubjectivity is thus built into the cognitive work of the module that houses the
ability. The modular view is strengthened by the weakness of alternative
options. *Learning* is not a very plausible option. How would an infant learn

to recognize attention over and above recognizing gaze? And if gaze recognition and gaze following are innate in primates, as they seem to be, why wouldn't the recognition of attention be as well? Which it appears to be, on account of its tight ontogenetic schedule. The *theory-of-mind* approach (Gopnik and Wellman 1994, Gopnik and Meltzoff 1997) might not be much better off at this early phase. The reason is its vague mix of minimal nativism and learning. Whence a dilemma: if the theory-of-mind view places too much emphasis on learning, it inherits the faults of the latter; but if it builds too much into the innate basis (e.g., by assuming the innateness of gaze and person recognition), then it may sing a modular song, after all. There are still other accounts that construe child interpretation in general as metarepresentation (Leslie 1988, 1991) or simulation (Harris 1993). Whatever their merits for later stages, these accounts seem literally premature for infants and young children and not particularly apt to handle shared attention in ways much different from the foregoing alternatives.

The modular account is not without its problems. Positing modules may be justly feared as an ad hoc way to find a home in the mental architecture for every new function that looks specialized and innate. The fear grows in this case because the neuroscientific evidence for a shared-attention module is not very compelling, at least so far. Since the modularity of joint-gaze recognition is better established, one may conclude that it is the *sharedness* of attention that remains unaccounted for in modular terms.[1] Baron-Cohen (1995, 46–50) takes the shared-attention mechanism to exploit "inordinately" the gaze-following mechanism; it could also so exploit the joint-gaze mechanism. How much inordinateness is that? Isn't shared attention, after all, joint gaze plus intersubjectivity?

To sum up, all we have so far are gaze-tracking skills, perhaps modular. The sharedness of attention and its intersubjectivity are still up for grabs. So the thought arises that instead of a shared-attention module mysteriously infused with intersubjectivity, there could be the good old gaze-recognition devices tapping a *separate* family of skills that secure mental sharing. (Not a rarity in evolution.) The proposals sampled next suggest *noncognitive* bases for mental sharing. I begin with an account of motor projection, which goes in the right direction but not far enough. Then I consider and opt for the sentimental line.

Motor Props
According to the *motor planning imitation* view, specialized sensorimotor skills are tapped for interpretive duties. The idea, developed by Andrew Meltzoff and Alison Gopnik (1993), is that the interpreter's motor plans and

later more calculative plans are mapped into the subject's behaviors, thus giving rise to the categories of simple desire and later intention. (Along this route may also lie the strategy of simulating the attitudes of others.) The infant's movements and postures, monitored internally by proprioception, may thus be treated as equivalent to the movements and postures noticed in others. The projection would then map the perceived behavior of a subject into the interpreter's impressions of internal states (such as pains and feelings) and of motor plans and desires. In this way the sensorimotor imitation establishes a "like-me" bodily equivalence that allows transfers of mental conditions or experiences. The earliest such transfer may be facial imitation, which is innate and operative no later than one hour after birth. Facial imitation may be the avenue by which the emotional state of an adult can be transmitted to the infant and then mapped on her own emotional states (Meltzoff and Gopnik 1993; Mundy, Sigman, and Kasari 1993; Russell 1996, part 3).

This interesting view proposes an early *noncognitive* mechanism for inter-subjectivity. The like-me equivalence could be an index of intersubjectivity. The reciprocal imitation between infant and adult, resulting in taking turns in imitation, could also anticipate the taking of turns in protoconversation. Yet, by themselves, these do not seem to amount to the *right* sort of intersubjectivity and turn-taking that my analysis is after. For they do not yet explain mental sharing and topical predication. As far as I can tell, the *affective* like-me equivalence has better chances to capture the mentally shared intersubjectivity than do bodily or behavioral equivalences, even though the latter may possibly underpin the former. Yet even an affective contact built on behavioral imitation does not go far enough. The intersubjectivity I am after must expose the *topical-predication* roots of reflexivity, in their ontogenetic growth, and also fit other contributing factors of cognitive development at the right joints. There is another line of explanation which meets these conditions plausibly and better than the alternatives just surveyed (while probably building on them). I introduce it by tracking its gradual ontogenesis and then offer a general defense of it.

Just You and Me

The notion of promentality was introduced (in chapter 4) to capture an instinctive, pre-conceptual realization by infants that others are mindful because they are mentally related or oriented to them rather than to the world. As Gomez (1996a, 1996b) suggests, there may be uniquely specialized skills for recognizing second person or I-You relations, different from recognizing subject-world relations. Eye-to-eye gaze is an example of bidirectional interpretation that evolved in primates. As practiced by nonhuman primates, eye-to-eye gaze is necessary but insufficient for recognizing promentality. Eye-to-eye gaze is tied too tightly to behavior, whether in signalling aggression, reconciliation, or an intent to act in some way, and thus is outward-oriented and too utilitarian, almost always pressuring or requesting others to do things (Gomez 1996b, 1998a). It is as though the gaze of the other, even when directed at self, is a window that reveals only the visible push-and-pull world of action, which one can influence, move or manipulate. By contrast, in the gaze (or vocalization) exchanges between human infants and adults, the gaze (or voice) seems to open a different sort of window and provide a different sort of access. It is an access that reflects the participants' dispositions toward each other, as manifested in their emotions, feelings, and other expressions of experiences, and in the dynamics of their exchanges and sharing. So textured, this I-You contact begins to display the intersubjectivity required for the recognition of promentality and to that extent forms the *noncognitive* core of mental sharing by way of sentimental bonding. Although other primate species display and communicate such noncognitive dispositions, and possibly use them for an affective like-me equivalence, it is unclear and (judging from their behavioral signals) rather unlikely that they recognize and share these dispositions as mind-revealing, irrespective of immediate behavioral implications (Cheney and Seyfarth 1990, chapter 8; Trevarthen 1993).[2] To count in the construction of a reflexive mind, the I-You bidirectionality must ground an ability to engage the outside world in ways that afford topical predication and its triangular mind-world-mind patterns of interpretation. Although apes appear to use a triangular I-You-It format more flexibly in ostensive communication (witness the Gomez's already-noted study in chapter 2, section 4), it is doubtful that this format is a genuine version of the mind-world-mind triangle found in human interpretation and communication, for reasons canvassed in chapter 3, section 3.

Thus the analysis loops back on to the argument of chapter 3 about sentimental minding as intersubjective interpretation and its development out of sentimental bonding and interpersonal regulation. Sentimental minding emerges as the basis on which infant and adult minds negotiate, step by ontogenetic step, forms of interpretation and communication that afford topical predication, language learning, and so much more, including mental reflexivity. Relevant to the ongoing analysis are some key ontogenetic steps in this process and their emulation moments.[3]

Interpersonal Relatedness

Interpersonal relatedness characterizes the intersubjective and sentimental version of the I-You contact, what Trevarthen (1979) calls "primary intersubjectivity." It is bidirectional exchange and coordination by sharing experiences, some vague (feelings), others more focused (emotions), operative in the first eight to nine months of infancy. The resulting two-way traffic opens a window on the other's mentality. This is why interpersonal relatedness is more likely than other factors to weave the parameter of promentality into the fabric of the metaintentional scheme, thus leading to the following (figure 5.5):

Fifth emulation   The category of promental relatedness emulates interpersonal relatedness.

At this early stage the affective exchanges between child and adult need not have a specific goal or target and hence a distinct *cognitive* value. This targetless communication was said (two chapters ago) to be essential for the fine-tuning of protoconversation as a flexible give-and-take of protocomments before topics are introduced through the cognitive routes of interpretation (joint gaze and the like). Soon enough, though, such bidirectional sentimental protoconversation acquires shareable topics and interpersonal relatedness enters in triangular arrangements, which is when topical predication, still prelinguistic, takes off. Intriguingly, this may happen when the physical distance between infant and mother increases and breaks the confines of cozy and topicless I-You bidirectionality. It was noted that the frequency of looking in the direction of mother and checking with her (topically) about some action or object increases with distance and hence loss of proximity (Dickstein et al. 1984). It looks almost as if distally targeted interpretation begins to take over when the functions of bonding, such as attachment, protection, and interpersonal regulation, can no longer be handled proximally.

Social Referencing

Social referencing is a first major move in that direction. Faced with unknown or ambiguous situations infants look to adults for guidance. As in personal relatedness, the clues they first look for are facial expressions and the promental stance they display, mostly through emotions but also glances, gaze, bodily orientation, mood, and relevant clues of the situation. This is "secondary intersubjectivity" operative from eight or nine months (Trevarthen 1979). It changes dramatically the context and manner of interpretation. Social referencing is *triangular,* the first version of the mind-world-mind triangle but with a very proximal and still egocentric "world." Child and adult take the data exchanged interpersonally to bear *on something* out there, most often an action initiated by child or some event affecting her. Social referencing discloses one's capacity to perceive and respond to another's affective orientation

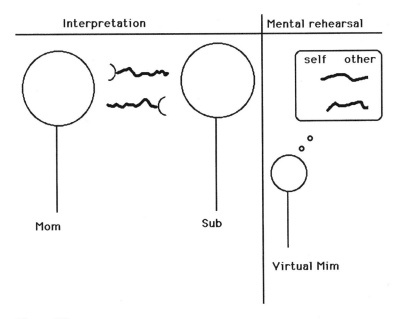

Figure 5.5
Sentimental minding. New symbols are in order to mark the dramatic turn to sentimental bonding and the intersubjective interpretation it affords. Thus:

'〰(' stands for sentimental interpretation, still situated, but now sensitive to how
mental conditions modulate person-to-person relatedness.

'〰' stands for a sort of protocommenting, just expressing some experience or mental
take, without an obvious and specific target.

It is hard to tell what exactly is virtual here, given that the infant may not have
developed any mental-rehearsal abilities and, with the exception of recognizing agency
and hence relatedness, probably has not yet matured other skills inherited (if any) from
earlier stages. Could it be the just some memory of mother's smile commenting on
infant's face or gesture? Bidirectional relatedness would make a revolutionary difference once it is fully coupled with the metaintentional scheme.

toward one and, at the same time, to one's relation to the world (Hobson 1993b, 38; Perner 1991, chapter 6; Rogoff 1990, 67). A well-known example is that of an infant approaching what appears as a drop-off and looking for a reaction from mother. If mother's face shows fear, the infant stops; if mother smiles, the infant proceeds across the clear glass suspended above the floor (Sorce, Emde, Campos, and Klinnert 1985). The mother's reaction is construed by the infant as an emotional comment on the target of their mutual attention (Harris 1989, 22–23).

To make the emulation road to metamentation more perspicuous, I propose to split the analysis of the work of social referencing in two parts. The first is about acquiring a sense of promental takes on something, the second about topical predication. Social referencing stimulates and sharpens the child's identification of mental relatedness to what is jointly referenced. This well-targeted relatedness is now perceived as somebody's *mental takes,* mostly affective in the beginning, on external items of interest. This is probably how the child comes to realize that fear or joy are emotions in others linked to what the child is doing in or experiencing about the world. The variability of actions and events linked to facial expressions or bodily postures revealing such mental takes may begin to individuate them as *types*—fear, joy, desire— and dimly suggest their directedness.

My reading of the data suggests that social referencing begins on a proximal note, being limited to actions and somewhat oblivious of their distal targets (in contrast to Hobson's more optimistic reading [1993b, 143–146], shared by other researchers as well). In that case, social referencing need not be semantically determinate, at least no more determinate than the kinds of actions it relates to. Echoing the first steps toward the metaintentional scheme, surveyed earlier, the targets of someone's mental takes may be supplied for a while subjectively by the child. As a result, the sense of mental take may be equally vague or incomplete at this stage. This would square with the noncognitive nature of the interpretive resources employed. It would also square with the fact that in early childhood the sharing of mental takes (to establish experiential contact and effect behavioral guidance with its help) is more imperative than sharing mental takes on well-defined targets. So what we have so far looks like this:

Sixth emulation   The category of a mental take on something emulates social referencing.

Yet the business of social referencing is not completed. Thus, the second part of its emulation job. Ordinary observation joins professional opinion in viewing social referencing as training ground for topical exchanges of experiences and information about shared topics. The topic may be an action or

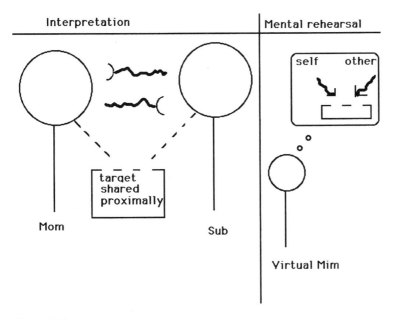

Figure 5.6
Social referencing. At this point Mom provides the virtual Mim with some resources to represent a mental take on something (proximal and perceptually transient). Even if internalized, turned inwards, and used in mental rehearsal (a big if), this representation is unlikely to afford any self-directed topical predication in the absence of other cognitive developments.

'⤳' stands for a mental take on something specific.

event involving the child, the comments could be expressions of emotion or of other experiences. As in the former scheme, the topic need not be sharply and objectively defined or even fully recognized as such at this stage (Rogoff 1990, 69). Nevertheless, a topical-predication version is now on the ontogenetic horizon (figure 5.6):

Topic-comment version   The recognition that a mental take comments on a topic as proximal target emulates social referencing.

Shared Attention
Shared attention, focused not only on actions but also on distinct objects and events in the world, becomes a form of "tertiary intersubjectivity." On the sentimental account, shared attention may inherit its mental sharing from interpersonal relatedness through protoconversation (and still further back, from neurophysiological regulation) and its categories of mental take and topic-directedness from social referencing and particularly its joint-gaze component

(Bruner 1983; Hobson 1993b, 1994). In that case, shared attention is joint gaze plus social referencing or joint gaze promentalized. Shared attention resembles joint gaze in its use of line of regard for determining direction and of exchanges of gazes to determine targets; it also resembles social referencing in the use of intersubjective experiencing to identify mental takes and read them as comments on shared targets. Through this combination, the category of mental take is invested with the full intentionality of direction and distal target (action, object, event in the world). Thus, the emulation log registers:

Seventh emulation   The category of directedness to target emulates shared attention.

The promental scheme now seems pretty much in place, at least as a possibility afforded by advances in interpretation. By making distal targets available as topics for mental comments, shared attention could also afford a topical-predication use of the promental scheme (figure 5.7):

Topic-comment version   The recognition that a mental take comments on a topic as distal target emulates shared attention.

The sentimental route to shared attention may begin to explain two important developments eventually leading to metamention. One has to do with infant solipsism. In early childhood the walls of solipsism surrounding the young mind begin slowly to crumble. Sentimental minding is better positioned than its purely cognitive competitors to bring this about. The matrices of intersubjective engagement provide the earliest *outside* frame of reference, someone else's, for the child's relations to the world.[4] A world about which emotional and attitudinal notes are compared with an adult is no longer a world tightly glued to, and almost indistinguishable from, a child's current perception and behavior. Such a development may prove as crucial as anything in disengaging the child's mind from its sensorimotor solipsism. Intersubjectivity through sentimental minding may provide grounds and opportunities for separating the world from mental takes on it. The interactive interpretation of apes fails on this score. Its best routine, joint gaze, cannot effect such a break from solipsism, insofar as it reveals only someone else's perceptual access. It takes a plurality of shared, exchanged, and mutually acknowledged mental takes—as in looking, smiling, frowning, expressing surprise—on items of mutual interest to begin to separate those items from the mental takes themselves, including one's own. It is a pattern of invariance similar to that noted in section 1 apropos of the direction and target of intentionality. In a word, sentimentally relating to another person, who so relates to you and to a shared world, can do wonders for your mind—in the long run, metamental wonders.

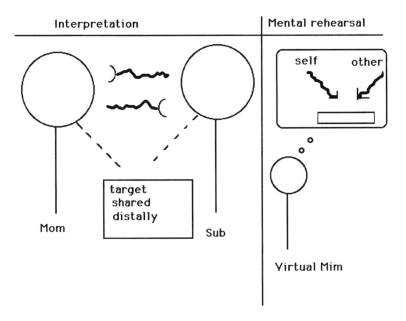

Figure 5.7
Shared attention. Since the mental life of a young Mom is situated and episodic, her social referencing and even shared attention may be implicit or, as Barbara Rogoff phrased it, "woven into the fabric of interpersonal relations and seldom the focus of explicit attention" (1990, 69). So may be the counterpart virtual representation in Mim's mental rehearsal (if any). Suppose it is. This could signal the onset of implicit metathinking. To see why, let us go back to chapter 4, section 1, and the text following figure 4.2. The example there was of metathinking imagistically, with the mental focus on what is imaged (as content) and only with an implicit sense of the imaging itself as mental relation to a scene. Shared attention is perception-driven and probably imagistic when reenacted in mental rehearsal. Implicit metathinking becomes possible when such reenactment joins the scene imaged with an implicit sense of imaging as mental relation.

The other important development concerns the format of explicit metathinking, whereby thoughts are thought about in relation to other thoughts. There is a good chance that the seeds of that format are planted in shared attention. Let us look back at Mom's column in figure 5.7. The child interpreter, Mom, represents an item in the world and expresses the representation sentimentally or behaviorally, and the subject (an adult) reacts by smiling or frowning or doing something—a sentimental or behavioral comment on a shared topic *and* the child's relation to it. Anticipate that, courtesy of later advances in interpretation, Mom's representation of a fact graduates to the metarepresentation of a thought and the adult's comment on it is internalized by Mom (on the model of the left column, that of virtual Mim) as thoughts that are about or comment upon or otherwise relate to the thought metarepresented. That would approximate Mim's metamentation. The rest of this essay endeavors to show how Mom, by internalizing and mixing in her thinking the counterpart roles of interpreter and subject in a mind-world-mind format, gradually becomes a reflexive Mim.

Checking on Further Contributions

As it works its way toward metamentation, interpretation is massively implicated in the development of a number of other mental skills, such as communication by shared meaning, acquisition of word reference, imagination and hypothetical thinking, executive control, and reflexive consciousness and selfhood.

I think that the implication of interpretation in the formation of various mental skills comes in different formats and degrees. Interpretation can be an *enabler* by inserting its contribution in an already existing skill and thus enhancing its power, widening its range, and redesigning some of its applications. This could be the case of communication and executive control. Interpretation can also be a *facilitator* by pressuring and stimulating the development of some mental skills, such as imagination or memory. Finally, in the strongest sense of implication, interpretation can be a *designer* of mental skills, such as acquisition of word reference, metamentation or reflexive consciousness. The latter skills would simply not exist without interpretation. For, in the design sense, the tasks of interpretation come to inhabit and structure those of the other (designed) skills.

Although focused on the design of metamentation, this book also means to convey a more general sense of how much the human mind owes to (intersubjective) interpretation and how many of its unique skills were built on its shoulders. The facilitator role of interpretation in the emergence of imagination and mental rehearsal was already evoked in chapter 2, section 4. The designer role in the emergence of reflexive consciousness and reflexive self-hood will be briefly discussed in chapter 7, section 3. There is a growing literature that touches on these and other contributions of interpretation. In some recent papers Josef Perner and colleagues have argued that executive control is also much indebted to interpretation (e.g., Perner and Lang 1999). It has also been known for a while that the prelinguistic communication between infants and adults follows the Gricean script of relying on reciprocal attributions of mental states (mostly emotions) and that children learn many if not most new words in the context of sharing with adults attention on particular targets linked to the words being introduced (see P. Bloom 1997 for a recent survey). Researchers who studied this phenomenon most closely regard the ontogenetic chain leading up to the mastery of word reference as going (in my terms) from sentimental bonding to intersubjective interpretation, protoconversation, topical predication, and shared attention (L. Bloom 1993; Bruner 1983; Hobson 1993b, 1994; Lock 1980; Tomasello 1995, 1996). In the context of this chapter, it is interesting to note that the first words are generally acquired around the first birthday (when social referencing is in place) with a tentative and imprecise reference (consistent with the vagueness and proximality of social referencing); the acquisition process accelerates and delivers improved reference around 18 months, which is when shared attention takes over. It is not simply that the acquisition of word reference would be impossible outside a social interaction negotiated through interpretation. The tasks involved in understanding word reference largely match those involved in prelinguistic communication based on shared attention (Akhtar and Tomasello 1998).

An interesting pattern emerges from these contributions. The very design of the reflexive mind owes a good deal to these various contributions of interpretation. Metamentation would be literally unthinkable without language, as a new medium of internal representation, and language would be internally unrepresentable and impracticable without word learning. Nor would metamentation work without executive control. And so on. The reflexive mind is a remarkable outcome of a tree-like development during which the trunk grows new branches that expand into further branches that prop and cross with still other branches until a uniquely textured crown emerges. That crown is the reflexive mind; the trunk is interpretation.

A quick summary before moving on. After distinguishing between minds that engage the world (all minds) and minds that recognize such an engagement (interpreting minds), this chapter has surveyed the first ontogenetic steps in the emulation saga, taken only by the interpreting minds. The metaintentional scheme emulated the earliest and most basic interpretive categories of agency, gaze following, and joint gaze. The domain was that of interactive interpretation. Topical predication and the promental scheme developed out of a sentimental sharing of mental states, culminating in shared attention. The latter in turn opened new opportunities for communication by shared meaning and language acquisition, which in turn propel interpretation to higher levels of internal representation from where it steers the child's mind toward metamentation.

Chapter 6

Unsituated Metaminding

Apprised of why and how situated interpretation built the basis for metamentation, it is time to turn to the unsituated superstructure erected on that basis. The impact of the superstructure on metamentation is going to be stronger and more direct than that of the basis. Yet, as before, it is an impact made of distinct but interacting developments. According to section 1, two such developments lead to the category of unsituated attitude. One is the metasemantic recognition of misrepresentation. The other is a naive functionalism that construes attitudes in terms of internal relations, perspectivality, and other such features. As a result, the interpreter comes to envisage the world unsituatedly and according to the subject's mind. Section 2 speculates about how these two developments, converging on the category of propositional attitude, end up emulated by a new and basic metamental counterpart, the category of explicit metathought. Several key developments made this emulation possible. A critical one, taken in up in section 3, is the turn to self interpretation. Other important developments, resulting in mind unification, are discussed in the next chapter.

1 Two Routes to Attitudes

A watershed development in child interpretation, perhaps the most studied and debated, is the recognition that minds relate to the world *representingly*. (This is the relation accessible to interpreters, not the one studied by philosophers or cognitive scientists.) Psychologists take the recognition of false belief to be the epitome of this development but disagree about its timing and nature. An externalist account focuses on the ability to monitor and evaluate the information traffic between mind and world (Leslie 1988; Wellman 1990; Wimmer, Hogrefe, and Sodian 1988). An internalist account focuses on the ability to spot internal constraints on mental representation (Astington and Gopnik 1988; Flavell 1988; Forguson and Gopnik 1988; Gopnik and Meltzoff

1997; Perner 1991). I see these as distinct rather than competing exploits, emerging for different reasons, at different stages, and employing different resources. If this distinction holds, then it points to different interpretational influences on metamental thinking. This is the agenda of this section. It begins with the first, metasemantic gambit.

Metasemantic Gambit: False Belief

Here, to begin with, is the classic Maxi-and-the-chocolate experiment on recognizing false belief. I paraphrase the description of the test from Perner (1991, 179):

Plot Maxi (the subject) puts the chocolate into a *green* cupboard, for later use, after which he goes out to play. In his absence mother takes the chocolate out of the *green* cupboard, uses some for her cake, and then puts it back in a different *blue* cupboard. She leaves the room while Maxi comes back to get his chocolate.

Test question for the interpreter Where will Maxi look for the chocolate?

Results Four-year-old and older interpreters correctly predict that Maxi the subject will look in the *green* cupboard, whereas three-year-olds predict that Maxi will look in the *blue* cupboard.

On the metasemantic account, the interpreter exploits her situated grasp of direct access but shows new sensitivity to the origins and causes of mental states. Gopnik and Wellman (1992, 151) note that the metasemantic gambit may be modeled on an earlier situated grasp of perception and desire, which are seen as direct and immediate links between subject and situations: desires as mental causes of external changes, perceptions as mental effects of external changes. Wimmer, Hogrefe, and Sodian (1988) estimate that only four-year-olds begin to see sources of information as causal origins of a subject's belief and use these sources to understand from where and how the subject got his beliefs. Prior to that age, children do not see perception and communication as information sources for belief, nor do they see the causal origins of that information as specific facts to be believed.

Witnessing the perceptual access of others allows young interpreters to know when others get information but not necessarily where they got it from and how. The causal origins of the access remain obscure. As a result, children fail to grasp that seeing or remembering a fact (e.g., the chocolate in the green cupboard) could be the causal origin for believing that fact. The causal origins and routes of perceptual contact provide the reference frame that distinguishes between true and false belief. On the metasemantic diagnosis, then, three-year-olds fail the false-belief test because they do not see how causal coordinates, such as origin and information route, provide the subject with, or deprive him of, the right beliefs about specific items.[1] These are the coordinates that constitute the early metasemantic understanding of attitudes.

On this diagnosis, the fact that children younger than three fail to recognize false belief because they fail to understand its causal formation jibes with the observation that the recognition of one's own false beliefs is more difficult, and appears to emerge later, than the recognition of false beliefs in others (Astington and Gopnik 1988). Fully immersed in what one perceives and does, one has little opportunity or need to see oneself as cause or effect of an intentional relation. That need not be true of someone else. To notice that one saw something or didn't, or notice that one has formed a false belief, can be full of consequences. Children around three to four come under increased social pressures to recognize the access of others to information and do something about it (Bogdan 1997, chapter 6).

The metasemantic diagnosis is not without its critics (Forguson and Gopnik 1988, Perner 1991). They point out that the difficulty young children have in understanding their false beliefs cannot originate in the failure to track their causal formation "since children can internally experience their own beliefs without having to understand how they are formed" (Perner 1991, 186). The failure must therefore be of another nature (the next gambit), in which case so must be the failure to attribute false beliefs to others. This argument need not be as compelling as it appears. Self-attribution of false belief may require new skills for identifying attitudes but the attribution of false beliefs to others may still begin on a metasemantic note, consistent with the young children's focus on gaze, attention, and other directly observable forms of access. I see no contradiction here. Nor should one exclude the possibility that young children do actually compute their own false beliefs by remembering or imagining themselves in a visual mode as having been related or not to an event. After all, how does one (at any age) decide whether one has seen or not something: often it is not just the internal experience (say, an image) stored in memory but also some correlative determination (no matter how indirect) that one was there, in a position to see. It is this latter determination that calls for representing one's own access along external and perhaps causal routes, which is something young children may have problems with, for a while. For all these reasons I am inclined to give the metasemantic gambit a fair chance.

So I conjecture that for a while the mastery of the metasemantic gambit remains largely situated, being anchored in external points of reference. What the child apparently does at this stage is keep fixed a situation currently perceived and remember or imagine access relations of the subject *other* than the ones currently perceived. The result is the metasemantic category of *situated attitude.* It is metasemantic because the content of the attitude is determined in terms of what it is about in the world; it is (almost) attitude, as type of cognitive access, because it can be identified independently of its current content; it is situated because its identification has one foot firmly set in a current context of perception. The determination of the attitude involves a comparison between two access relations, one current, the other past or imagined, and may go like this: 'Subject first had perceptual access to *p* but now has access to *r*, and hence he believes (falsely) that *p*.'[2]

To sum up, the reason the interpretation of a situated attitude, such as perceptual belief, counts as metarepresentational is that it provides the first realization that an intentional relation or mental take represents, in the narrow but decisive semantic sense that it can be on target or not, true or false. The metasemantic gambit affords an external determination of the contents of attitudes in terms of what they represent and an external categorization of the attitude as the intentional relation or mental take that can represent or misrepresent. This, then, is another crucial moment in the history of mental reflexivity emulating interpretation (figure 6.1):

Eighth emulation   The recognition that mental take represents semantically (that is, the category of situated attitudes) emulates the metasemantic gambit.

This recognition is only the first step in setting up the metarepresentational scheme. The other step is understanding the internal constraints on representing. Such understanding seems to result out of a largely distinct set of developments in child interpretation. These developments in turn allow the metasemantic gambit to acquire a more abstract and less situated scope.

Naive Functionalism

An attitude interpreted metasemantically is not yet a full blown propositional attitude, for it is neither unsituated nor thoroughly desubjectivized. It takes several new insights to get there. They enable the young interpreter to view situations according to, and often in terms of, the subject's attitudes to them (Forguson and Gopnik 1988, Perner 1991, Wellman 1990). I baptize these insights *naively functionalist.* They are about mental conditions whose interaction is taken to reveal what and how others mentally represent. I construe them as 'functionalist' because the work and often identity of one mental condition is viewed as a function of other mental conditions and also because how people represent the world is viewed as an internal (in-the-head) affair. It so happens that functionalism is the name of a philosophical doctrine that classifies mental state types, including propositional attitudes, as patterns of

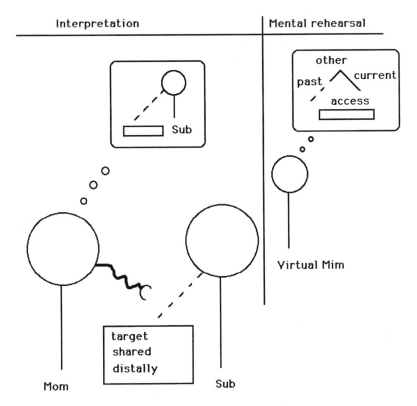

Figure 6.1
Metasemantic interpretation. Mom can now see a subject's current perceptual access
to a target, at the same time mentally compute his past or imagined access to a target,
and notice a discrepancy, in case there is one. Internalizing this new ability and turning
it toward her own thoughts, Mim could (for the first time) metarepresent mental takes
directed at perceived targets and hence metathink explicitly but semantically. According
to the account given in chapter 4, section 1, this is not yet the explicit metathinking
that animates the thought-to-thought metamental routines. As in figure 5.7, Mim's
metathinking might be mostly imagistic and to that extent not really about thoughts.

interacting mental conditions. In a naive and unreflective form, functionalism is also thought to be at the heart of the commonsense psychology of propositional attitudes (Fodor 1987, D. Lewis 1972, Loar 1981). Among the new insights of naive functionalism the first (internal interaction and interdependence) seems to underpin most of the others. Here is a sample of these insights (Astington and Gopnik 1988, Flavell 1988, Forguson and Gopnik 1988, Perner 1991, Wellman 1990):

Internal networking The interpreter becomes aware that attitudes are interdependent mental conditions influenced and shaped by their links to memories, perceptions, preferences, and other mental conditions, including other attitudes.

Opacity The interpreter switches from her perceptual and self-centered identification of the targets of the subject's attitudes to how the subject may represent them. (The notion of opacity captures the fact that reference depends on how it is represented.) In so doing, the interpreter comes to realize that her representation of the target may differ from the subject's or that different subjects may represent the same target differently. This realization affects how she predicts and explains the subject's attitudes and actions.

Mental diversity and change The interpreter realizes that different people can have different desires or beliefs about the same things; or that some desire or believe what others do not; or that some may desire or believe or act better or more accurately or more realistically or more successfully than others. Also noticed now is that people may change their attitudes to the same situations, relative to new evidence and changes in other mental conditions.

Perspectivality The realization of mental diversity implies that attitudes can depend on point of view—first visual, later extended to memory, learning, expertise, and so on.

Appearance versus reality The interpreter realizes that, because of position, access or available data, the subject may take things and situations to have properties different from how they really are.

Futures, pasts, and hypotheticals The interpreter sees the subject as having desires and beliefs oriented toward the future or past and thus toward things and situations that do not exist.

Whether the young interpreter stumbles from one naively functionalist insight to another or gets them in a package, the result is that interpretation enters a new and radically different stage, when attitudes are construed as unsituated mental takes on propositions. Thus:

Nineth emulation The recognition that a mental take represents opaquely, perspectively, etc. (that is, the category of unsituated propositional attitude) emulates naive functionalism.

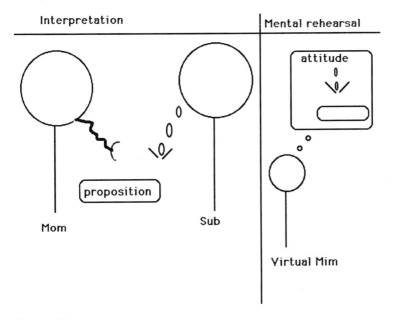

Figure 6.2
Metarepresentational interpretation. A dramatically new form of interpretation, the metarepresentation of propositional attitudes, calls for a new symbol. Thus:

'ₒₒₒₒₒ>' stands for an unsituated attitude to a proposition or some mental object.

Mom now masters the category of propositional attitude on naive-functionalist terms, which is what Mim can represent and mentally rehearse.

This recognition provides a finer-grained and richer grasp of how minds relate to the world. It is the grasp that new constraints, reflecting mental conditions and their interactions, *further* modulate how attitudes represent— just as, at an earlier phase, emotions and experiences were understood to modulate intentional relations in a promental fashion. The ontogenesis of interpretation could therefore be viewed as a sequence of insights into successive and finer-grained intramental modulations of subject-world relations (figure 6.2).

Divided Labors
There are reasons to think that the metasemantic gambit and the naively functionalist insights are distinct developments in interpretation, with distinct consequences for metamentation. I begin this diagnosis on a conceptual note, add some philosophical reflections, and close with a look at a relevant psychological debate.

Conceptual Reasons   Ascertaining the truth or falsity of a proposition is not the same as grasping its logical structure or how this structure bears on truth value. The semantic facts needed to individuate a structureless proposition and to follow the logical links among such propositions are different from the facts needed to individuate a structured proposition and to follow the logical links among such propositions. These differences are borne out by logic and its pedagogy. Propositional calculus is not the same as predicate calculus. Nor are they taught and understood in the same way. The former draws mostly on metasemantic intuitions, the latter also on understanding formal structure and expressive resources. To stretch this analogy a bit further, still later in conceptual and pedagogical order come specialty logics, such as the modal logic of necessity and possibility and the epistemic logic of belief, perception, and knowledge. These specialty logics add new operators and new formal constraints on propositions, their structure, and form of representation.

On this conceptual analogy, it makes sense to think that the young interpreter begins with a metasemantic grasp of situated attitudes to structureless propositions that are true or false in perceptual contexts. Such a grasp fits situated and perception-bound interpretation because the interpreter, in observing the subject's cognitive access, does not have sufficient data and constraints to estimate what exactly it is, in fine grain, that the subject perceives and believes. The interpreter may supply the grain subjectively, in terms of her perception and her topical-predication parsing of the situation; all that her interpretive categories afford may be the grasp of a structureless event. Only her naively functionalist insights open up the propositional content believed (or perceived or desired) to a structural estimate and a new sensitivity to how the content is represented because new evidence and new constraints get noticed.

Philosophical Reasons   Philosophers have long known the distinction between a metasemantic (or mostly external) and functionalist (or mostly internal) reading of propositional attitudes, and have used the distinction to argue for opposite conclusions. The behavioristically-minded and those attuned to ordinary language argue that attitude attributions are metasemantic and public, with little if any concern for mental innards (see Austin 1961 and Wittgenstein 1953 for classical statements; see Collins 1987 for a more recent restatement). Other philosophers argue, as forcefully, that attributions reveal a more penetrating and structure-sensitive grasp of mental links, and hence that interpretation takes the naive form of a functionalist theory of mind (D. Lewis 1972, Loar 1981). Mindful of the force of both positions, still other philosophers compromise on a dual-track theory of mental content in attitude attributions, one metasemantic and another functionalist (McGinn 1982, Stich 1983) and try to harmonize the two tracks (Fodor 1987). What matters here is that these positions provide further rationale and ammunition for distinguishing between the metasemantic and naive functionalist gambits of interpretation. The former is mostly concerned with the external ascription of attitudes, the latter with explanation and rationalization in terms of mental factors. This difference fits the ontogenetic picture drawn earlier in this chapter. In early childhood the attitude ascriptions made from outside (perceptual access versus lack of it, true versus false belief) seem preeminent, not only as a matter of conceptual mastery but also for the prediction of action. Later the explanation or justification of what others do, and why, gains importance and calls for further sensitivity to the structure of and internal links among attitudes. This line of speculation brings us to psychology.

Psychological Reasons   Evidence from, and debates in, psychology bestow further plausibility on the distinction between the metasemantic and naively functionalist perspectives. I begin with an evolutionary pointer. One could expect the young interpreter, under new pressures to recognize attitudes and their possible mismatch with reality, to try to put old tricks to new uses. It is a game evolution plays often. Checking information access is an old and well-tested gambit going back to the interpretation of gazing. The metasemantic interpretation of situated belief may not be that different, at least in its early phases. This evolutionary expectation comports with a minority but forceful view in developmental psychology which is unimpressed by the majority view that (false) belief recognition pops out between three and four, and sees earlier signs of such recognition (Chandler 1988, Chandler and Hala 1994, C. Lewis 1994, Mitchell 1994). The metasemantic-functionalist distinction may accommodate this line of dissent, for it suggests that it is the *metasemantic* interpretation of *situated* (just true or false) belief that emerges earlier, drawing on skills already used in shared attention and in interpreting visual access. In contrast, the majority view, which insists on a tighter timing of belief recognition, is preoccupied with the *naive functionalism* of *unsituated* attitudes, not just true or false belief (Astington and Gopnik 1988; Gopnik and Ferguson 1988; Perner 1991; Wellman 1990). So there may be no conflict here: these could be rather distinct developments that result in distinct (though eventually overlapping) categories of attitudes.

2   Explicit Metathought

Is there a metamental counterpart to the category of propositional attitude? Almost. It is the category of *explicit metathought,* anticipated in chapter 4, section 2, as the core unit of metamentation. The anticipation was that explicit metathinking categorizes thoughts as mental structures represented in relation

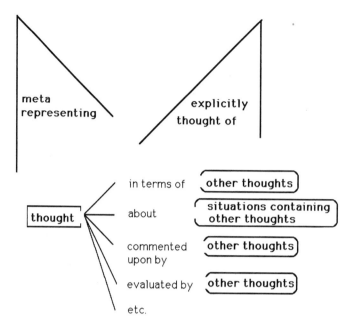

Figure 6.3
Explicit metathought.

to other such structures. The upshot is that a thought's identity, relation to a content, and content itself are all explicitly represented. The blueprint for such explicit representation comes from interpretation and in particular from that of propositional attitudes. One could not think explicit metathoughts unless one were an interpreter of propositional attitudes. Yet other developments are also needed to give shape and substance to the final result. So argues the rest of this chapter and the next. I begin with an intuitive model of the tasks involved, and then, drawing on empirical facts and theories surveyed so far, explore the developments in child interpretation most likely to have bestowed cognitive reality upon this model. I conclude with some critical remarks against the popular views that the category of explicit metathought could originate in an inside look at one's mind through self interpretation or self awareness.

Intuitive Model
Figure 6.3 is a graphic rendition of what is meant by the category of explicit metathought. One explicitly metathinks when one represents a thought whose content is specified by reference to other thoughts, such as being about, commenting, defining or evaluating. Two things may be noted right away.

First, the content of an explicitly metarepresented thought is parsed in *relation*—actually several kinds of relations—to other thoughts in patterns corresponding to different metamental tasks and routines. These thought-to-thought relations are modeled on the relations of attitudes to propositional contents and, like their models, build upon and distill the mind-world relations represented in interpretation and particularly the mind-world-mind relations of intersubjective interpretation, ranging from simple intentionality and topical predication to metarepresentation.

Second, there is a *left-right format* in the graphic display of metathinking. Compare figure 6.3 with figure 4.2 from chapter 4 (p. 87). Figure 4.2 depicts implicit metathinking as consisting in representing a fact (left side) implicitly thought of (right side). In contrast, explicit metathinking brings into the representing slot a thought (on the left side) whose content is thought in relation to other thoughts. The point of this display is to suggest a division of labor among metamental tasks: the left side feeds thoughts in mental rehearsal whose contents are spelled out on the right side in relation to patterns of other thoughts. In the emulation story the left side fingers the (child) interpreter and the right side the subject who relates to, represents, reacts to, comments on, or evaluates what is shared with the interpreter. This ego-world-alter or mind-world-mind pattern is uniquely intersubjective and human and solely responsible for metamentation evolving out of interpretation. The left side in both figures is that of the ego. The right side internalizes the subject's role; it is the voice of the *other,* the *alter,* merely social at the outset, later cultural as well. Phrased poetically, the inner voice of the (right side) metathought echoes the outer voice of the subject. The interplay between left and right, between ego and the socio-cultural alter, may reflect actual stages in the ontogeny of metamentation. In the early stages the young child merely registers another person's awareness of what is shared. That would be an implicit sense of a subject's (pro)mental relation to what the child relates to (as in social referencing or shared attention). Internalized, that is more or less what figure 4.2 illustrated. Later developments and notably the mastery of propositional attitudes change dramatically the rules of mental game played internally on both sides and particularly on the right side, that of the alter (Tomasello 1993). The tasks involved are worth spelling out, while the stages in which the tasks become available to the child's mind will be taken up in the next section.

The Tasks

To represent an explicit metathought is to (a) categorize a mental condition *as* a structure that represents and (b) specify its content in relation to other thoughts.

Mental Representing

The category of propositional attitudes thus does double duty: it categorizes attitudes as mental representings and—assuming other developments, such as attitude iteration and reconstruction—specifies their contents in relation to other attitudes to contents. The first role relies squarely on naive functionalism. The second relies on the same and sundry later developments. What is important to note now is that it is the unsituatedness that naive functionalism bestows on interpretation which makes possible the category of explicit metathought. This category is unavailable to a situated mind. To represent an explicit metathought is to be able to think of a thought as a mental representing. The situated categories of intentional relation and mental take cannot sponsor this ability because they cannot represent mind-world relations *separately* from their targets and surrounding contexts.

A chief reason why situated cognition cannot generate the category of explicit metathought is its domain-dependency: its sensorimotor procedures are perceptually cued to landmarks of the surrounding ecology and cannot operate in their absence (chapter 1, section 2). Calculated ecologically, under perceptual rules, mind-world-mind relations cannot be represented outside a perceived context. Moreover, perceptual representations, typical of situated cognition, tend to be analog or imagistic—a type of coding unfriendly to an invariant and detached attitude interpretation and thought explicitation. It is only when the child begins to grasp unsituated attitudes in *naively functionalist* terms that she acquires the category of propositional attitude. This acquisition need not be explicitly coded, and probably isn't, at least not in its early stages, but it has the effect of systematically tracking attitudes as mind-world *relations* with semantic and mental properties. This systematic tracking turns out to be also essential to the handling of the second and as important task of explicit metathinking—the relational specification of its content.

Relational Specification of Content

In a rudimentary but discernible fashion, the relational specification of content begins in earlier forms of world-sharing intersubjectivity such as social referencing and more clearly in shared attention. The child interpreter, Mom, represents an action, event, or object out there as something-the-other-mentally-relates-to-and-comments-upon (e.g., smiles at or says something about). The hypothesis, then, is that the in-relation-to-other-thoughts format developed out of what-the-other-relates-to format. The latter is an older format that reaches back to the basics of intersubjective interpretation, the mental sharing at work in social referencing and shared attention. But at the metasemantic stage Mom seems able to do two new things. She begins to distinguish between a relationally specified content (what-is-desired or believed) and actual fact. This is how she forms the category of unfulfilled desire or false belief. This is one new and momentous acquisition. The other is that Mom can now coordinate two or more such situated attitudes whose contents are relationally specified. Imagine Mom observing two subjects, John and Harry, who witness the same situation. Mom specifies what John sees in the explicitly relational terms of what Harry sees. That is, Mom forms the representation that John sees what Harry sees. Later Mom uses the same trick with unsituated attitudes in attributions like 'John believes what Harry remembered' or 'John desired the thing that Harry noticed'.

These are relational identifications of content in terms of *mind-world-mind* relations. The content is represented as something-that-is-mentally-represented. Turned inwards, this format of content specification is uniquely positioned to provide a model for specifying the content of explicit metathoughts. If I represent my believing a proposition that I used to believe years ago, which is an instance of explicit metathought, I employ the same relational gambit in specifying what I believe as Mom did in the earlier example. My ego, now believing something, is on the left side of figure 6.3 and my earlier ego, who used to believe the same proposition, is on the right. Ego and time aside, this is what the concept of explicit metathought is all about: it specifies the content of a thought in relation to other thoughts. But our little Mom is not yet there. She still has some way to go before mastering all the parameters of the category of explicit metathought (figure 6.4).

I noted at the beginning of this section that the category of explicit metathought *almost* emulates that of propositional attitude but not quite. The gap is in the relational specification of content. A normal attribution of a propositional attitude—e.g., that Pipa believes that crows are smart (she heard that they may be tool users)—need not relationally specify the content (that crows are smart) in mind-world-mind terms. The content is specified as a fact or situation; that is all. By itself, such a specification is not conducive to the category of explicit metathought. Why not? Because the relational specification of content cannot emulate the mere representation of a proposition, even when the attitude to a proposition is self attributed. Emulated, a self-attributed attitude allows one to represent and be aware of one's believing a fact (the implicit metathinking of figure 4.2) but *not* the fact of one's representing a thought in terms of other thoughts (the explicit version of figures 6.1 and 6.2). Emulated and self-directed, the category of attitude to a proposition allows one to represent the thought that crows are smart, full stop; it does not allow one to represent the thought that one's thought that crows are smart is what Pipa believes or what other people need to be convinced of or the like. Only

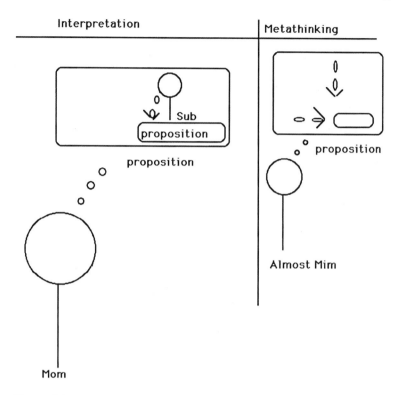

Figure 6.4
Relational specification of content.

the latter are instances of explicit metathoughts and therefore have the right format for metamentation.

So much for the conceptual analysis. It is now time to map its insights on to the ontogenesis of the interpretational acquisitions leading up to the category of explicit metathought. With respect to the tasks involved in explicit metathinking—recognizing mental representing and managing a relational specification of content in terms of other thoughts—I see the transition going from the interpretation of the other to self interpretation and from there (given further developments noted below) to metamentation.

Alter before Ego

The first step is to give some substance to the idea that the attitudes of others are interpreted *before* one's own and therefore that self-directed attitudes are not the first targets of metarepresentation. There is a lively debate over this matter, both in terms of what the evidence warrants and how interpretation actually works, whether as simulation (self to other) or as initially other-directed. This is not the place to engage the debate, although I will note a few arguments and facts here and there, which on balance seem to me to favor the primacy of alter over ego interpretation.

Consider some observations first. A very young mind remembers past events but not past access *relations* to such events, hers or others'. The past access of *others* is identified and remembered *before* one's own. Construed as causal access (in the sense discussed in section 1 above), one's understanding of (false) belief in *others* appears to emerge *before* that of one's own (false) belief. When the child eventually understands that her beliefs can be false, that understanding appears to originate in *naively functionalist* and other-directed rather than metasemantic (access) insights (Astington and Gopnik 1988, Perner 1991, Wellman 1990). The last fact also suggests that overriding perceptual access to a current situation, in order to compare it with access to a past or possible situation, is beyond situated interpretation and doable only through naive functionalism. Taken together, these facts suggest that situated interpretation cannot handle explicit relations between self and world, not until they are first spotted in others. In general, as Josef Perner wrote, "children do not come to understand the relevant aspects of their own mind any earlier than they understand the relevant aspects of other people's minds" (1991, 270). This diagnosis backs up the idea (not uncontested but increasingly plausible) of a developmental sequence going from interpreting others to interpreting self.

An alter-to-ego sequence also makes *evolutionary* sense. Given the social, epistemic, and political pressures of childhood, it is the other, not the self, whom one must deal with and figure out first. This asymmetry fits the expectation, taken seriously in this work, that causal categories, such as those of interpretation, represent targets of causal manipulation. In the social domain causal manipulation *begins* with the other, not with self. This is why first recognized are other-world relations, such as visual access or propositional attitude. The priority of other over self interpretation finally makes *cognitive* sense. Identifying another person's access (as an explicitly recognized relation) to situations is easier than identifying one's own. Unlike the latter, the former is out there, relata and relation, ready to be noticed in its entirety. Immersed in what one perceives and does, one has little opportunity, reason, or means to represent oneself in relation to the world, let alone as cause or effect of an access relation. The same is true of one's memory: one remembers past events more easily than and before one remembers one's access to them as a distinct relation. Someone else's access, in full view and graspable in its entirety, can be registered and stored. When cognition and interpretation are situated, it is hard to get around these limitations. Although harder to document empirically, there may be a similar developmental asymmetry in the relational specification of content, for largely the same reasons. The young interpreter may fail to see the facts she believes or remembers explicitly *as* what-I-believe or remember (as a prelude to a more abstract content specification as what-this-thought-means or how-it-relates-to-other-thoughts or the like). She may remember a house and recognize it as such, yet fail to represent the house explicitly as what-I-remember. She may relationally identify the house that someone else remembers as what-that-person-remembers, yet again fail to so identify the house she remembers, in the first person. The turn to self in the relational fixation of content is as critical for the category of explicit metathought as is the turn to self in attitude ascription. Hence the next topic.

3   The Turn to Self

The self is a delicate and much debated topic in philosophy and more recently in the psychology of animal and human interpretation. Far from me the wish or temerity to enter its still mysterious territory and get lost in the process. All I need to show here is that there are good reasons for a turn to self interpretation, modeled on and following that of the interpretation of others, and that these reasons are decisive in setting up the format of explicit metathinking. I also want to show that one's representations of one's mental goings on cannot, without interpretation, be a basis for representing explicit metathoughts, and that if interpretation is such a basis, it cannot begin at self.

Reasons for Self-Importance

Why would an interpreter need to ascribe explicitly attitudes to self and individuate their contents relationally? Recall that mental rehearsal, the other partner in the metamention deal, is where interpretive resources do most of their mental work (in prediction, planning, deliberation) and therefore where intramural pressures on interpretation show up, reflecting those in the social domain. Mental rehearsal is also where the explicitation of thoughts is effected, as one scrutinizes, evaluates or plans one's thoughts. So, what's happening in mental rehearsal to explain the turn to self interpretation? The short of it is that the ego must be factored explicitly into the calculations about the alter and that such factoring calls for new tasks, executed by new categories and schemes. I think that these developments build up the category of explicit metathought.

Now the longer story. The child is a busy social agent, increasingly busier as she grows up. Her interpretations are fed into her off-line social calculations, which call for long-ranging hypothetical calculations about future and past interactions with others. Attitude ascriptions enable her to imagine social scenarios and plan what to say or do to others. So far the familiar script, just more intense and complex. But there are also qualitatively new pressures with far-reaching implications for metamentation. To understand these new pressures, it is important to see why the old and basic ego-*world-alter* (or mind-world-mind) pattern of intersubjective interpretation is not enough. In that pattern the ego is implicit, not focused on explicitly. Interpretation is directed at the other. Graphically, the pattern reads: ego-*world-alter;* it's the subject-world relation that matters most. This is what is changing now. The ego is also focused on, made explicit, fully aligned to the other two variables. Making sense of others needs to be mixed with making sense of *self to others,* in communication, play, education, child politics, and so on. Self justifications and rationalizations of actions or attitudes become frequent, and so does self regulation in terms of what others would think of self and how self would respond to that (Dunn 1988; Rogoff 1990; Tomasello, Kruger, and Ratner 1993). Making sense of self to others also requires making sense of *self to self.* This is vital. If one wants to rehearse mentally how one should present one's sayings, actions, decisions, motives or preferences to others, then one has to represent them explicitly to self, reason and talk to self about them, which is a self-to-self interpretation, thoroughly mixed with interpretations of others.

To play this new game, the child must be able to ascribe attitudes to others and to self and to represent the two types of ascriptions in *comparable* if not common representations. Not only must the child iterate attitude ascriptions by embedding some in the content of others (a development discussed in the next chapter) but she must also be able to *mix* self and others in the relational determination of contents ascribed—a development noted to be vital for the mastery of explicit metathought. With this mastery acquired, the interpreter can represent such mixed attributions as 'I now remember what he said he used to believe' or 'I believe what she believes' or, solely in the first person, 'I believe what I hope will happen'. The young interpreter can play a mental chess, as it were, with representations of other- and self-bound attitudes on the *same* mental board, with the same pieces, following the same rules (figure 6.5).

Such sameness of treatment of self- and other-directed attitudes points to the emergence of a *common* denominator, the category of explicit metathought, when mind-world-mind relations or representings are mentally rehearsed in a common format and across various domains, as the next chapter explains. What we have so far, prior to these developments, is a parallelism of format, which can be parsed as in table 6.1.

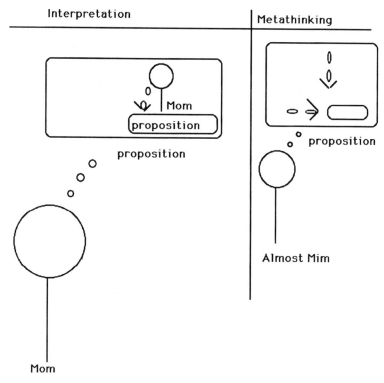

Figure 6.5
Relational and self-directed specification of content. This is the same as figure 6.4 except that Mom is also in the position of subject. The emulation saga is now moving fast. Although still virtual, Mim is almost a protoreflexive thinker, in that the format of his explicit thoughts is now pretty much in place.

Table 6.1
Explicitly Representing

	Interpretation	Reflexive thinking
Mental act of explicitly representing . . .	attitude to a proposition relationally defined	explicit metathought
Relation	Mind-world-mind relation (or attitude that)	Thought that
Content	What is attitudinized by self and others	What is thought in relation to other thoughts

If anything is emulated at this stage, it would probably be a generic *format* of representing explicit metathoughts but not yet the full blown category of explicit metathought. The emulation log could mark this interim moment as follows:

Tenth emulation   The format of explicit metathought emulates the category of attitude to a content relationally specified.

Before examining (in the next chapter) two major developments that bring this emulation to completion, let me fortify my analysis against some popular alternatives. Time to get critical.

Self-Representing Mind

The first alternative I want to argue against is the notion that, viewed from inside, one's mentation could be a basis for representing explicit metathoughts. A first thing to note is that even though ground-level thoughts operate in mental rehearsal and can be conscious, their kind is different from the higher-level or reflexive kind. 'Different' means not just 'unlike in structure and function.' It also means that reflexive thoughts cannot be generated with the resources and from the perspective of conscious ground-level thinking. The argument develops a distinction made in chapter 5, section 1, between minds that do and minds that don't interpret.

A ground-level thought is a data structure representing a target in the world in virtue of (a) causal or lawful or some other sort of regular (including normative) connections between target and data structure and of (b) the way these connections are encoded in the data structure and assumed by the programs that generate it. The facts expressed in (a) and (b) are truths available to cognitive science but not to an individual mind. As perceiver, I have no way to grasp lawful or causal connections between my visual images and their targets; I simply see the latter as represented by the former; that is all. As perceiver, I have no handy formula to figure out how lawful or causal connections between targets in the world and my perception end up encoded in my visual images. The same is true of other sorts of ground-level representations, such as mental images, sentences, memories, and so on. In short, neither (a) nor (b) provide grounds for metarepresentation, as required by the category of explicit metathought, since neither can be explicitly reenacted internally. This was a conceptual point. There is also a developmental point. When a child acquires the ability to represent herself *as* perceiving something, as being in that distinct relation to the world, it is thanks to *interpretation,* which is a mode of cognition different from perception. Merely perceiving something won't do. One cannot discern the perceptual relation in what one perceives without switching to interpretation and first to the interpretation of others and of their perceptual relations to the world. The same is true of other ground-level kinds of mental representation. This is why in general none of these kinds can underpin the category of explicit metathought, which is built around the representation of distinctly discernible relations between other minds and the world.

What about the *conscious* awareness of ground-level thoughts? Could it represent explicit metathoughts? I think not. A conscious thought is not yet an explicit metathought. The former is defined by access, the latter by its *form of representation*. Access does not determine form of representation, certainly not that needed for explicit metathought or for self-ascribed attitudes, for that matter. Access or awareness do not *classify* ground-level structures relationally *as* mental representings. One may be aware of what a thought represents but not *that* the thought represents. Although ground-level thoughts covary with or are caused by properties of their targets, which is why they represent, these (as just noted) are not relational truths explicitly and consciously represented by their thinker. As in the case of perception, the thinker represents the target of the thought, not *that* the target is represented in thought. It is the latter relation that is essential to explicit metathought.

Two forms of conscious awareness get top attention nowadays. One is hot or phenomenal, the other cool or metarepresentational. I do not take a stand on this distinction but simply use it to make a critical point. On the hot side, *phenomenal* awareness is said to provide internal signals of having attitudes or thoughts, of being in those kinds of states. The signals can be feels, sensations, perhaps an immediate sense of what it is like to be in a mental state. Some philosophers think that phenomenal awareness could categorize attitudes (Goldman 1993), and therefore (on my analysis) be a basis for the category of explicit metathought. On the cold side, *metarepresentational* access is what a higher-level representation provides to a lower-level one. It is believed that such access could also be a basis for metathinking. Some philosophers view metathinking as introspective (Armstrong 1968, 94–107; Sellars 1963, 177–196); others allow for nonintrospective access to lower-level states, so that the accessed state is conscious but the accessing one need not be (Carruthers 1996, chapter 7; Mellor 1978; Nelkin 1995, chapter 8; Rosenthal 1986, 1993).

In my view, the symptomatic notion in all these accounts is that of *state.* The notion of state picks out a *nonrelational* entity that cannot deliver a representation of explicit metathought. For the following reason. On the hot side, phenomenal data may signal the presence of a type of mental state and may provide a sense of *having* it. Yet this internal sense cannot yield the recognition of the *relations* that the state has to the world. Sensing one's goals, feeling one's desires or noticing one's beliefs as states (assuming this is possible) is not yet recognizing them *as* instances of mind-world relations. Since one normally identifies desires or beliefs as mind-world relations, one is unlikely to identify them as mere states. Conscious reflexivity presupposes the representation of mind-world relations and therefore cannot emerge from merely having and registering internal states.

On the cool side, a lower-level state is represented by a higher-level state as a mental event (experience) or formal configuration (structure made of interrelated elements) or in terms of its content (what it represents). Neither of these representations is about the *relation* required by the category of explicit metathought, which is the representing relation between a mental state and its target. The content gambit alone may look relational but actually isn't. Unlike the other two, which are internally specified without mention of a target, the content is about a target, but it does not *explicitly relate* the target to its representation; the content simply captures what is represented, a fact or situation, not *that* it is represented. In short, hot or cold, conscious access offers no avenue to the category of explicit metathought.

Self-Interpreting Mind

One may grant my criticism that the self accessing its mental *states* cannot represent explicit metathoughts but insist that interpretation *begins with self* and that, from there and in its terms, so does the representation of explicit metathought. It is true that, as just argued, the category of explicit metathought owes much to self interpretation. Yet it is false that interpretation begins with self. Among the arguments that it does, two are popular. One construes self-bound attitudes as mental states or other nonrelational episodes that one has immediate access to, in which case we are back to my just-concluded criticism. Indeed, the authors cited in that connection tend to construe the mental states introspected as propositional-attitude *states*. I take the argument of the previous subsection to show that this construal is misguided when propositional attitudes are viewed relationally, as they should (also Bogdan 1995, 1997).

Simulation is another way of arguing that interpretation begins with self and can ground the development of mental reflexivity in self knowledge. (See Davies and Stone 1995, for a survey of debates about simulation). I doubt both propositions. To explain why, I begin by distinguishing two conceptions of simulation, one narrow, another ambitious. *Narrowly construed*, simulation interprets others by using the interpreter's resources for practical reasoning: she feeds data about the subject's conditions into her practical-reasoning mechanism, runs the mechanism off-line (disconnected from her conation, cognition, and action), and comes up with an output that explains or predicts the subject's attitudes or actions (Gordon 1995). Simulation is thus a form of interpreting *others* by recruiting one's *noninterpretational* resources. Nothing in the narrow account entails that one begins by *interpreting* self or by interpreting self *before* interpreting others or by interpreting self first *in order to* interpret others. The projection from self to other need not use any interpretive gear (or indeed any form of internal experience). It does not proceed from one's attitudes, recognized as such, to those of others. Narrow simulation works along inferential or projective lines, as an answer to the question, how would I act in his place? Running one's practical reasoning off-line amounts to using one's conative and cognitive resources but not necessarily *recognizing* them, from an interpretive stance, *as* desires and beliefs. In short, one can simulate narrowly without making explicit self attributions of attitudes.

And there is a further point to consider. Narrow simulation operates as some sort of mental rehearsal of what one would do or expect or think if one were in somebody else's shoes. This is mental rehearsal in the *social* domain. Narrow simulation may have evolved as a mental-rehearsal strategy in the social domain, as a form of social imagination. In that case the narrow simulator must *already* know that those who are simulated are *intentional* agents who harbor desires and beliefs on which they act. The same conclusion seems to emerge from studies of child development (Perner 1991, 270). The point may sound trivial but is important because simulation works only because some prior *interpretive* knowledge is available. This knowledge need not determine what a subject's action or desire would be in a *particular* case, which is precisely the job of simulation, but it secures the very possibility of simulation. In other words, narrow simulation as social imagination evolved to handle the *particulars* of a subject's intentionality or world-relatedness, from the interpreter's perspective; it did not evolve as a strategy of representing a subject's intentionality *as such,* in all its forms. This diagnosis is further firmed up by the hypothesis (entertained in chapter 2, section 4) that mental rehearsal itself may have first evolved in the social domain as a form of social imagination. For all practical purposes, narrow simulation may have been one its versions.

An *ambitious* account of simulation wants the conceptualization of attitudes to begin at self. If this gambit is supposed to link up with one's awareness of inner states, then I already said enough against this possibility. If the gambit is learning in social contexts how to categorize mental states (Gordon 1995, Harris 1991), then it must be stressed that social learning presupposes interpretation and that children operate in the social domain by already possessing a minimal interpretive knowledge of what others are (namely, intentional agents) and how they relate to the world. Which leads to a more general point. When one takes a longer evolutionary view of the matter, one would recognize that a few interpretive categories, such as agency, gaze or attention, seem innate, initially other-directed, and employed by interpreters, such as apes and human infants, who do not appear to simulate, may fail to be self conscious or introspective, and may even fail at self recognition. Why would the evolutionary story suddenly change in older children and adults with the successor categories of belief or intention? As far as I can tell, it doesn't, for reasons discussed earlier in this work and elsewhere (Bogdan 1997). And even if some of the later categories were learned, then the question is why they would be learned from inside, while their innate predecessors were consistently other-directed. So, in the company of other critics sympathetic to narrow, predictive but not category-building simulation (Perner 1991, chapter 11; Stich and Nichols 1993), I conclude that the simulation account does not have a plausible story of the interpretive categories and thus of the sources of mental reflexivity.

Time now for a brief recapitulation. The category of explicit metathought is at the heart of metamentation. This chapter has examined its immediate interpretational sources, the metasemantic category of situated attitude and its successor, the naively functionalist category of propositional attitude. When the latter category is turned to self-interpretation, the category of explicit metathought is almost within reach. Almost but not quite. Some further developments await. Hence the next chapter.

Chapter 7
Mind Unification

Another key development in interpretation that allows the category of explicit metathought to do reflexive work is the ascription of attitudes to many interacting subjects who interpret each other or still further subjects. It is the ability to hold many minds in one's mind, as I like to phrase it, and it is the topic of section 1. Equally important are the common format of interpretive categories and a cross-domains integration of the data they represent. That is the topic of section 2. Both developments are complex and not yet fully understood, which is why my analysis is selective and sketchy but, I hope, sufficiently detailed to portray them as essential to the completion of explicit metathinking and the maturation of metamentation. Section 3 comments on some by-products of these developments, particularly mind unification and reflexive consciousness, both symptomatic of metamentation and rather unexpected from an evolutionary point of view.

1 Holding Minds in Mind

My account has so far registered two major contributions made by interpretation to the category of explicit metathought: an explicit representation of other- and self-regarding attitudes and a relational determination of their content. In isolation, however, an explicit metathought—a thought related to another thought—is almost an abstraction, rarely operative as such; normally, it is part of much larger sequences of thoughts required by the metamental routines. So the question arises as to whether the contributions made so far by interpretation, together with the combinatorial possibilities afforded by language and logic, are enough to generate sequences of explicit metathoughts. I think not, for several reasons.

The Evolutionary Why
Not often asked is a simple but important question: Why would the child link explicit metathoughts with other such thoughts and iterate the process? From

the adult angle, it looks like a normal and good thing to do; which it is. But this need not be the child's angle. It is not adult competence that the child cares about or (even if she did) knows how to emulate. The perspective of the adult forms was shown to yield a distorted explanation of their development. So, to switch perspectives, let us think of adult forms as becoming possible because (and intelligible in the light) of pressures during childhood. What sort of pressures and in what domains?

The data suggest (below) that older children progress slowly in envisaging two or three moves ahead in solving a problem, even when the problem is framed in figurative terms. So why would the child think iteratively and abstractly about *thoughts* about (say) birds, and not, more easily and pleasingly, about situations with birds or pictures of birds or even visualizable stories of possible birds? The child could think of various possibilities without having to think explicitly of thoughts *inhabiting* these possibilities, and certainly not in embedded or extended iterations. Since the cognitive cost of doing so is high, what could be the incentives and benefits or, alternatively, the costs of not doing it? It will not surprise the reader that my answer favors interpretation.

Whether one likes it or not, one *must* interpret other people, who in turn interpret other people (often) interpreting still other people, and so on. Interpretations of others interpreting still others are not a matter of choice or chance (as can be problem solving in the physical domain) but of daily necessity. It is because one so frequently and spontaneously interprets other people in multiply embedded and iterated sequences of attitudes that one comes to think of explicit metathoughts in similar sequences. In many ways, the argument echoes the old story of multilateral relations among conspecifics, played first in imagination before being acted upon socially (chapter 2, section 4), but at a higher level of abstraction and complexity. Or so I propose to look at the matter.

The proposal may be conceptually plausible, yet its theoretical articulation and empirical defense remain problematic. For one thing, the role of interpretation in generative metamentation has not been much studied empirically, so far as I know. The data I found are scarce, indirect, and mostly symptomatic. Perhaps echoing the philosophical focus on the static and isolated propositional attitude, developmental psychologists have shown less interest in studying interpretation beyond the metarepresentation of discrete attitudes, with the notable and laudable exception of research on narrative interpretation (Bruner 1990; Bruner and Feldman 1993; Carrithers 1991, 1995), on which more below. These empirical limitations render my dossier incomplete, more speculative than I wanted, and inevitably detective. Yet the tactic of my argument remains the same. It is to show the following:

• It is in the social territory patrolled by interpretation that the child first and most often finds patterns of relations calling for iterated ascriptions of propositional attitudes. The pressures on her interpretive imagination to range over many interinterpreting minds call for iterated and multiply embedded ascriptions of attitudes, which in turn are emulated by generative deployments of explicit metathoughts.
• The generative forms of metamentation are close to and often isomorphic with iterated and multiply embedded attributions of attitudes.
• The ontogenetic schedule of the interpretation of many interrelated minds seems to be ahead of, yet fairly consistently correlated with, that of generative metamentation.

The Need for Reconstruction
If the handling of sociocultural life calls for sequences of attributions ranging over many minds, how is interpretation going to manage such new tasks? It turns out that metarepresentational interpretation is as incomplete on its developmental track as is having isolated metathoughts on the reflexive track. The building blocks, attitude attributions, may be in place, but the know-how for their iteration is not. It does not take much professional acumen to note that preadolescent children often interpret choppily, in small, brief, and isolated bursts, without much continuity, relatedness or sensitivity to complex and evolving plots. Their attitude ascriptions remain heavily biased toward situatedness, are not very good at handling the intricacies of adult minds or at guessing derived or interlocked attitudes, and, importantly, are not yet good at interpreting many subjects who interpret each other. (Except, of course, the younger versions of the present readers and the ones they love.) The cultural training of the interpreter, through instruction, discussion, and story telling continues apace throughout late childhood and into early adolescence (Bruner 1990; Bruner and Feldman 1993; Slobin 1990; Tomasello, Kruger, and Ratner 1993). I read these developments as evidence that *further* interpretive skills are being groomed along the way.

   There are good reasons for such new skills. The whole system of socialization, instruction, and enculturation depends on the child's ability to hold many minds in mind. Self-regulation and social planning are telling examples. Imagine the older child planning her reactions by asking herself, 'What would mother think if I tell her that I read Derrida late into the night?' Or to push the complexity one notch up, 'What would the teacher think of my parents' reaction to the news that I first read fragments from Derrida in a funny book written in French by a theoretical physicist from New York?' (Push the complexity still further by adding a grandmother's conservative thoughts to

this sequence of worries.) Other examples can be found in planful communication, whereby one often has to foresee chains of reactions by others and
then contemplate her reactions to theirs. The others are far-seeing and far-
reaching social planners, schemers, problem solvers, and communicators, who
may hold in mind many other minds when making a decision or communicating something. They are the sort of thinkers who could ask someone
(primary subject) to do something by considering in advance, as the primary
subject would, what others (secondary, tertiary, *n*-ary subjects) would think
and say and how the primary subject would factor their reactions into his
thinking before accepting, or not, to do what asked. The same challenges
emerge when the child accepts adult truths (a full-time job at this age).
Imagine a child who witnesses a heated metaculinary discussion between her
multiethnic Swiss parents, and remembers, 'It must be true that the French
eat better than the Germans because the teacher said it, with exasperated envy
in his voice, being from the plain-eating village of Schwartzenkniffeln, and
what the teacher says must be believed, particularly when prefixed by der,
die, das'.

   In short, as they grow up, children come under increased pressures to master
the intricacies of the more sophisticated adult minds. It is as a result of being
challenged by such complex minds—who constantly mind other minds in
what they think, say, and do—that children develop new interpretive skills
that will help turn them into reflexive thinkers. I group these new skills under
a competence for *reconstruction* (Bogdan 1997, chapter 8). It is a competence
that does several jobs. It allows the interpreter to identify attitudes and social
roles from a cultural distance, as it were, when visual, behavioral, or directly
verbal signposts are not available. It also enables the interpreter to adjust the
representations of the attitudes and roles of others, thusly identified, to her
own interests and practical concerns. And finally, reconstruction manages to
format the practically adjusted representations of attitudes and roles of others
so as to mesh smoothly with the interpreter's own thoughts, attitudes, plans,
and actions. It turns out that it is precisely during the lengthy initiation into
reconstruction that the older child is faced with and gradually comes to master
the iterations and multiple embeddings of propositional attitudes, which is the
part that matters in the present discussion.

   I cite next two indirect but symptomatic pieces of evidence that support
the notion that, as an ability that enables one to handle multiple iterations
and embeddings of attitude ascriptions, reconstruction is under way in late
childhood and early adolescence. One such piece of evidence is narration, the
other (more controversial and indirect) is problem solving in the physical
domain.

Narration

Narration offers evidence of progress in mastering reconstruction and gradually turning it into metamentation. Narration also suggests that generative metamentation is not just the mastery of the category of explicit metathought plus formal algorithms of iteration or embedding. It is a fact that the child has and employs such algorithms before she can reconstruct attitudes or narrate properly. The narration I have in mind is *interpretive* narration, of the sort found in story telling, gossip, elaborate lies, justification of actions, and recounting complex events involving many people interpreting each other. In later childhood narration alone has the imaginative sweep to project across space, time, and possible worlds extended and ramified sequences of situations populated by agents related interpretively to other agents. It turns out that interpretive narration is not fully mastered before early adolescence. Despite lively protestations from friends fondly recalling their golden intellectual development, I side with what I hear around and with the professional data suggesting that younger children seldom narrate in a continuous and coherent fashion (Bruner and Feldman 1993; Leondar 1977; Nelson 1996, chapter 7; Slobin 1990). Older children, even as old as nine, can tell stories but in a stereotyped and mechanical way. These are stories of the sort 'He did that, and she did that, and then he went there and looked for, etc.' (Many college students narrate like this and even some adults, particularly on cellular phones used in implausible places.)

As training ground for new skills, narration may gradually reframe the child's reconstruction from an intuitive, visual, self-centered, idiosyncratic, and situated interpretation to one that is abstract, public, unsituated, and mapped on the shared grid of culture. Imagine the process as a transition *from* interpreting visualizable people interpreting other such people in directly accessed, vividly represented, situated contexts (early childhood) *to* interpreting (rather disembodied) minds interpreting other (rather disembodied) minds in indirectly accessed or somewhat more abstractly represented contexts (late childhood) *to* interpreting independently individuated and unsituated attitudes about other attitudes (adolescence). This is a transition rather well reflected in the verbal, illustrated, and later written stories that children progressively understand, compose, and enjoy.

There are several reasons for looking at the transition in this way. One is that the interpretation of sequences of relations among visualizable people and later of somewhat disembodied minds may be easier, since closer to the mental situatedness of younger children, and hence may emerge earlier than the interpretation of unsituated attitudes. Although six or seven-year-olds master the category of unsituated attitude, it need not follow that they can easily sequence such attitudes abstractly and unsituatedly. The evidence cited earlier points that way. This is probably why older children (and even adults) still understand and produce stories about other people in a visualizable and quasi situated manner. In such stories children may go first (the default option) for situated attitudes, such as seeing, remembering, simple desiring, or, with extra effort, for half-situated attitudes, such as lack of perceptual access as false belief—a possibility generally documented by Perner (1991). Since older children already possess the categories of propositional attitudes, one may reasonably infer that their narrative incompleteness has to do with the generative abilities to link and embed such attitudes rather than understanding them individually.

Meantime, in Other Domains

There is another and intriguing line of experimental and clinical evidence suggesting that advances in interpretation correlate significantly with, and may be responsible for, advances in various forms of thinking, such as sequential means-ends analysis and problem solving, even outside the social domain. This serious possibility reinforces the general argument of chapter 2 (section 4) to the effect that social cognition and interpretation may have stimulated and shaped the evolution of mental rehearsal. The same pattern may be at work in child development. A recent body of experimental literature (surveyed and analyzed by Perner and Lang 1999) shows from different perspectives that, when turned toward oneself, interpretation provides or facilitates the following:

• A better understanding of the child's own mind and thus a better control of her mental processes
• Inhibition of distracting alternatives
• An ability to represent instructions as intended, thus affording metarepresentational control over executive functions
• Possibly, an ability to embed multiple sequences of conditionals (Frye, Zelazo, Palfai 1995)
• In general, an increased ability of executive control, which seems to progress hand in hand with advances in child interpretation

Interestingly, older children become progressively better at means-ends analyses by getting better at keeping in mind simultaneously larger numbers of increasingly more complex subgoals. The progress is indicated by the number of moves required to advance from an initial arrangement to a goal. Each year after three adds two or more moves to the means-ends analysis. Nevertheless, even six or seven-year-olds are not yet accomplished means-ends analyzers who can contemplate alternatives to short-term subgoals or long or ramified trees of subgoals (Siegler 1991, 267–268; see also Bjorklund 1995, 137). This study has focused on means-ends analyses in the *physical* domain but one might expect similar data in the social domain. The progress in means-ends analyses, very marked in the period from three to six, takes place during the critical period when interpretation turns to basic propositional attitudes and when more complex attitudes, such as intention, hope or regret, appear to be gradually assembled out of basic ones. The problems that six or seven-year-olds have envisaging extended means-ends sequences seems to parallel the pressures to mature the generative abilities needed to construct ramified and extended sequences of attitudes across many and interrelated possible worlds populated by agents who interpret each other.

There is also neurological and clinical evidence in support of the parallel between interpretation and means-ends thinking. On the neurological side, it is known that brain areas involved in social regulation also do planning and decision making (Damasio 1994, chapters 4 and 8). Specifically, interpretation and executive functions are believed to draw on the same or related brain structures (Ozonoff et al. 1991; Perner and Lang 1999). On the clinical side, autism is known to be a mental impairment manifested both in interpretation and executive functions involved in means-ends thinking. The deficit in interpretation seems more basic and, in the light of what was just said, likely to be responsible for deficits in executive functions (more in chapter 8, section 1).

There could and will be objections to this entire line of inquiry. One objection may be that what is responsible for advances in sequential means-ends analyses is simply a development in the memory capacity (Bjorklund 1995, 137). But then, I ask, what would drive memory development and the ability to sequence goals and subgoals. It is a fact that communication and social interaction force the older child to engage constantly in anticipatory planning and problem solving, in which attitude attributions *are* causally treated as means to ends. Children do play a sort of mental chess with people's attitudes and actions before they do it with mechanical actions on physical objects. The mental chess increasingly involves possible social scenarios in which possible moves are contemplated in terms of attitudes, before a course of action is selected. It is also conceivable that the abilities for mental rehearsal in the physical and social domain draw on the maturation of distinct abilities or of deeper and domain-neutral computational abilities. Nevertheless, there is little in the child's mind which appears domain-neutral, at least not in the early stages (for the pros and cons, see Hirschfeld and Gelman 1994, and Karmiloff-Smith 1992). The tight schedule of maturation of most abilities also speaks against domain neutrality. But even if there were domain-neutral computational resources, tapped by various programs for use in different domains, it could still be true that strong pressures in the social domain, together with its rich texture of relations, make interpretation, particularly at the reconstructional phase, the first and most potent exploiter of these resources and a model for use in other domains.

Thus Far
Such is the inductive dossier I could assemble for the claim that reconstructive interpretation has the reasons and evolves the means to mix, iterate, and embed other- and self-bound attributions of propositional attitudes. Without question, it is a dossier in need of further theory and empirical backing. Yet I think it stands a fair chance to be plausible and support the notion that the tasks of generative metamentation emulate those of reconstruction (see figure 7.1). Hence:

Eleventh emulation   The ability to generate and track iterations and multiple embeddings of explicit metathoughts emulates generative reconstruction.

Analytically, however, we are not quite there. Mim is not as generative as it may seem. She now has the tools but not yet all the material to work with. Perhaps better said: the material is not yet organized in the right way for the tools to do their job properly. The mastery of the new tasks of iteration and embedding of explicit metathoughts awaits two other crucial developments, intimately involved in the turn to self interpretation and reconstruction, but left unanalyzed so far. These developments round up the design of the category of explicit metathought and its dynamic deployment in metamentation.

2   All Together Now

Explicit metathoughts have a uniform mental identity, recognized as such, which is that of mental structures that represent (no matter what). As for content, they operate across various domains, whether physical, biological, numerical or social. To do that, explicit metathoughts draw on many sorts of categories, schemes, and databases. This ability is puzzling because this is not how animal minds are supposed to work. Such developments are not in the evolutionary cards, as it were, at least not on currently influential accounts (see Barkow, Cosmides, and Tooby 1992; Cummins and Allen 1998; Donald 1991; Mithen 1996; and Tomasello and Call 1997 for surveys). So the question is how these developments came about and why. They could, but do not seem to, reflect maturational processes built into the genetic design of the child's

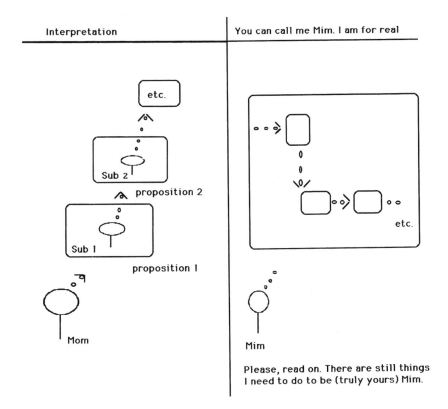

Figure 7.1
From reconstruction to metamentation. The iterations of attitudes that design the category of explicit thought and its metamental work are the ones whose propositional contents are specified relationally. For example, when Mom interprets Pipa as believing that Boba hopes that crows are smart, the relational specification of the contents involved can be represented as follows: Mom interprets Pipa as believing what Boba hopes, which is that crows are smart. The virtual Mim who mentally rehearses such iterations relationally specified is, all things considered, very close to a reflexive Mim. That is why this is the last figure. Mom and Mim bid you farewell and urge you to stay reflexive as long as you can and to treat other people as you treat your own thoughts. If you see what I mean, you saw the point of this essay.

mind and scheduled to come off under the right stimulation. Nor do they seem to reflect tasks that the child's mind learns how to handle on its own, through individual exposure to the world. Assuming that the primate mind does not begin as a *tabula rasa,* it is hard to see how such a mind could learn to connect its categories across domains and break the walls separating its specialized databases. So we must look elsewhere for an explanation. Like earlier developments in metamentation, the common format of explicit metathoughts, the isolated bits of knowledge they integrate, and the different domains they engage simultaneously suggest the conceptual hand, evolutionary rationale, and ontogenetic schedule of interpretation. So argues this section.

The Puzzle
Primate minds, including apparently those of young children, are not expected to format their mental structures and what they represent in various domains in commensurate, let alone common terms. Such is the expectation of the modularity view of the mind (Fodor 1983) and is embraced by many evolutionary psychologists (Alexander 1990b, Cosmides and Tooby 1987, Rozin 1967, Sperber 1994, Tooby and Cosmides 1990). This expectation could also be extended to those positions, equally influential, that view mentation in terms of naive and domain-specific theories or even of learning strategies, as long as these are functionally specialized and domain-specific (Carey 1985, Gopnik and Meltzoff 1997, Karmiloff-Smith 1992). In short, an integrated mentation that formats its data uniformly across databases and domains is puzzling. This is because, on any of these views, animal minds are partitioned with respect to domain, database, and categorization skills. When an animal acts on the physical domain, it recognizes aspects and recalls details that are different from those recognized and recalled in the biological domain. The partitioning of animal minds is not limited to cognition. It also applies to emotion. There seem to be no single "emotion faculty" but rather so many distinct and specialized types of emotions, such fear, defense, mating, and so on, dedicated to specific domains of behavior (LeDoux 1996).

Primate minds are no exception. Consider their interpretation. It has its domain, its database with information about typical patterns of social interactions and relevant details about individuals, and its specialized categories of intentional relations. These categories may have their specialized domains and databases within the larger ones. The gaze-recognition category, for example, tracks only eyes, line of regard, and head posture, as features of the larger domain of conspecific behavior and interaction, but may ignore other features, such as bodily postures or specific patterns of behavior, and may access some types of data about conspecifics, such as eyes and facial expressions, but not others (Baron-Cohen 1995). Like all animal minds, those of the primates are not expected to mix apples and oranges. Yet some do.[1] It isn't clear when this gambit makes its phylogenetic appearance. It may show timid signs among apes, although the evidence is inconclusive, but is clearly at work in human childhood. I focus on two aspects of this puzzling gambit: common format and knowledge integration. They are instrumental in producing a unified mind that thinks reflexively, which is perhaps the greatest puzzle of them all.

Common Format

Explicit metathoughts are represented *as mental structures related to contents specified in relation to other thoughts,* whatever the content or manner of representation. The italicized part constitutes the *generic* form of representing explicit metathoughts. Consider these examples of explicit metathoughts I now entertain, for your sake:

• I vividly remember now that the water I was looking at in Corsica (for hours, while listening to philosophical papers) was cobalt blue. I want to go back.
• Catalina feared that others would believe that the cover design she made for a book on interpretation was too iconoclastic to be accepted by the press, but it was.
• Some people think that I hold that the widespread attraction of deconstruction, postmodernism, and other intellectual fashions is the price paid for having an industry-sized faculty in the humanities that is constantly in frantic search of new ideas to fight for and convert into tenurable security while they cheerfully irritate the bourgeoisie (including, alarmingly, that part which pays the tuition of its offspring). Those people are onto something.

My representations of these explicit metathoughts are differently structured, pick out different types of mind-world relations, originate in different cognitive modalities (perception, memory, emotion, reasoning), and therefore draw on different databases. Nevertheless, the representations have this much in common: they categorize and compute *mental relations to contents* containing further such relations, irrespective of the specifics of the relations and contents in question. It is as if the metamental programs first scan for such common patterns before filling in the details. There is a problem, though. In its early phases, interpretation *itself* is thought to be partitioned and specialized. The modular view takes these partitions to be tightly sealed (Baron-Cohen 1995; Leslie 1988, 1994). The liberal theory-of-mind view has a more fluid conception but acknowledges the self/other asymmetry and the developmental distinctness of the categories of different attitudes (Gopnik and Wellman 1994,

Meltzoff and Gopnik 1997, Perner 1991, Wellman 1990). On either view, the common format of representation of other- and self-bound attitudes and of different types of attitudes in each class remains something of a puzzle. What could explain it? It is a long, complex, and unfinished story. But some of its contours, which matter here, can be discerned and briefly sketched.

In an earlier work I argued that interpretive categories evolved as practical procedures of engaging subject-world relations (Bogdan 1997, chapter 5). These categories are made of conditional rules that segment and sequence subject-world relations in patterns that afford effective strategies of causal engagement. The categories have their domain of application and a database that stores facts known about the domain. For example, one may assume that the category of gaze has rules such as 'If eyes are open and line of regard has a discernible direction, then expect the subject's interest and behavior in that direction, so get involved', or that the category of belief has rules such as 'If different subjects have similar desires but different access to a situation, then subjects might act differently, so get involved accordingly', and so on. These examples are not meant to shine in precision or comprehensiveness but simply to make a point.

The point is that such rules do not actually pick out gaze or belief *as such*. The latter categories *simplify* and *unify* larger families of rules that in turn simplify and unify various action patterns and observable conditions of subjects. All primates seem to evolve such hierarchies of increasingly economical representations that operate as "intervening variables" over lower-level attributions, as Andrew Whiten has proposed (Whiten 1993, 1994, 1996; Whiten and Byrne 1988b). This gambit is a response to deeper evolutionary pressures for taming complexity through economic packaging of data and speed of access and processing (Dawkins 1976). On this model, interpretation computes top-down: from generic types (intentional relation, propositional attitude) to narrower categories (desire, belief) to conditional rules (such as those illustrated a paragraph ago). At each level, when available, phenomenal indices and linguistic markers may further simplify the access to categories and rules (Bogdan 1997, 142–148).

It is only in the metarepresentational interpretation of propositional attitudes that this complexity-taming tactic yields a consistent policy of common formatting, thanks to several developments. Naive functionalism, for one, encourages a uniform representation of attitude types across contexts and contents. Belief, for example, can be uniformly categorized as a mind-world relation caused by information access, influenced by other attitudes, leading to action when coupled to desire, and so on. So categorized, belief is discerned as an attitude type that is *invariant* across different modalities that identify it, such as perception, memory or imagination, also across variable contexts in which it occurs, and relative to an immense variety of contents. The same is true of other attitude types, such as desire or intention (Astington and Gopnik 1988, Perner 1991, Wellman 1990).

All this still leaves attitude types distinct, with common formatting inside but not *across* types. Yet the representation of explicit metathought is *attitude-neutral*. How come? Any primate interpreter can join the recognition of what a subject sees and wants, but this, as noted below, is a matter of joint access rather than common format. Mixing and jointly computing distinct attitude types is different and much harder (Wellman 1990, Whiten 1994). Several developments may have had a hand in bringing about such attitude integration. Naive functionalism, again, reveals features that different attitude types *share*, such as mind-world relatedness, opacity, perspectivality, mutual influence, embedding and iteration, and so on. In these shared respects, the interpreter could form a *common* sense of attitude. Another development could be the turn to *self* interpretation, noted at the end of last chapter to extend the representation of other-bound attitudes to those of the self. In order to operate over and mix self- and other-regarding attitudes, mental calculations need a common format. And so would the representation and computation of iterations and multiple embeddings of propositional attitudes. The point is not that the attitudes, so calculated, lose their identity but rather that their neutral and generic format is represented before type-specific differences are factored in. Once represented neutrally and generically, the category of propositional attitude begins to look more and more like its later emulator, the category of explicit metathought. When the latter is fed into mental rehearsal, two things happen: the metathought is explicitly represented as a mental relation to a content; but being hypothetical, off-line, imagined, the representing itself need not be subject to any attitude. One comes to entertain or imagine thoughts, which one need not believe. What matters is that one imagines mental representings of something or other; one just thinks about thoughts.

Knowledge Integration
The common format of attitudes is only part of the story. The other part concerns the *contents* of the attitudes. Attributions of (attitudinized) contents can range over many domains and tap many databases. So does the reflexive traffic with metathoughts. This development would not be possible unless the knowledge accessed by the interpreter-turned-metathinker becomes integrated, instead of being partitioned in tightly sealed boxes. Yet again, this is surprising. Like all organisms, humans are thought to inherit and develop specialized faculties (whether modules or naive theories) for distinct domains. Their

knowledge is therefore expected to be domain-specific and serviced by distinct and uncommunicating categories that access unshared and equally domain-specific databases. For a while, this may be the sort of knowledge the infant actually has. But not for long. Something happens later, resulting in a cross-domain integration of data over which mental rehearsals are run. Two interpretation-driven developments, already examined, seem instrumental in bringing this about: mental unsituatedness and holding many minds in mind.

A comparison with the partitioned knowledge of situated minds may explain why knowledge integration depends on mental unsituatedness and on what interpretation has done to make it possible. Suppose an animal sees a predator near a tree. It recognizes biological and physical items in some relation. This may look like knowledge integration: different domain-specific categories (biological, physical) tap distinct databases (what the animal knows about predators and trees) but fuse these categories and data in perception. This is *not* what I mean by knowledge integration.[2] Joint perceptual recognition indicates *access* of control and motor routines to the *outputs* of various sensory and memory systems and domain-specific categories. The brain's intermodal integration of various kinds of data, mostly sensorimotor, is the larger phenomenon. For convenience, I call it 'fused output access'. Rare an organism that could manage without it. Yet it need not follow (a) that a fused output access comes together as a unified body of data represented explicitly in a common format, or (b) that this unified body of data is subject to mental rehearsal. But (a) and (b) *are* conditions for knowledge integration and they cannot be met by situated minds. The fused output access is perceptual, short-lived, and available to action alone, *not* to further higher-level processing.[3]

Consider now interpretation. Alone among cognitive abilities, it ranges systematically over two distinct information spaces mapped together: one space is populated by conspecifics as subjects, the other is populated by whatever in the world subjects relate to—physical events, biological organisms, you name it. Call these the 'subject space' and the 'world space'. Interpreters constantly commute between these spaces along subject-world routes. Since a subject can have successive and changing relations to distinct domains in the world or to several domains at once, the interpreter must also engage these domains, often simultaneously. This *is* unprecedented. First among cognitive faculties, interpretation is strongly pressured to handle such a multi-domain engagement and become ever better at it. Yet the result is different in situated from unsituated interpretation. The difference bears crucially on knowledge integration (Alexander 1990b, Rozin 1976).

By sharing perceptually a world with the subject, the situated interpreter can supply her *own* representations of the domains to which the subject is related. This is a subjective, egocentric solution to the problem of cross-domain integration of knowledge. As noted in chapter 5, section 2, an ape interpreter, following the gaze of another ape, may provide her own determination of what the target of the gaze might be and in what domain; she does it through her perception, not through *specialized* interpretive skills. If the target is a physical object, her mind goes into a physical-knowledge mode; if another organism, it goes into a biological-knowledge mode; and so on. Whatever the dominant mode at the moment, all forms of sensorimotor cognition (and situated interpretation is one) call for fused output access, when properties or targets from different domains are joined together. If, for example, a conspecific plays with a banana, the dominant mode would be that of interpretation (targeting a conspecific), the subordinate mode that of naive biology (targeting fruits or edibles), and the output access (prior to action) would fuse the discriminations made in the two modes. Such fusing, however, falls short of knowledge integration.

Unsituated interpretation is different. The unsituated interpreter often does not have perceptual access to the domains engaged or imagined by the subject. And the interpreter often needs to represent facts in those domains *as* the subject does, irrespective of the domain the interpreter happens to engage at the time. If the subject's attitude engages two domains (say, physical and biological), then the interpreter must *mix* those domains when ascribing a content to that attitude. The interpreter must do so objectively, by specialized skills and from a cognitive distance, as it were, without the benefit of her own perceptual access to those domains. Such content ascription calls for knowledge integration across distinct domains and databases. Suppose that, lacking perceptual access to what she interprets, a child takes a subject, a father, to believe that there was a cat in the garden and that another child noticed and started playing with the cat. To ascribe to father the integrated belief content that a child noticed the cat and played with it, our interpreter must conjoin data about distinct domains (conspecifics, biological kinds, mechanical activities). The belief attributed to father integrates these different data in the content slot. The representation and processing of that belief *in the interpreter's mind* calls for such integration, if a content is to be ascribed (Tian 1996). The objectivity and cognitive reach of the integration suggest specialized skills at work.

The point, then, is this. If one must represent the world *according to* the mind of someone else but without direct access to that world, then one must be prepared to cross domains mentally, open up distinct databases, and integrate their information, in order to track what the other mind represents. This is why unsituated attributions act as a knowledge integrator in the *interpreter's* mind. If the category of explicit metathought emulates that of propositional attitude, then a similar gambit may be at work: to represent the world *according to* one's further thoughts, one must cross domains mentally in order to represent the various relations of those further thoughts to the world. The parallel makes sense, at least intuitively: if one developed the ability to think of the world as represented by somebody else, then one might just as well use that ability to think of the world as represented by further thoughts of one's own. In its earliest child versions, pressured by demands for self regulation or learning by perspective-taking, this self-directed exercise may have started by mimicking what somebody else would have thought, then transferring that role to self, and continuing with a self-to-self (and later thought-to-thought) dialogue.

Isolated attitude attributions are a prelude to knowledge integration, just as the interpretation of such attitudes is a prelude to generative reconstruction. The outputs of reconstruction are in turn fed into the interpreter's mental rehearsals and goal policies. These further utilizations add their pressures and rewards for knowledge integration. Think, for example, of a detective who must solve a case involving several interconnected suspects who say and do things to incriminate each other. The detective must cast a wide web of interpretation over these sayings and doings, which range over many domains, and also extend the web to their motives, thus opening up further worlds populated by other people, other attitudes, other domains, other motives. To make up her mind, the detective must deploy her attitude ascriptions over all the domains involved and access different databases. Sensitive to all these facts, her reconstruction must also sequence the ascriptions in the right patterns. The outcome of this laborious process must then be fed into her plans, projects, and inferences, with their domains and databases. Since life does not stay put, such a dynamic reconstruction also requires constant update from various databases, quick shifts from one domain to another or from one mixture of domains to another.

What detectives do professionally, explicitly, and carefully, folk psychologists do as a matter of course, most of the time, and spontaneously. The very possibility and efficacy of such reconstructions depend on free and multiple access to whatever bodies of data are needed for mental rehearsal. According to the emulation story, what is true of the interpretational handling of attitudes in mental rehearsal is likely to be true, mutatis mutandis, of the metamental handling of explicit metathoughts. Once such knowledge-integration tasks are in place, emulation may translate them into patterns of explicit metathoughts and make them available to metamentation. Thus, finally:

Twelfth emulation   The full category of explicit metathought emulates the category of an attitude to a content relationally specified, commonly formatted, and integrated across databases and domains.

3   Afterthoughts

The official argument of this essay is just about over. Having journeyed so far, I cannot resist a few pertinent though largely subtextual remarks about some further and equally intriguing by-products of the mastery of explicit metathought—explicit afterthoughts, really, which further glue the reflexive mind together.

Jack of All Trades

I said that mind unification by common formatting and knowledge integration looks like an evolutionary puzzle. If this essay is on the money (meager as it is, given the academic royalty rates), then a unified mind evolved out of a mind that minds other minds. The latter (interpreting) mind begins as functionally specialized and domain-specific, maybe modular, in its early phylogenetic and ontogenetic versions. Yet, according to this chapter, a unified mind seems neither functionally specialized nor domain-specific, let alone modular. On the standard notion (Fodor 1983), it is hard to see how a battery of modules would behave like a unified mind and even harder to understand why. (To a lesser degree, the same may be true of naive theories that are domain-specific and tied to exclusive databases.) A module is a mental reflex that does its narrowly specialized job, no matter what else happens or is available as information in the larger system. The module does not have access to the domains of other modules or to their databases. Why would it, if it is a wired-in adaptation good at doing a specific job? Why would such access and its unifying effects be selected for?

One way out of this puzzle is to take it to invalidate the modularity or functional specialization of the mind. I would not bet my (already shaky) pension plan on this solution. Once popular with empiricists, behaviorists, and learning theorists, the notion of an open-ended and general-purpose mind has recently become less attractive and explanatory, in the light of what is now suspected about evolution and mental development. A more realistic but challenging option is to explain mind unification *out of* its initial modularity or functional specialization and domain-specificity. Some evolutionary thinkers view mind unification as a response to the pressures of socialization

(Alexander 1990b; Damasio 1994; Humphrey 1986). I share this view and take the tasks involved in common formatting and knowledge integration to respond to social pressures on interpretation and its role in mental rehearsal.

How the transition from a modular or functionally specialized partition to mind unification works *architecturally* is still a mystery, although some light is getting through. There are several proposals around. Some see the hand of language (Rozin 1976) or of language involved in dialogue with self and in public relations (Dennett 1978, 1991). Others look at a general development across mental faculties which takes the form of a "representational redescription" of implicit procedures into explicitly representable structures (Karmiloff-Smith 1992). This could be a way of looking at the gradual emergence of the category of explicit metathought out of earlier implicit and procedural categories, such as those of intentionality and even propositional attitudes. I join other theorists (Sperber 1994, Tian 1996) in the estimate that, as the eminent ability to metarepresent, interpretation is responsible for mind unification, either alone or in a dominant position. It so happens that the most critical ontogenetic changes in representational redescription, 18 months and 4 years (cited by Karmiloff-Smith 1992, 167–168), happen to be closely associated with critical developments in interpretation that play a major role in unsituating and eventually unifying the mind: counterfactual imagination, shared attention, and false belief, respectively. Equally critical in this process are developments in late childhood (surveyed earlier), when interpretation becomes unsituated, turns to self, moves beyond metarepresentation to reconstruction, and comes increasingly under the spell of culture.

Puzzling is not only the unified mind itself but also what it can do. It can mimic a general-purpose mechanism or open-ended learner (Alexander 1990b, Rozin 1976), while possibly remaining deep-down modular (Sperber 1994), or can bootstrap itself into such a mechanism or learner (Karmiloff-Smith 1992). By letting beliefs die in our stead, in Popper's phrase, it can also painlessly mimic the work of natural selection (Bonner 1980, Dennett 1991). Perhaps the greatest puzzle of all is consciousness. The evolutionary theorists, who see social life as supplying the strongest selective pressures for mind unification, also see the outcome of this selection as taking the form of consciousness (Alexander 1990b, Humphrey 1986, Rozin 1976). What sort of consciousness could that be?

Reflexive Consciousness

It could be a form of *reflexive* consciousness and its developmental midwife could be interpretation. Cognitively speaking, consciousness means *access*. If it turns out that reflexive access is the product of self-directed metarepresentation, *then* interpretation is a reason and cause of that form of access. This is the conditional argument I am about to sketch in rough outline.

I borrow its premise from the literature on consciousness (but see chapter 6, section 3, for caveats). A mental representation provides *conscious access* if it is used in reasoning and in the rational control of action and speech (Block 1995, 231) and, I add, in other forms of mental rehearsal. If a mental representation is higher-level and provides access to another, lower-level mental representation, then the access is *conscious*. If the higher-level representation is itself conscious, then the consciousness is *introspective,* that is, conscious at both ends. Quite often, however, the higher-level and access-providing representation need not be conscious in order to make the lower-level one conscious. Think (heuristically) of a distinction between a stage lit from the dark (nonintrospective access) and a stage lit from an illuminated area (introspective access). The stage here is an ongoing deployment of representations.

Suppose this is a plausible way to look at conscious access. The first thing to note is that ground-floor thinking and even implicit metathinking can do with just conscious access (illumination only at the lower level). Explicit metathinking, however, requires *introspective* consciousness (lights at both ends). It is hard to metathink explicitly without knowing *what* you are doing (forming thoughts related to other thoughts) and *that* you are doing it. I find it empirically significant that introspection is counted by many developmentalists as a late development in childhood, perhaps as late as seven or eight. One of them writes, "We are not born with some sort of inward eye that informs us about our own mental processes. We learn about these gradually" (Lunzer 1979, 12). In the same sense, John Flavell and colleagues note that although capable of a "primary consciousness" of percepts, feelings, or thoughts (mere conscious access in my sense), preschoolers display "very limited introspective skills" of the metacognitive sort, they "do not think about thoughts very often spontaneously," and thoughts appear to them to be "isolated and largely inexplicable mental happenings, not linked to preceding causes or subsequent effects" (1995, 74–75, 84). These conclusions fit nicely with the observation (made earlier in this chapter) that there is a parallel limitation in the preschoolers' ability to narrate interpretively and interpret by reconstruction. After all, what interpretive narration and reconstruction do is link up propositional attitudes in various causal patterns and thus, on my hypothesis, provide a blueprint for linking up one's own thoughts in such patterns. Like exercises in narration or deliberate means-ends analyses, formal schooling and other forms of regimented enculturation may enhance the youngsters' ability to reconstruct and track their trains of thought (Flavell et al. 1995, 90–91).

Let me now bring in the conclusion of an earlier argument (chapter 6, section 3) to the effect that conscious access cannot individuate the *relational* form of mental representing needed in metamentation. It should follow that conscious access explains neither metamentation nor, perhaps more surprisingly, introspection as reflexive consciousness. It is the other way around: metamentation, trafficking in explicit metathoughts, explains how conscious higher-level mental representations are about lower-level representings and, as a result, provide introspective access. Since interpretation introduced the primate mind to conscious metarepresentation and metamentation, interpretation must also be a (if not the) source of and reason for reflexive consciousness. (It is in this light that I construe some arguments in Carruthers 1996, chapters 5 and 7; Olson 1988; Pylyshyn 1978; and particularly the pioneering work of Wilfrid Sellars 1963, chapter 5). Being indispensable to metamentation, introspection may have been pressed into service by the development of interpretation, in its later stages, and its conversion to metamentation.

Another interesting implication is that implicit metathinking (let alone ground-level thinking), even when accessed consciously, does not seem to have the resources or reasons to bootstrap itself into metamentation. Implicit metathinking recognizes thoughts implicitly and individuates their contents semantically as facts or situations. Meta-ascent in representing contents as facts does not make much sense (a fact is a fact is a fact!), because it tends to collapse into the representation and consciousness of a first-level content as fact—a conclusion apparently drawn by many philosophers since Descartes and Locke (Rosenthal 1993). It is only when mental *relations* to contents are *explicitly* represented and when, in addition, the contents themselves are *relationally specified,* that metamental ascent and reflexive consciousness make distinct sense. That happens only in explicit metathinking. Since one cannot do metamental ascent without reflexive consciousness, it may well be that the former instigated the development of the latter.

This has been an admittedly sketchy preview of what I suspect to be a plausible and promising story of reflexive consciousness. I encapsulate its point by playing with a developmentally sensitive sequence of Cartesian-like slogans which goes from 'I interpret; therefore I metathink' to 'I metathink; therefore I am conscious reflexively.'

How did reflexive consciousness evolve and why? It is too late in this project to engage such tough questions, assuming one (not me) would know how to answer them. But let me venture this much. One option, explored by Nicholas Humphrey (1986), takes the simulation line on interpretation and argues that, in order to simulate others, one must first access the contents of one's mind. Humphrey's position does finger interpretation as the evolutionary stimulus for reflexive consciousness, which is fine with me. But, as noted in the last chapter, I have reservations about simulative interpretation in this role. Apes and very young children interpret to some degree but do not appear to simulate or enjoy reflexive consciousness. Their mental situatedness does not seem to favor off-line mentation and perspective taking, which are essential to simulation. And even if simulation were an option, it could not lead to conscious reflexivity, for reasons canvassed in the previous chapter, chief among them the absence of the categories that would capture subject-world relations. Simulation is as blind to such relations as is mere conscious access.

My option is more ecumenical. I expect the explanation of how reflexive consciousness came into being to integrate several developments. One is the turn from alter to explicit ego interpretation and the resulting mental rehearsals with self- and other-regarding ascriptions. This is a most potent development because it forces the young interpreter to conceive of herself as *explicitly related* to the social world and to conceive of others as acknowledging and representing this relation. Before that, interpretation was probably self-un-reflective, even when shrewdly calculational, because it focused solely on others, not on self, and only from the perspective of the interpreter. Now the opposite happens: interpretation turns to self because it is forced to take the perspective of others on self (what would others say? and how would I respond to how they see me?). The self thus becomes illuminated (explicitly inter-preted) from outside, by others. Internalized (the voice of the other becomes that of the alter ego) and factored into mental rehearsals with self- and other-regarding attitudes, this outside perspective individuates, in the inner eye of the beholder, a detached and explicit self related to others and others related to this new self. Thus re-represented from inside but in socially relational terms, the self becomes a *reflexive self,* a self that looks at its mental exploits *as* others would, from their (interpretive) perspectives. Reflexive selfhood promotes reflexive consciousness because it provides the *relational* perspective of others on self which, emulated within, becomes the "inside look" with which people scan their mentation (the right side of figure 6.1 in the previous chapter).

Still other developments are likely to pitch in. Other acquisitions in inter-pretation may help the cause of reflexive consciousness: by further articulating and extending early propensities for mental rehearsal, particularly through mimagination and scenario-building about other minds, the narrative resources of reconstruction are thought by some researchers to firm up one's reflex-ive consciousness (Alexander 1990b; Humphrey 1986). Last but not least, language enables a deliberate and publicly encoded dialogue with self and thereby provides the means through which the mental contents one is reflexively conscious of can be explicitly represented and manipulated (Carruthers 1996; Dennett 1978, chapter 9; Sellars 1963, chapter 5).

In conclusion, the last chapter focused on how interpretation evolves the category of propositional attitude and how further pressures and developments (responding to these pressures) initiate its gradual metamorphosis into the category of explicit metathought. This chapter looked at how the continuing interplay between interpretation and mental rehearsal creates the conditions in which explicit metathoughts get iterated and embedded in dynamic and generative sequences that acquire a common format of representation and integrate knowledge across domains and databases, thereby bringing about an evolutionarily unexpected mind unification and consciousness at the reflexive level.

Chapter 8

Parting Thoughts

Thus concludes this essay: the development of metamentation emulated that of interpretation; Mom begat Mim; or Mim gradually internalized Mom and put the internalized expertise to new uses. Far from over, the argument for this conclusion is in its early stages, an incitement to further thinking on these matters. This chapter takes the measure of what was done and what still lies ahead. It begins with a clinical confirmation provided by autism—a mental impairment that seems to translate deficits of interpretation into deficits of metamentation along the developmental paths charted in earlier chapters. Section 2 reviews the journey from interpretation to metamentation and highlights those junctures where the road took rather unexpected turns that still await explanation. Which is why, in a critical but forward-looking spirit, the concluding section 3 acknowledges problems still outstanding.

1   Hints from Autism

The main themes and conclusions of this essay find clinical support in autism. An autistic mind can operate in different domains, including those of mechanical action and interactive socialization, but not at all or not well in that of intersubjective socialization. The missing link is intersubjective interpretation. As a result, the autistic mind fails to develop normal metamentation. Thus goes the argument of this section.

The Condition Itself

Autism is a complex mental condition, much studied in the last few decades but still far from fully diagnosed and understood. I sample here only aspects relevant to this essay, on which there is reasonable diagnostic consensus. There are several and often conflicting accounts of autism. Most agree about abnormalities in social interaction and communication, in emotional reactions, interpretation, reasoning, and reflexivity. Autistic people tend to think in concrete, stereotyped, and inflexible ways, and cannot adjust their thinking to fast changing contexts of activity, communication, or social interaction. Autistic communication is utilitarian, limited to orders and requests, and indifferent to exchanging information and experiences. This latter handicap is visible early on when autistic children fail to engage and share attention with others. Juvenile play, which is a training ground for many cognitive skills, is impoverished in autistic children, who show little imagination, versatility or ability to pretend. Autistic pretense and imagination are minimal, inflexible, repetitive, and largely tied to the sensorimotor domain (Baron-Cohen and Bolton 1993, Harris 1993).

As for interpretation, these signs point to a largely interactive sort of mind, deficient in topical-predication and reflexive skills. Autistic children do not show the ability, needed in shared attention, to bring different and alternating perspectives on a topic (Hobson 1993b, 200). It is not clear that they always distinguish clearly between topic (as object of attention or interest) and comment (attitude or reaction to it) and therefore have a hard time following the give-and-take of conversation. They fail to maintain the topic of conversation across shifts of comments and additions of new information, and thus fail to regard communication as exchange of relevant information (Hobson 1993a, 1993b; Tager-Flusberg 1993). Failures of communication are apt to resurface as failures of metamentation, not because communication shapes metamentation (which it might, in part, if metamentation actually builds on the inner dialogue between self and others) but because the design of both abilities is indebted to intersubjective interpretation. Like conversation, metamentation also operates in topic-comment formats and unfolds by maintaining topics through long sequences and changes of comments. If autistic individuals fail these tasks in conversation, it is unlikely that they would handle them better in metamentation. Such topical-predication and reflexive failures seem linked also to the inability to integrate first- and third-person stances, as, for example, in representing 'I see A seeing B'. Autistic children also confuse the pronouns 'I' and 'you', cannot easily track the contextual shift in their meaning, and thus cannot understand the listener-speaker roles and their interchange in communication (Baron-Cohen 1995, 1996; Barresi and Moore 1996; Tager-Flusberg 1993). As a result of these handicaps, not only topical predication but mental stancing, and hence self regulation and self evaluation, may be beyond the reach of most autistic children, and so may be the mind-world-mind format of interpretation, so essential to the development of metamentation.

If they fail at joint attention and mental sharing of topics and experiences, and also fail to distinguish and integrate different comments and perspectives, including first and third person, then (according to chapter 4) autistic people are prone to have a poor sense of *mental* metarepresentation and hence an equally poor ability to metathink. Yet they can metarepresent in a *public* sense. They recognize that a sentence or photograph is a representation and know what it represents but cannot do the same with mental representations. They can recognize when a photograph misrepresents but not when a belief does. As Leslie and Roth note, "a picture does not *believe* what it depicts" (1993, 93; see also Perner 1991, 97–101). Autistic children understand depicting but not believing. They can form many concepts and understand the meanings of many words but fail to master the concepts and language of interpretation and particularly of the meanings of mental-states words (Baron-Cohen 1995; Frith 1989, 120–130; Hobson 1993a, 1993b; Tager-Flusberg 1993). These contrasts vindicate the notion (first evoked in chapter 4, section 2) that interpretation is not public metarepresentation, that understanding the semantics of public representation is not the same as understanding mental representing, and that understanding photographs or sentences is not the same as understanding beliefs or intentions. These are failures of intersubjective interpretation that become failures of reflexive thinking.

Poor Interpretation, Poor Thinking

Autism does not fare much better in the other half of the metamentation deal—mental rehearsal. Autistic people tend to be poor at innovative planning, problem solving, and counterfactual reasoning. If a current context evokes a habitual plan, then they may do fairly well. I stress 'current' and 'habitual' because autism is predisposed toward the situatedness of thinking and the repetitiveness of its strategies. Autistic people encounter problems in overriding the control exercised by contextual or habitual factors and formulating new plans to meet changed or unforeseen circumstances. In particular, they seem unable to think ahead about hypothetical situations as bridges from a current to a desired situation (Baron-Cohen and Bolton 1993; Frith 1989, 1997).

This planning deficit is reminiscent of the ability of chimpanzees to plan ahead what tools to take (stones) to handle a future situation (breaking nuts at a distant location) but only from the standpoint of *current* desires and beliefs about this sequence of events; but they cannot envisage future changes in desires and beliefs, brought about by changing circumstances. Symptomatic is also the fact that the object manipulations of most autistic children are reminiscent of the mental limitations often attributed to ape tool use: rigidity, lack of flexible hierarchy, serial memorization and rote sequencing, and need for spatial or temporal contiguity (Wynn 1993). Add to this list of parallels the fact that apes and autistic people seem to share a capacious and almost photographic memory, sensitive to the smallest details (Baron-Cohen and Bolton 1993, Tomasello and Call 1997). This sort of memory may be a handicap when it comes to the development of abstraction and counterfactual imagination.[1]

These parallels between autistic and ape thinking look less fortuitous, and could be explained, when the interactive interpretation they share is taken into account. It is an interpretation that is situated, on-line, anchored in the here and now, utilitarian, and almost mechanical in its handling of others. Autistic interpreters can hold a current situation fixed and imagine different intentional relations to it (such as seeing or not seeing something) but cannot set aside a current situation and imagine instead a hypothetical one toward which others (or themselves) can have different intentional relations (Harris 1993). On some views, autistic individuals are no better interpreters than apes or even monkeys (Gomez, Sarria, and Tamarit 1993; Happé and Frith 1992; Tomasello, Kruger, and Ratner 1993). The autistic limitations in interpretation may explain related limitations in mental rehearsal: autistic thinkers cannot extricate themselves from ongoing mental involvement in a current situation in order to envisage alternative involvements in possible situations. Chimpanzees may share some of these limitations in both interpretation and mental rehearsal (Tomasello and Call 1997), perhaps for some of the same reasons. The complicity between interpretation and thinking and its impact on autism resurfaces in the debate about the causes of autism, a debate that sheds further light on the positions taken in this essay.

Causes of Autism

Where do the autistic deficits come from? It is hard to find a single cause, if there is one. Most experts take a confluence of causes to be more likely. Two families of causes compete for explanation. Reflecting the contrast between mechanical and social agency, one explanation looks at executive functions, another at interpretation. The executive functions point mostly to thinking as mental rehearsal. The explanation is that autistic individuals fail at planning, problem solving, and inhibition of response because of impairment in the prefrontal cortex dedicated to executive functions (Ozonoff, Pennington, and Rogers 1991; Russell 1996, 1997). This explanation may appear to invalidate the story told in this essay. The invalidating argument would be that the autistic mind fails to be reflexive because it fails to handle the executive functions involved in mental rehearsal. Interpretation is not in this picture, either as source of reflexivity or as cause of autism. In contrast, my conjecture is that autism is largely (though not exclusively) a deficit in interpretation which prevents the autistic mind from turning reflexive.

I do not think the invalidating argument invalidates too much. I begin on a conceptual note. This essay has argued that metamentation evolved out of an interplay between mental rehearsal and interpretation, and that metamental tasks concern patterns of relations that could emerge only in the domain of interpretation. So, whatever the role of the executive deficits in mental rehearsal, they cannot alone account for metamental failures. There is a structural isomorphism of tasks between metamentation and interpretation which no alternative account can match, including that of executive functions.

There is also a comparative story that has not been sufficiently explored in the debates over the sources of autism. Congenitally blind children show failures similar to those found in autism, particularly in handling mental sharing, personal pronouns, pretense, and producing and understanding narratives. The reason suggested is that blind children do not have the visual access needed to engage in shared attention and in the forms of topical predication that the latter affords (Hobson 1993b, 203–207). Yet the congenitally blind children studied are normal in other capacities, including those for executive functions. They are also normal in sentimental bonding and emotional sharing—premises of intersubjective interpretation—which is probably why, through some compensatory mechanisms, not yet fully understood, blind children seem to solve most of their interpretational problems by seven or so. This story suggests the mosaic-like pattern in which existing mental capacities come together to generate new mental capacities (Hobson 1993a, 1993b). It also suggests that executive functions are *not* part of the mosaic shared by autistic and congenitally blind children. Autistic children are (as it were) blind to sentimental bonding and emotions, thus lacking the framework in which to do, and build upon, topical predication and the mind-world-mind pattern it affords; blind children have the sentimental resources to do both (as their later recovery indicates) but are literally blind to the initial visual contents with which to fill in the slots. Since visual imitation is inaccessible to congenitally blind children, one would assume that sentimental bonding and emotion sharing may be the only initial avenues to like-me intersubjectivity. Also notable is the fact that the clinical record registers forms of executive dysfunctions that do not result in autism (Perner and Lang 1999).

Finally, to return to a theme pursued in several chapters and most recently a chapter ago (section 1), executive functions could have first evolved in the *social* domain, as part and parcel of primate social cognition and interpretation, and may even have driven the evolution of mental rehearsal in other domains. The first and most pressing problems a primate kid faces, plans about, solves, imagines, and acts on are social and hence interpretational. This is why the social domain could be the first to force the gregarious primates to sharpen their executive functions and keep them well oiled. Defended at length in this work, this hypothesis has some neurological grounding: there are prefrontal areas *jointly* involved in planning, decision making, and social regulation of behavior (Damasio 1994; Ozonoff, Pennington, and Rogers 1991; Perner and Lang 1999). Couldn't the executive deficits responsible for autism be located precisely in those areas? If so, why not talk of executive functions *of the social sort,* permeated with interpretation, and allow for the possibility that this is where autism fails initially? If plausible, the hypothesis entertained a chapter ago, to the effect that advances in counterfactual imagination and means-ends analysis built on advances in interpretation, could explain the link between autism and executive deficits without pitting the latter against interpretation.

One should not exclude the possibility that primate minds have dedicated and domain-specific faculties for solving problems and planning actions (Harris 1993), so that solving a spatial problem (e.g., how to reach an object) need not draw on the same skills and databases as solving a social problem (e.g., how to fool a conspecific). One may figure out how to place a large piece of luggage in a narrow trunk, and plan an action accordingly, by drawing on resources, such as mental imagery, which have nothing to do with those needed to guess one's intentions and planning to do something about them. In that case, demonstrating deficits in planning or problem-solving abilities in one domain need not say much about executive deficits in other domains. But it still remains a lively and robust possibility that executive deficits of the social sort are most basic and are the first to explain autism. This is an estimate backed by further facts, as noted next.

Asocial Normality

Autistic cognition may occasionally operate well in *nonsocial* domains, such as physical, numerical or biological, or at least better than in the social domain. The autistic mastery of formal skills for logic, mathematics, and grammar at times approaches normality. This would be expected if one takes the Piagetian line that mastery of formal skills evolves out of sensorimotor schemes of mechanical action. Not very far apart from the Piagetian line, as far as the preeminence of formal thinking is concerned, a classical and still potent rationalist tradition—going back to Plato, Descartes, and Leibniz, and nowadays embodied in the computer (or pure intellect) model of the mind—further assumes that metamentation may be the output of abilities for logical and mathematical reasoning. Also attractive is the view that language and its public semantics are not only enablers of metamentation (which they surely are) but are actually responsible for it (Clark 1998). The preceding chapters endeavored to show that many of the patterns in which thoughts link up reflexively with other thoughts cannot be found in the formal patterns of logic or mathematics and that such patterns emulate categories and representation schemes that precede language and are not exhausted by its rules and constraints, whether semantic or syntactic. Autistic people may handle well logical and mathematical tasks as well as large fragments of the semantics and syntax of language yet fail to metamentate precisely because they fail to handle, as interpreters, the prelinguistic mind-world-mind patterns emulated in metamentation. Also telling is the fact that young children master language years before they metamentate. This diagnosis gets further support when we look at how logical skills and public semantics are used to compensate for the natural failures to interpret and metamentate.

Unnatural Compensation

Children with Asperger's syndrome—near normal in intelligence and language use but socially almost as awkward as autistic children—do as poorly as autistic children on planning and problem-solving tasks of the mechanical sort, yet are better on interpretation tasks (Frith 1997, Harris 1993). It is thought that Asperger children may reconstruct in nonintuitive or nondedicated ways some of the psychological insights needed for interpretation. This compensation strategy has also been documented in a few cases of intelligent and articulate autistic persons. They make up for interpretational deficits through a *logical reconstruction* of aspects inaccessible to them by normal routes. A well known example is that of Temple Grandin, Ph.D., accomplished agricultural scientist, lucid writer, and autobiographer. Oliver Sacks (1994) reports from discussions with Grandin that she had to *infer* social signals among people but could not perceive them, nor participate in this "magical communication" nor "conceive of the many-leveled, kaleidoscopic states of mind behind it." As for making sense of the social life around her, with its communicational and interpretational dimensions she most often misses, Grandin says that she "had built up a vast library of experiences over the years . . . , like a *library of videotapes,* which she could *play in her mind and inspect* at any time—'videos' of how people behaved in different circumstances. She would play these over and over again, and *learn,* by degrees, to *correlate* what she saw, so that she could then predict how people in similar circumstances might act. She had complemented her experience by constant reading. . . . 'It is strictly a *logical* process' she explained" (my emphases; see also Baron-Cohen 1995, 139–143; Bruner 1995, 11; Frith 1989, 128–129, and 1997). The notions emphasized in Grandin's account—mental videotapes played and inspected, learning to correlate in order to predict, logical processes—indicate a deliberate recruitment of various resources to solve the interpretational problems of the intersubjective sort arising in communication and socialization. Although about social behaviors and encounters, the resources thus recruited are noninterpretive since they do not actually track subject-world relations the way interpretive categories do. Photographs about what people do in standard situations are no substitute for reading their intentions and beliefs.

Autistic people have similar problems figuring out a speaker's intentions by normal interpretational routes. A compensation strategy seems, again, the way out. According to Francesca Happé (1994), they try to understand what was being said from the words alone by means of logic, grammar, and a basic public semantics devoid of meanings of mental-states terms. The compensation would use the code model of communication, which I construe as a model for public metarepresentation, instead of the normal inferential model (Sperber and Wilson 1986), which I construe as a model for mental metarepresentation. The code model presupposes that communication works by encoding a message at a source and decoding it at a receiver by means of logic, grammar, and public semantics. The code model is not normal for human communication. Its gravest problem is the wide gap between the semantics of public utterances and the thoughts they convey. The gap cannot be bridged by coding and decoding. It is a gap somewhat related to that between interpreting others interactively and intersubjectively. This is how I read Uta Frith's suggestion (1989, 180–181) that in communicating with autistic persons one should adopt a literal and behaviorist (i.e., interactive) posture toward information and spell out carefully (i.e., in terms of public representations) the topics pursued, what is relevant, and the implications of what is said. This strategy may allow an autistic person to carry out a logical or codelike reconstruction, at least to some extent. These sorts of reconstructions are beginning also to acquire therapeutic value. Juan Carlos Gomez (1997) reports on research intended to exploit the autistic understanding of public representations, such as photographs or diagrams, to compensate for the failure to understand mental representations (see also Swettenham et al. 1966). Autistic children fail the false-belief test formulated in normal terms of interpretation but pass it when the test is reformulated so that the subject is portrayed as forming in her head photographs of situations, including "false photographs."

How far can such compensatory tactics go? Hard to tell but probably not very far. The ability to generalize to new situations remains problematic, and so does the power of such generalizations to mimic genuine interpretation (Gomez 1997). Here is a cautionary tale from a different but relevant area. Hobson (1993b, 5) reports a case of a man diagnosed with Asperger's syndrome. The man was unable to grasp what a friend is. He would ask again and again, "Are you a friend?" "Is he a friend?" Despite the efforts of the ward staff to teach him the meaning of 'friend' by giving instances of the concept and by having someone act as a befriender, the man was unable to grasp the concept of friend. What is so elusive and special about 'friend'? After all, the man had little difficulty with other concepts. As Hobson suggests, friendship is unlike most other concepts learned by ostension, inference or public stipulation. It is more like interpretive categories (e.g., attention or desire) that are innate or built up in tightly framed contexts of interpersonal interaction out of numerous clues, such as gaze, bodily posture, smile, shared experiences, and the like. In either version, such categories cannot be easily reconstructed logically and publicly and might not be reconstructible at all.

The moral for our story is that friendship, as a type of interpersonal phenomenon, grows out of intersubjective interpretation. So does reflexive thinking. If one lacks the right interpretive gear, one would not grow into a friend or a reflexive thinker. The question, then, is what sort of metamentation is accessible to autistic persons. If the pragmatics of normal conversation is inaccessible to them, wouldn't the same be true of metamentation, since both grow out of intersubjective interpretation? Should we conclude that, if possible at all, autistic reflexivity might also be a feat of logical reconstruction in terms of formal algorithms over public representations? (Does this sound somewhat like the rationalist model of metamentation?) And should we also conclude, by analogy with normal communication or the normal sense of friendship, that a logically reconstructed metamentation would have major limitations mirroring those in interpretation? Here are some clues to possible answers.

Mental Unity Revisited

A vital contribution of interpretation to mental reflexivity was shown (a chapter ago) to be the common formatting and integration of knowledge, resulting in a unified mind. How does the autistic mind fare in this respect? Backing the argument of this essay, what is known so far suggests deficits in unity and integration, to various degrees. Some of the symptoms are there: restricted interest, attention limited to specific features and details (surfaces, colors) often uninteresting to normal people, rote memory, and repetitive tasks—in short, a "preference for segmental over holistic information processing" (Frith 1997, 76; see also Baron-Cohen and Bolton 1993). A deeper physiological story backs up the symptoms. Brain-imaging studies (by Happé and colleagues) show that autistic people have less brain activity for processing meaningful stories versus meaningless text than normal people, which is consistent with their apparently related inability to integrate information to derive contextually relevant meanings (Frith 1997). These findings are interesting not only because processing meaningful stories is a good test of knowledge integration and common formatting but also because narration is a training ground for the reconstruction-based ability to hold many minds in mind and mimagine possible worlds according to those minds. Mental reflexivity is incomplete without this ability and practically impossible without common formatting and knowledge integration. By failing to reconstruct, most autistic people are likely to fail to mimagine and metamentate in a full sense.

Missing Joints

The comparative analysis of autistic versus normal minds thus comes back full circle to mirror at key joints the conceptual and developmental story of mental reflexivity. Chapter 4 argued on conceptual grounds that metamentation begins with and builds on topical predication. It turns out that most autistic persons have problems with topical predication in normal conversation and most probably in their own (dialogical) metathinking. Chapter 5 argued on evolutionary and psychological grounds that a plausible mental surround, enabler, and scaffolder of topical predication is an intersubjective interpretation based on sentimental bonding. It turns out that autistic persons are not good at intersubjective interpretation and do not much bond sentimentally with others. Similar correlations hold later in development: autistic children are late and limited in their recognition of propositional attitudes, with likely implications for their mastery of explicit metathought; and to the degree that they do not reconstruct well the mental life of others, and how others interpret the mental life of still others, they also miss the opportunities and means to develop a unified mind.

Suppose (as I did) that mental reflexivity results from separate developments in sentimental bonding, topical predication, language learning, and mental rehearsal, under the guiding hand of interpretation. Suppose also that human interpretation itself is built up in such a convergence pattern, relative to sundry developments and resources, partly mapped out in this essay. It would then be unproductive to think of autism as a *single* mental handicap, and as unproductive to look for a single genetic expression of this handicap. In its developmental drama, autism may be the perfect mirror image of how the interpreting mind of a child is assembled (or not, or not entirely) at each ontogenetic turn and how, as a result, her metamind is assembled (or not, or only in some degree) and expressed in reflexive consciousness and a reflexive sense of self.

Having added the perspective and evidence provided by autism to the story of how metamentation evolved out of interpretation and mental rehearsal, it is time to wrap up by looking first backward, at how the main story went, and forward, at what still remains to be done.

2 Adding Up

The background story, told in the first part of this essay, was about the selective pressures most likely to have spawned a reflexive mind. They were found to emerge among primates from an intense social life (rather than work and mechanical agency) and the resulting socialization of primate minds. Mind socialization is effected by interpretation. It is by playing this role that interpretation becomes the evolutionary stimulus and shaper of mental reflexivity. Why and how this happened was the foreground story told in the second part of the essay. Two major themes were pursued in the foreground story. One was the constant and fruitful evolutionary interplay between interpretation and mental rehearsal. The latter is the major employer of interpretation, passing on to it the pressures posed by primate social life and exacting from it, as adaptations, ever novel categories and representation schemes. The other theme focused on the triangular pattern of mind-world-mind relations which interpretation alone can lend to metamentation. The two themes converge when mind-world-mind relations, mentally rehearsed, turn into patterns of metamentation. That is what the foreground story was all about.

With these themes in mind, I propose to steer this overview toward some evolutionary highlights that marked the contributions of interpretation to mental rehearsal and, through them, to metamentation. Up to a point, it looked like the straightforward work of natural selection. I am thinking of the mastery of the metaintentional scheme, in particular of the categories of relatedness, direction, and perhaps target, shared by ape and human interpretation. In both versions the mastery seems universal, well scheduled developmentally, and functionally specialized. This is as far as the interactive interpretation of apes goes and it may overlap with fragments of the interpretation of very young children and that of autistic people. It is a bilateral interpretation focused on subject-world relations. Human children also have an ability, absent in apes and apparently in autistic children, to share emotions, experiences, and mental takes on the world with others and to communicate in such terms. I attributed this ability to sentimental bonding, whose initial functions may have been selected for interpersonal regulation and attachment. This intersubjective ability opens the way to a triangular form of interpretation, of the mind-world-mind sort, which generates radical novelties in interpretation and, through them, in other areas of mental life.

The starting point of these radical novelties, sentimental bonding, may be a first evolutionary juncture where distinct developments come together, rather unexpectedly. After all, the offspring of many species, including prehuman primates, cry, twist faces, and employ all sorts of tricks to get food, protection, and other goodies. Yet they do not seem to factor these tricks into their interpretation (if any) and, unlike human infants, do not seem to exploit the resulting interpretive gear for new uses, such as sharing information about the world. The meeting between sentimental bonding and interpretation, resulting in triangular mental sharing, creates the premises for intersubjectivity and topical predication. The latter makes two vital contributions to the development of reflexivity: it provides the topic-comment format needed for representing thoughts about thoughts, a format that allows child and adult interpreters to engage in a cultural game without evolutionary precedent and genetic pedigree. Learning symbolization and word reference are among the remarkable outcomes of this new game, and they in turn help intersubjective interpretation along toward metarepresentation. It is through the mastery of metarepresentation that the child begins to form the category of explicit metathought by emulating the category of propositional attitude. This is a crucial step forward but not enough. Culture, again, steps in to steer interpretation toward dynamic and complex deployments, through iterations and multiple embeddings of attitudes. That was interpretation by reconstruction, whose main contribution to reflexivity was to allow holding many minds in mind, thus scaffolding the ability to relate thoughts to other thoughts across distinct domains and databases. At each turn in this ontogenetic journey, the novelties in interpretation show up in mental rehearsal until, eventually, they come to represent and manipulate explicit metathoughts.

All this goes to show that interpretation designs metamentation by recruiting various abilities—most notably for mental rehearsal, sentimental bonding, topical predication, and language—each with its own functions and *raisons d'être*. Many evolutionary outcomes emerge in this way. What is rather surprising is that the abilities so recruited are choreographed by interpretation into a well-timed and tightly interlocked dance that does not seem to follow a genetic script written by natural selection. Nor does the dance seem to follow genetic instructions mutated by some unprecedented accident, a sudden quirk of evolution, as some theorists view the irruption of grammar in the human brain. Whatever its origins, mental reflexivity does not seem to be an innately determined process, certainly not entirely and not thoroughly. So one can say that the human mind was not destined by nature to become reflexive. Yet the emergence of reflexivity is not anarchic, arbitrary or variable, either. A reflexive mind is the norm, a psychological universal among normal humans.

They all metamentate, roughly in the same ways, thanks to a well-scheduled and uniform mental development. This looks like an evolutionary surprise. How is it possible and why? This question gives the tone for the last section.

3 Subtracting: Outstanding Questions

Being work in progress, this essay leaves many questions unanswered and raises many others. I count the following among the most challenging and worth pursuing of the outstanding questions. The question that just ended the previous section heads the list.

More on Development

Needless to say, I do not have answers to the question of how, unassisted by natural selection, interpretation manages to design metamentation as a psychological universal. And even if I fancy some answers, I do not yet know how to demonstrate and document them empirically. (Grant suggestions or at least a summer house in Provence will be much appreciated.) But I nurse a hunch that a promising tack would be to look afresh at child development and at how interpretation—serving the different and often diverging interests of children, adults, and culture—takes advantage of development in socializing and enculturating the young mind. I discern two distinct but ultimately converging lines of inquiry packed into this hunch. One, outlined in chapter 3, is to look at the uniqueness of development in the light of the child's evolutionary interests. That could explain how, in order to survive and prosper, the helpless and dependent child engages in reciprocal coordination with adults, effected through sentimental bonding and intersubjective interpretation, and how, as a result, the child is inducted into the rules of Humean coordination and acquires a Humean mind—premises of mental reflexivity. This analysis could also explain how the child's mental proclivities and biases select for those cultural practices that are adaptive for, or at least manageable by, the child at particular ontogenetic stages. From the opposite direction of adult society and culture, another line of inquiry would explore how sociopolitical forces and cultural practices guide interpretation in weaving together intersubjectivity, mental rehearsal, language, and other resources in patterns that, although not scheduled genetically, manage to yield metamentation rather uniformly.

Cultural Design

These lines of inquiry raise the more general and intriguing question of the cultural design of the human mind. The question calls for a better understanding of how cultural evolution works and how it came to universalize practices that end up designing the human mind (Dennett 1995, chapter 12; Janicki and Krebs 1998). Pending such an understanding, there are at least three (complementary) angles from where to approach the cultural-design question in more specific terms. The *technological* angle would focus on cultural tools as mind designers. I am thinking of universal narratives, folklore, schooling, writing, books, computers, other external memory systems, and the like. These cultural tools assist and often reconfigure the operation of mental skills (Dennett 1996, Donald 1991). Mental reflexivity may have been aided and stimulated by such cultural tools, particularly in late (school-bound) childhood (Flavell et al. 1995).

Another approach, sensitive to what may be called *cultural regimentation,* would focus on cultural practices, such as scripting routine activities and social interactions, affording collaborative learning or training narrative skills, which have the effect of developing, extending, and refining mental abilities (Nelson 1996; Rogoff 1990; Tomasello, Kruger, and Ratner 1993). One relevant example discussed a chapter ago was the generative interpretation or reconstruction of propositional attitudes leading up to mimagination, common formatting of explicit metathoughts, and knowledge integration. That was mostly a cultural accomplishment. The third and most basic approach, *psychocultural* in nature and initiated by Vygotsky, would explore the cultural design of the earliest mental faculties, such as joint attention, mastery of word reference, communicating by sharing meanings, and the like. There is already significant work in this direction (Bruner 1983, 1990; Hobson 1993b; Nelson 1996; Rogoff 1990; Tomasello, Kruger, and Ratner 1993; Tomasello 1996). The present essay was strongly influenced by this recent work.

What about Programs?

From the very outset this inquiry has favored tasks over programs. I share with many cognitive scientists the expectation that in many (though not all) areas of cognition the inquiry benefits from discerning the tasks first and letting them offer guidance to the nature and operation of the executing programs. I also share with some evolutionary psychologists the view that adaptations can be fruitfully analyzed in terms of tasks and the latter then fed into the top-down (task to program) approach of cognitive science (Cosmides and Tooby 1987, Dennett 1995, Tooby and Cosmides 1992; see also Bogdan 1994, chapter 10; Bogdan 1997, chapter 3). In some (though not all) areas of mental life a study of the forces of selection and the resulting adaptations, in phylogeny as well as ontogeny, can go a long way toward discerning the tasks that illuminate the work of programs. There are domains of mental activity—

interpretation among them—whose tasks may be intelligible *only* in terms of the forces that selected for them as adaptations (Bogdan 1997, chapter 3). Given its umbilical chord to interpretation, the same could be true of metamentation. These are some of the pluses of adopting a top-down analysis that begins with tasks. What they add up to (at least in this essay) is the notion that the tasks of metamentation emulated those of interpretation, executed in mental rehearsal.

But there are minuses as well. One of them is that the task angle on emulation leaves open the question of what the metamental programs look like and how they came about. Were they borrowed wholesale from interpretation and turned inward? Were they retooled here and there to fit the new domain? Or were the metamental tasks actually mixing different resources to do the job? If so, what resources? One way to understand the metamental architectures is to look at the literature on consciousness; there are some proposals there in terms congenial to this inquiry (Carruthers 1996, chapter 8; Dennett 1978, chapter 9). Also noted often in this essay was the fact that the models furnished by interpretation are unlikely to be emulated in metamentation without lots of props and enablers from language and other areas of cognition. About them my account was also silent. Equally open and untackled remains the question of when and how distinct metamental categories and schemes become operative. Some of their early versions may be building blocks of metamentation but never at work as such, in which case they would be hard to detect by observation or experiment.

On Its Own
This essay was about why and how metamentation, a new competence, evolved out of interpretation and mental rehearsal, older competencies. It was not about how metamentation takes off and operates *on its own*. There is some (not much) work on that topic (e.g., Lehrer 1997) and indirectly one can draw insights from the larger literature (already cited) on reflexive consciousness, self knowledge, and propositional attitudes (at least their psychologically realistic portions). It is an open question whether 'operating on its own' means 'without any (or any residue of) interpretational props built into its modus operandi' and, if it means that, whether metamentation actually grows into a competence *entirely* distinct from interpretation-in-mental-rehearsal. If it does, then interpretation would be the ladder, discarded after use—as it was in acquiring word reference and other mental skills. The alternative is that metamentation remains at heart mentally rehearsed interpretation (same competencies, more or less) but shifts its focus inwards, formats its subject matter uniformly as explicit metathoughts, which it turns loose on whatever domain

and topic it fancies at the moment. In other words, the choice is between distinct though historically related competencies, with distinct tasks and utilizations, versus a single competence with largely similar tasks but distinct domains and utilizations. On either option, to metamentate is to bring ground-level representations in a mental-rehearsal mode, target them for further representation, and represent them as explicit metathoughts, under some reflexive relation. This essay had nothing substantive to say about how these conditions of the metamental competence are met in actual performance. Its job was to analyze the competence in terms of what it takes to form thoughts about thoughts and carry out metamental tasks and to explain how and why the competence might have come about.

4 In Sum

While counting the pluses and minuses of this investigation, the reader is invited to retain and judge the central hypothesis that, operating in mental rehearsal, interpretation served as emulable blueprint for reflexive thinking. Interpretation alone was found to have the evolutionary reasons and opportunities as well as the cognitive means to do it. To prove this central hypothesis I assembled an inductive dossier—both enumerative (piling up evidence in support of the emulation thesis) and at times eliminative (ruling out worthy competitors)—which mixed the evolutionary ruminations of the first three chapters with the conceptual dissections and psychological theories and data cited in the next four. If the dossier was persuasive, then it honored the leitmotif of this essay: as in interpretation, mentally rehearsed, so in metamentation, *mutatis mutandis.*

Notes

Chapter 1

1. For a fair sample of opinions in the evolutionary literature, see Byrne and Whiten 1988, Gibson and Ingold 1993, Lock and Peters 1996, Tomasello and Call 1997, and Whiten and Byrne 1997.

2. According to Weber, it was the Protestant ethic of northern societies that stimulated and rewarded hard work and thriftiness. Is it fortuitous that these colder societies put a lesser premium on social interaction and fun—particularly fun—than the warmer Mediterranean societies? Or that Western civilization, like good food, started in the latter, not the former?

3. The trend favoring social life over physical work has now spread wide across ethology, cognitive anthropology, as well as comparative and developmental psychology (see Byrne and Whiten 1988, Tooby and Cosmides 1992, Goody 1995b, Lock and Peters 1996, Quiatt and Reynolds 1993, Tomasello and Call 1997, Whiten 1991, and Whiten and Byrne 1997 for representative surveys).

4. Even scientists who find primate work and specifically tool use much more frequent than the ones cited in the text recognize that there is no obvious connection between these phenomena and advanced mentation (McGrew 1993).

5. In Bogdan 1997, I distinguished the two kinds of interpreting minds as psycho-behavioral (now interactive) and psychosocial (now intersubjective).

6. To see why left, imagine you are an ape who wants to evolve into a metathinker. You have to make choices. You are on top of the diagram looking down to the tree of options. From that position, socialization and later intersubjectivity are to your left. You may end up as a metathinker, if the argument of this essay is right. If it isn't, it was worth the try, wasn't it? It was also fun. Check your political inclinations, too, for history shows that in general the left is socially minded and the right work-minded. You draw the conclusions.

7. The overall portrait of the situated mind is distilled from the literature on animal and child cognition and interpretation, ranging from Piaget 1960 to Donald 1991, Humphrey 1988, Perner 1991, Povinelli and Eddy 1996, Tomasello and Call 1997, and Wellman 1990, among others.

8. Mead's and Vygotsky's were not the first attempts in this direction. Vygotsky credits the turn-of-the-century French psychologist Pierre Janet for having seen as "the

fundamental law of psychology" the fact that "children begin to use the same forms of behavior in relation to themselves that others initially used in relation to them" (Wertsch 1981, 157). Vygotsky and his school also saw in Marxism a theoretical framework that grounds the priority of society over the individual mind and the role of the former in shaping the latter, particularly along the cultural lines that interested Vygotsky most.

9. There is already a vast literature on Vygotsky's work, extending from A. R. Luria's autobiographical account of Vygotsky's life and work (1979) to James Wertsch's monographs (1985a, 1991) and edited collection (1985b). There are also several volumes of Vygotsky's work translated into English, beginning with his monograph *Thought and Language* (1986) and collections of articles reprinted in Wertsch 1981 and van der Veer and Valsiner 1994. I rely on these sources in what I say about Vygotsky in this section.

10. "The internalization in our experience of the external conversations of gestures which we carry on with other individuals in the social process is the essence of thinking; and the gestures thus internalized are significant symbols because they have the same meaning for all individual members of the given society, i.e., they respectively arouse the same attitudes in the individuals making them that they arouse in the individuals responding to them: otherwise the individual could not internalize them or be conscious of them and their meaning" (Mead 1934, 47; see also Mead 1963 for earlier papers).

11. In contrast, Piaget saw these activities as carried out by the representational capacity required to manipulate objects, which is why he viewed internalization in terms of schemas for physical action. Piaget's angle leads to a conception of thinking centered around formal abilities for logical and mathematical reasoning and action-oriented planning and problem solving. This, I argue throughout this essay, is an angle that cannot account for reflexive thinking.

12. The notions marking this distinction—mind socialization and mind encultura-tion—reflect a different and more basic angle than the more familiar notions of social cognition and enculturation. The latter notions are about types of cognitive and practical interactions, whereas the former are about the formation of mental skills that make social cognition and enculturation possible in the first place.

13. The account of Tomasello, Kruger, and Ratner goes in the direction I want to go, which is interpretation. For they too note, "Though it is likely that the cultural learning experiences that depend on the concept of person [i.e., interpretation] comprise only a small minority of all learning experiences in human ontogeny, it is our contention that they are absolutely crucial for the acquisition of many of the most important cultural skills, including language and many of the basic skills in which youngsters receive intentional instruction from adults" (1993, 502).

14. To repeat, semiotic or gestural mediation will not do, because the issue is how they too manage to engage the child's mind and align it to the adult's. Perhaps there are other internalizing factors I have missed. It wouldn't surprise me. After years of unnecessarily worrying about skepticism and the mind-body problem, the tired brain of a philosopher tends to miss the obvious or reinvent the wheel.

15. Christopher Sinha (1996, 402–403) begins with a criticism similar to that made in this section, to the effect that Vygotsky's notion of internalization fails logically

because it does not account for what is initially responsible in the child for the internalization. To say that internalization is biological is not to explain what it is about the child's biology that accounts for internalization. Sinha's criticism strikes closer to home when he notes that accounts of intersubjectivity, and hence interpretation, suffer from the same failure to explain the biological basis for intersubjectivity and interpretation. Before addressing this criticism, I suggest that Sinha's own solution too begs the question. He states that the biology of human development is a product of the interaction of biological and cultural evolution at the specific site of ontogenesis, where the cultural contributions come mostly in the form of canonical rules of object and symbol manipulation. This may well be the case, but still unanswered is the question of what enables the child, in interaction with adults, to absorb the rules and internalize the cultural contributions. We are back to square one. My own proposal is that the child evolves (noncultural, innate) interpretive skills of intersubjectively engaging others and does so for her own evolutionary reasons, such as regulation, metabolism, and defense. These skills are later exploited by cultural indoctrination.

16. An instructive phylogenetic parallel here would be to look at the evolution of the human mind, spanning the Pleistocene, from the later perspective of its literate and scientific employment. Pleistocene evolution had literacy and science not as formative pressures but rather as tardy and incidental outcomes. True, in development, unlike in history, the adult society knows what it wants the child's mind to become, but the fact remains that adult guidance exploits mental resources that may have evolved to handle problems inherent in development.

17. The child's mental activism is precisely where Barbara Rogoff (1990, 16–18), a careful student of child-parent interaction, parts company from Vygotsky. She does so on psychological grounds, largely because of recent evidence about the mental equipment of infants that was not available to Vygotsky (see also Wertsch 1985a, 44–45). The same is true about the comparative evidence about primates. Yet it is worth insisting that, such evidence notwithstanding, it stands to evolutionary reason that socially complex organisms, such as apes and human infants, are bound to be active in their survival strategies and therefore to require commensurate mental abilities.

Chapter 2

1. In an earlier work (Bogdan 1997) I attempted to document systematic correlations between the epistemic, communal, and political patterns of interaction among primates, on the one hand, and forms of interpretation, on the other hand, in an effort to check whether the former can be viewed as evolutionary forces selecting for the latter. On a more modest scale here, I go one step further in this metaevolutionary inquiry and check for links between forms of interpretation and kinds of socialized minds to see whether the need for interpretation generated pressures for novel mental skills and also whether, in so doing, interpretation contributed to the design of those skills.

2. The ethological and animal-psychology literature rarely makes this distinction, which is why so many animal species are regarded as tool users (Beck 1980, Vauclair 1996). Some primate psychologists, aware of the conceptual basis of the distinction, are more skeptical and frugal about who counts as tool user (Kummer 1995, Tomasello and Call 1997). It is not my aim or competence to decide what is a tool and which species use tools. My argument simply needs the idea that a tool is an implement

which meets the generality and separability conditions and whose use requires causal knowledge. The implement/tool distinction can make sense of the fact that most primate species, including human infants, use implements in the physical domain and tools in the social domain, thus having some causal knowledge of the latter but not of the former. Perhaps human adults alone acquire the causal knowledge required to use tools in the physical and other nonsocial domains.

3. The idea that causes are means or tools used to bring about effects is not that new. Collingwood (1940) is credited with an early defense of it and so is Gasking (1955) and other more recent authors. My analysis is not committed to an exclusive tool-like or agency reading of natural causation, although it may be true that the *intelligibility* of causation may be heavily indebted to the notion of manipulating events to generate other events. On this notion, causation is understood in terms of possible manipulation, even when such a manipulation is impossible or impracticable. So viewed, the issue is not about causation in the world actually *being* tool manipulation (an ontological claim) but rather, closer to my discussion, about its *intelligibility* and *knowledge* (a psychological claim). My analysis is committed to the latter aspects and in particular to the ontogenesis of the category of causality.

4. As far as I know, few students of interpretation have linked the understanding of causality specifically to that of intentionality; and among those few Michael Tomasello (1998) may be the first to take an interventionist view of that dual understanding and to speculate about its role in mental rehearsal.

5. One may wonder whether in the interval between developing the sense of agency and that of full intentionality as relatedness + direction + target (according to chapter 5) the causal knowledge of infants is rather subjective and proximal, in the sense of being limited to getting others to do whatever the infant attends to perceptually. With the recognition of full intentionality in the picture, a child may use causal knowledge (like the gorilla in Gomez's story) to influence an adult to do something that is publicly shared and distal.

6. Even skeptics about nonhuman causal knowledge like Kummer concur that "primates are considered to be experts in the detection of social causality" because many patterns of their social interactions, such as threats, reconciliations and alliances, ranging over extended space-time regions, could not be handled by contiguity-based learning (1995, 34). Tomasello (1998) explicitly connects the understanding of causality with that of intentionality, thus concluding that the former must have first emerged in the social domain.

7. I follow here Stephen Levinson's insightful discussion (1995), which alerted me to the differences in mental gear generated by representing and computing zero-sum interactions versus non-zero-sum coordinations. See also Trevarthen 1993, 128.

8. Nonhuman primates may have evolved specialized skills for interpretation which can handle the common core of their epistemic, communal, and political relations. Judging from their social behavior and communication, it is a core defined by thoroughly utilitarian proclivities. In this respect Andrew Whiten notes that the asymmetry of emphasis between the politics of nonhuman primates and the epistemic and communal interactions of human primates is reflected in the focus of current research on interpretation: nonhuman primate interpretation is usually studied "in the cut and thrust of severe social competition," where it is expected to be best manifested, whereas

"human infant intersubjectivity is typically analyzed in the cozy, protective context of parent-infant preverbal games and conversations" (1993, 369). As Whiten notes, this asymmetry is misleading, for nonhuman primates cooperate on a large scale, and human infants-parents relations are rife with competition and exploitation. Still, as I see it, the question concerns the specialized skills involved in these distinct types of activities. In order to reexamine the asymmetry more should be known about the earliest stages of ape and monkey mental and interpretational development and their impact on their way of life.

Chapter 3

1. The more technical wording has it that "the evolutionary payoff under conditions of r-selection is that those individuals who reproduce most rapidly, and/or in the greatest number, are disproportionately represented in future generations by virtue of their headstart in filling available niche space" (Chisholm 1988, 81; see also Bonner 1980, 48–50). In this subsection, I mostly follow Chisholm's excellent survey.

2. Prolonged development, in the form of delayed social maturation, seems to be achieved through selection for regulator genes that delay the switching on of structural genes coding for the production of endocrine substances, such as growth hormones, that determine the timing and rate of development (Chisholm 1988, 82).

3. A few evolutionary reminders can place this epigenetic story in a larger perspective. One is that flexible adjustment to environment is a sign of adaptation throughout the living world. Williams writes, "The boundary between the somatic and ecological environments is not entirely distinct. Sometimes a major phenotypic difference may result from a minor and transient ecological factor, largely by a triggering of a critical change in the somatic environment. A minor dietary change early in development makes a bee a worker rather than a queen. . . . The presence or absence of metamorphosis in urodeles may be similarly decided by a dietary threshold. The settling and metamorphosis of marine larval stages is contingent upon sensory stimuli emanating from suitable attachment sites." He concludes, "It is the ecological environment that determines how well adapted a soma will be and what sorts of morphogenetic change are possible" (1966, 67). Another reminder, analyzed by Changeux (1985), is that there is a progressive decrease in the impact of the genotype on the neural phenotype from invertebrates to vertebrates, from lower vertebrates to higher, and from nonhuman primates to human (see also Chisholm 1988, 83). It may be no accident that this progressive decrease in the power of the genotype is associated with an increase in the texture and complexity of the social life of the species involved. Adaptation to a social environment calls for a high degree of freedom in setting the environment-sensitive values of the parameters present in the genotype.

4. One is tempted by a phylogenetic analogy at this point. The mental equipment of the human species evolved during the Pleistocene, and that evolution was completed some 35,000 years ago. This, as often noted, means that the evolutionary pressures responsible for the design of the human mind have little, if anything, to do with the more recent history of the species and its intellectual accomplishments. Advanced human culture, based on literacy, technology, and science, has been created and fueled by a mind designed for illiterate and prescientific hunters and gatherers. So the analogy would be that the cultural mind may be an incidental effect of selection during

Pleistocene for high intellectual capacity in illiterate hunters and gatherers (Tooby and Cosmides 1990), just as, ontogenetically, the sophisticated adult mind may be an incidental effect of selection for high intellectual capacities during child development (see the references on page 72).

5. Affects and emotions are known to be effective binders capable of gluing cognitive and sociocultural innovations to the child's mind (Damasio 1994), in the same way in which at a more basic level the chemical properties of the pleasure effects bind biological and behavioral innovations (Morillo 1995).

6. In a series of very interesting articles (1994, 1996a, 1996b, 1997, 1998a) Juan Carlos Gomez explores the phenomenon of mutual awareness and estimates that apes (though not monkeys) also display it, most notably in communication through eye contact. But it appears to be a mutual awareness with utilitarian topics—things to be done and the like. I return to this matter in chapter 5, section 3.

7. Akhtar and Tomasello (1998) define predication (a) in topic-comment terms when (b) effected through joint attention and (c) the comment, though not neccessarily the topic, is linguistically specified. I follow them with respect to (a) but not (b) and (c) by allowing the notion of predication to operate prelinguistically and also prior to the development of joint attention.

8. It is worth noting that the pressures to figure out goals and targets that are less vital, obvious, and egocentric increase tremendously for the nonhuman primates brought into cultured captivity and forced to handle new intellectual and behavioral challenges. A few researchers noted that the mental abilities of these primates, usually apes, may stretch beyond their natural range (of the social bush) and show surprising innovations (Humphrey 1988, Premack 1988). One can look at such cases for brief but so incomplete glimpses into how evolution could have gone, or actually went, when our distant ancestors first encountered manifestations of culture or similarly novel challenges, and, as a result, took a turn toward a new type of mind.

9. One could fantasize that apes almost got to the interpretive grasp of topics, through their incomplete grasp of intentionality (as noted in chapter 5, section 1) but failed to get a grip on commenting, because of their failure to evolve sentimental bonding and its interpretational version of sentimental minding. Failure to comment in turn may have prevented apes from completing their grasp of intentionality and hence of the category of topic, on which to build a new sense of symbol reference in general and word reference in particular, on which the interpretive understanding of propositional attitudes and metarepresentation rests, which understanding in turn is essential to mental reflexivity. This is another way of looking at the mind-design pattern that evolution built on the shoulders of topical predication.

Chapter 5

1. Both Baron-Cohen (1995) and Leslie (1994) are careful to specify the empirical evidence for the modules they posit, and Baron-Cohen in particular is on lookout for neuroscientific data. Yet, as far as I could determine, there is little specifically on shared attention. The empirical data are typically about gaze following and joint gaze.

2. As Cheney and Seyfarth point out (1990, 235–236), animals can behave with compassion toward others by recognizing the physical impairments or needs of the

others but still failing to recognize the mental conditions of others, including their experiences or feelings. This is why evidence for compassion is not evidence for *recognition* of mental conditions and hence cannot indicate intersubjectivity by mental sharing. The two authors cite experiments suggesting that monkeys and chimpanzees might communicate and thus share some basic emotions, such as fear or excitement, by recognizing their facial or behavioral expressions. They note that these accomplishments may emerge out of repetitive associations between behavioral patterns and specific types of events (1990, 238–239). But even if there were a fearful-face recognition instinct, it does not follow that what is recognized is the experience and its specific connection to the world, as opposed to its external expression as an alarming Gestalt. The human infant, who recognizes fear on mother's face, registers not just an alarming Gestalt but also a dramatic change in what mother communicates and shares. Crucially, this change is expected by the infant to have some intentional force, to point to something that mother always shares, for example, the infant's ongoing behavior.

3. The emulation story was supposed to be about tasks, not programs. The sentimental route to shared attention and other interpretive skills may suggest a commitment to programs. It should not be read that way. Revealing and exchanging emotions and other experiences is a matter of what is done, not of how it is done, by what specific means. Mother may regulate infant behavior, by expressing her regulatory emotions, through mere vocalization, facial expression, bodily posture, or articulate speech— same tasks, different ways of carrying them out. My argument is that it is through what it does and accomplishes that the sentimental route looks best poised to deliver intersubjective interpretation and mental sharing, so crucial to the development of reflexive thinking.

4. As Bakeman and Adamson (1984) note, mothers socialize reference to objects by embedding it within the interpersonal sphere well before infants can structure this integration by themselves. I think the point can be generalized to other, earlier and later, achievements such as reference to action, comments on mutually experienced topics, and so on.

Chapter 6

1. Wimmer, Hogrefe, and Sodian (1988) talk mostly of knowledge and lack of it but often mean belief and false belief as well. The metasemantic gambit can be construed in this liberal or inclusive manner because it merely establishes and evaluates, on external and typically causal grounds, whether information has been received from a source.

2. It is worth noting that the attribution of perceptual access (or lack thereof) need not be treated as one of belief. Younger children and even great apes master such access, can factor it into their goal policies, and can causally manipulate it (Gomez 1991, Povinelli and Eddy 1996). Perceptual access *becomes* a variable in the belief equation only when other computations, such as memory or imagined comparisons with other access relations are brought in. Also worth noting is that attributions of iterated *perceptual-access* relations need not count as *level* distinctions in attitude computation, as is often assumed in the psychological literature. I am thinking of cases where an interpreter notices that a subject sees another subject seeing a third doing something of interest to everybody present. Many theorists are tempted to see this as

a case of *higher-order* interpretation of attitudes about attitudes. I think this temptation should be resisted. Seeings or any other *situated* relations need not be interpreted *as* attitudes, to begin with, if they are not computed by isolating causal origin and information route, abstracting them from currently perceived situations, and checking them against remembered or imagined situations. It is this sort of attitude computation, not the sequencing of seeings, that makes the level distinction legitimate and explanatory. And there is a *reductio ad absurdum* in the offing as well. If seeing seeings and in general relating situatedly to other situated relations would count as higher-order interpretation, then (on the hypothesis pursued in this book) reflexive thinking might be thought to be in principle accessible to such higher-order interpreters as apes and young children. But the consequent is unwarranted, and so, therefore, is the antecedent. At least as I read the facts, the seeing-seeings sort of interpretation does not have much if anything to do with mental reflexivity. Since it is the latter that guides our sense of higher-order mentation, I conclude that the former is not genuine *higher-order* interpretation.

Chapter 7

1. My interest here is not in the architectures but rather in the developmental reasons for, and the tasks revealing, mind unification. My thoughts on this topic have been stimulated by a penetrating paper of Dan Sperber (1994), the insightful work of my former doctoral student Ping Tian (1996), and the larger-scale developmental analysis of Annette Karmiloff-Smith (1992). Their interest, unlike mine, was mostly in the architectural issues surrounding the demodularization of the mind.

2. I thank Mia Zebouni, a doctoral student in psychology at Tulane, for pressing me to clarify this point. And I thank her in general for sharing her extensive knowledge of and insights into primate minds with me and my students in recent classes where I presented bits and pieces of this essay.

3. This diagnosis holds even if one does not buy into a modular view of the mind. Neither the naive-theory view nor a general-purpose view of the mind can get a situated mind to satisfy the two conditions. These views allow more flexibility as to how the accessed output data can be linked and revised, but that is far from providing a common format of representation or the opportunity and resources for mental rehearsal.

Chapter 8

1. A point made by Nick Humphrey in his talk at the 1998 New Iberia Conference on Human Cognitive Specializations.

References

Akhtar, N., and Tomasello, M. 1998. Intersubjectivity in Early Language Learning and Use. In S. Braten (ed.), *Intersubjectivity and Emotional Communication*. Cambridge: Cambridge University Press.

Alexander, R. G. 1990a. *How Did Humans Evolve?* Special Publication no. 1. Museum of Zoology, University of Michigan.

Alexander, R. D. 1990b. Epigenetic Rules ands Darwinian Algorithms. *Ethology and Sociobiology* 11: 241–303.

Armstrong, D. 1968. *A Materialist Theory of Mind*. New York: Humanities Press.

Astington, J. W., and Gopnik, A. 1988. Knowing You've Changed Your Mind: Children's Understanding of Representational Change. In J. W. Astington et al. (eds.), *Developing Theories of Mind*. Cambridge: Cambridge University Press.

Austin, J. L. 1961. *Philosophical Papers*. Oxford: Oxford University Press.

Baillargeon, R., Kotovsky, L., and Needham, A. 1995. The Acquisition of Physical Knowledge in Infancy. In D. Sperber, D. Premack, and A. Premack (eds.), *Causal Cognition*. Oxford: Oxford University Press.

Bakeman, R., and Adamson, L. B. 1984. Coordinating Attention to People and Objects in Mother-Infant and Peer-Infant Interaction. *Child Development* 55: 1278–1289.

Bard, K. A. 1990. "Social Tool Use" by Free-Ranging Orangutans. In S. T. Parker and K. R. Gibson (eds.), *"Language" and Intelligence in Monkeys and Apes*. Cambridge: Cambridge University Press.

Barkow, J. H., Cosmides, L., and Tooby, J. (eds.). 1992 *The Adapted Mind*. New York: Oxford University Press.

Baron-Cohen, S. 1991. Precursors to a Theory of Mind: Understanding Attention in Others. In A. Whiten (ed.), *Natural Theories of Mind*. Oxford: Blackwell.

Baron-Cohen, S. 1995. *Mindblindness*. Cambridge: MIT Press.

Baron-Cohen, S. 1996. Can Children with Autism Integrate First and Third Person Representations? *Behavioral and Brain Sciences* 19: 123–124.

Baron-Cohen, S., and Bolton P. 1993. *Autism: The Facts*. Oxford: Oxford University Press.

Barresi, J., and Moore, C. 1966. Intentional Relations and Social Understanding. *Behavioral and Brain Sciences* 19: 107–122.

Barton, R. A., and Dunbar, R. I. M. 1997. Evolution of the Social Brain. In A. Whiten and R. W. Byrne (eds.), *Machiavellian Intelligence II*. Cambridge: Cambridge University Press.

Bartsch, K., and Wellman, H. M. 1995. *Children Talk about the Mind*. Oxford: Oxford University Press.

Bateson, M. C. 1979. The Epigenesis of Conversational Interaction. In M. Bullowa (ed.), *Before Speech*. Cambridge: Cambridge University Press.

Beck, B. B. 1980. *Animal Tool Behavior*. New York: Garland.

Bjorklund, D. F. 1995. *Children's Thinking*. Pacific Grove: Brooks/Cole.

Block, N. 1995. On a Confusion about a Function of Consciousness. *Behavioral and Brain Sciences* 18: 227–247.

Bloom, L. 1993. *The Transition from Infancy to Language*. Cambridge: Cambridge University Press.

Bloom, P. 1997. Intentionality and Word Learning. *Trends in Cognitive Science* 1: 9–12.

Boesch, C., and Boesch, H. 1984. Mental Map in Wild Chimpanzee. *Primates* 25: 160–170.

Bogdan, R. J. 1985. The Intentional Stance Reexamined. *Behavioral and Brain Sciences* 8: 759–760.

Bogdan, R. J. 1987. Mind, Content, and Information. *Synthese* 70: 205–277.

Bogdan, R. J. 1988. Information and Semantic Cognition. *Mind and Language* 3: 81–122.

Bogdan, R. J. 1989a. Does Semantics Run the Psyche? *Philosophy and Phenomenological Research* 49: 687–700.

Bogdan, R. J. 1989b. What Do We Need Concepts For? *Mind and Language* 4: 17–23.

Bogdan, R. J. (ed.). 1991a. *Mind and Common Sense*. Cambridge: Cambridge University Press.

Bogdan, R. J. 1991b. Common Sense Naturalized. In R. J. Bogdan (ed.), *Mind and Common Sense*. Cambridge: Cambridge University Press.

Bogdan, R. J. 1993. The Architectural Nonchalance of Commonsense Psychology. *Mind and Language* 8: 189–205.

Bogdan, R. J. 1994. *Grounds for Cognition*. Hillsdale, N.J.: Erlbaum.

Bogdan, R. J. 1995. The Epistemological Illusion. *Behavioral and Brain Sciences* 18: 390–391.

Bogdan, R. J. 1997. *Interpreting Minds*. Cambridge: MIT Press.

Bonner, J. T. 1980. *The Evolution of Culture in Animals*. Princeton: Princeton University Press.

Bowlby, J. 1982. *Attachment*. New York: Basic Books.

Braitenberg, V. 1984. *Vehicles*. Cambridge: MIT Press.

Bremner, J. G. 1988. *Infancy*. Oxford: Blackwell.

Bruner, J. 1983. *Child's Talk*. New York: Norton.

Bruner, J. 1990. *Acts of Meaning*. Cambridge: Harvard University Press.

Bruner, J. 1995. From Joint Attention to the Meeting of Minds. In C. Moore and P. J. Dunham (eds.), *Joint Attention*. Hillsdale, N.J.: Erlbaum.

Bruner, J., and Feldman, C. 1993. Theories of Mind and the Problem of Autism. In Baron-Cohen et al. (eds.), *Understanding Other Minds*. Oxford: Oxford University Press.

Butterworth, G. 1991. The Ontogeny and Phylogeny of Joint Visual Attention. In A. Whiten (ed.), *Natural Theories of Mind*. Oxford: Blackwell.

Butterworth, G. 1995. Origins of Mind in Perception and Action. In C. Moore and P. Dunham (eds.), *Joint Attention*. Hillsdale, N.J.: Erlbaum.

Byrne, R. W. 1995. The Ape Legacy: The Evolution of Machiavellian Intelligence and Anticipatory Interactive Planning. In E. N. Goody (ed.), *Social Intelligence and Interaction*. Cambridge: Cambridge University Press.

Byrne, R. W. 1997. The Technical Intelligence Hypothesis. In A. Whiten and R. W. Byrne (eds.). *Machiavellian Intelligence II*. Cambridge: Cambridge University Press.

Byrne, R. W., and Whiten, A. (eds.). 1988. *Machiavellian Intelligence*. Oxford: Oxford University Press.

Byrne, R. W., and Whiten, A. 1991. Computation and Mindreading in Primate Tactical Deception. In A. Whiten (ed.), *Natural Theories of Mind*. Oxford: Blackwell.

Calvin, W. H. 1993. The Unitary Hypothesis: A Common Neural Circuitry for Novel Manipulations, Language, Plan-Ahead, and Throwing? In K. Gibson and T. Ingold (eds.), *Tools, Language, and Cognition in Human Evolution*. Cambridge: Cambridge University Press.

Carey, S. 1985. *Conceptual Change in Childhood*. Cambridge: MIT Press.

Carrithers, M. 1991. Narrativity: Mindreading and Making Societies. In A. Whiten (ed.), *Natural Theories of Mind*. Oxford: Blackwell.

Carrithers, M. 1995. Stories in the Social and Mental Life of People. In E. N. Goody (ed.), *Social Intelligence and Interaction*. Cambridge: Cambridge University Press.

Carruthers, P. 1996. *Language, Thought, and Consciousness*. Cambridge: Cambridge University Press.

Cartwright, N. 1983. *How the Laws of Physics Lie*. Oxford: Oxford University Press.

Chandler, M. J. 1988. Doubt and Developing Theories of Mind. In J. W. Astington et al. (eds.). *Developing Theories of Mind*. Cambridge: Cambridge University Press.

Chandler, M. J., and Hala, S. 1994. The Role of Personal Involvement in the Assessment of Early False Belief Skills. In C. Lewis and P. Mitchell (eds.), *Children's Early Understanding of Mind*. Hillsdale, N.J.: Erlbaum.

Changeux, J.-P. 1985. *The Neuronal Man*. Oxford: Oxford University Press.

Cheney, D. L., and Seyfarth, R. M. 1990. *How Monkeys See the World*. Chicago: University of Chicago Press.

Chisholm, J. S. 1988. Toward a Developmental Evolutionary Ecology of Humans. In K. B. MacDonald (ed.), *Sociobiological Perspectives on Human Development*. New York: Springer-Verlag.

Clark, A. 1998. Magic Words: How Language Augments Human Computation. In P. Carruthers and J. Boucher (eds.), *Language and Thought: Interdisciplinary Themes*. Cambridge: Cambridge University Press.

Clark, E., and Clark, H. 1977. *Psychology and Language*. New York: Harcourt Brace.

Collingwood, R. G. 1940. *An Essay on Metaphysics*. Oxford: Oxford University Press.

Collins, A. 1987. *The Nature of Mental Things*. Notre Dame, Ind.: University of Notre Dame Press.

Corkum, V., and Moore, C. 1995. Development of Joint Visual Attention in Infants. In C. Moore and P. J. Dunham (eds.), *Joint Attention*. Hillsdale, N.J.: Erlbaum.

Cosmides, L., and Tooby, J. 1987. From Evolution to Behavior. In J. Dupré (ed.), *The Latest on the Best*. Cambridge: MIT Press.

Costal, A. 1989. A Closer Look at "Direct Perception." In A. Gellalty, D. Rogers, and J. A. Sloboda (eds.), *Cognition and Social Worlds*. Oxford: Oxford University Press.

Cummins, R. 1986. Inexplicit Information. In M. Brand and R. M. Harnish (eds.), *The Representation of Knowledge and Belief*. Tucson: University of Arizona Press.

Cummins, D., and Allen, C. (eds.). 1998. *The Evolution of Mind*. Oxford: Oxford University Press.

Currie, G. 1996. Simulation-Theory, Theory-Theory, and the Evidence from Autism. In P. Carruthers and P. K. Smith (eds.), *Theories of Theories of Mind*. Cambridge: Cambridge University Press.

Damasio, Antonio, 1994. *Descartes' Error*. New York: Avon Books.

D'Andrade, R. G. 1989, Cultural Cognition. In M. Posner (ed.), *Foundations of Cognitive Science*. Cambridge: MIT Press.

Davies, M., and Stone, T. (eds.). 1995. *Mental Simulation*. Oxford: Blackwell.

Dawkins, R. 1976. Hierarchical Organisation. In P. Bateson and J. Krebs, (eds.), *Growing Points in Ethology*. Cambridge: Cambridge University Press.

Dennett, D. 1978. *Brainstorms*. Montgomery, Vt.: Bradford Books.

Dennett, D. 1987. *The Intentional Stance*. Cambridge: MIT Press.

Dennett, D. 1991. *Consciousness Explained*. New York: Simon and Schuster.

Dennett, D. 1995. *Darwin's Dangerous Idea*. New York: Simon and Schuster.

Dennett, D. 1996. *Kinds of Minds*. New York: Basic Books.

De Waal, F. 1982. *Chimpanzee Politics*. Baltimore: Johns Hopkins University Press.

De Waal, F. 1989. *Peacemaking among Primates*. Cambridge: Harvard University Press.

Dickinson, A., and Shanks, D. 1995. Instrumental Action and Causal Representation. In D. Sperber, D. Premack, and A. J. Premack (eds.), *Causal Cognition*. Oxford: Oxford University Press.

Dickstein, S., Thomson, R. A., Estes, D., Malkin, C., and Lamb, M. E. 1984. Social Referencing and the Security of Attachment. *Infant Behavior and Development* 7: 507–516.

Donald, M. 1991. *Origins of the Modern Mind.* Cambridge: Harvard University Press.

Dretske, F. 1972. Contrastive Statements. *Philosophical Review* 81: 411–437.

Dretske, F. 1988. *Explaining Behavior.* Cambridge: MIT Press.

Dretske, F. 1995. *Naturalizing the Mind,* Cambridge: MIT Press.

Drew, P. 1995. Interaction Sequences and Anticipatory Interactive Planning. In E. N. Goody (ed.), *Social Intelligence and Interaction.* Cambridge: Cambridge University Press.

Dunn, J. 1988. *The Beginnings of Social Understanding.* Oxford: Blackwell.

Dunn, J. 1991. Understanding Others: Evidence from Naturalistic Studies of Children. In A. Whiten (ed.), *Natural Theories of Mind.* Oxford: Blackwell.

Fernald, A. 1992. Human Maternal Vocalization to Infants as Biologically Relevant Signals. In J. Barkow, L. Cosmides, and J. Tooby (eds.), *The Adapted Mind.* Oxford: Oxford University Press.

Flavell, J. H. 1988. The Development of Children's Knowledge about the Mind. In J. W. Astington et al. (eds.), *Developing Theories of Mind.* Cambridge: Cambridge University Press.

Flavell, J. H., Green, F. L., and Flavell, E. R. 1995. *Young Children's Knowledge about Thinking.* Monographs of the Society for Research in Child Development, vol. 60, no. 1. Chicago: Society for Research in Child Development.

Fodor, J. A. 1983. *Modularity of Mind.* Cambridge: MIT Press.

Fodor, J. A. 1987. *Psychosemantics.* Cambridge: MIT Press.

Fodor, J. A. 1992. A Theory of the Child's Theory of Mind. *Cognition* 44: 283–296.

Forguson, L., and Gopnik, A. 1988. The Ontogeny of Common Sense. In J. W. Astington et al. (eds.), *Developing Theories of Mind.* Cambridge: Cambridge University Press.

Frith, U. 1989. *Autism.* Oxford: Blackwell.

Frith, U. 1997. The Neurocognitive Basis of Autism. *Trends in Cognitive Science* 1: 73–77.

Frye, D., Zelazo, P. D., and Palfai, T. 1995. Theory of Mind and Rule-Based Reasoning. *Cognitive Development* 10: 483–527.

Gasking, D. 1955. Causation and Recipes. *Mind* 64: 479–487.

Gibson, K. R. 1993. Tool Use, Language, and Social Behavior in Relationship to Information Processing Capacities. In K. R. Gibson and T. Ingold (eds.), *Tools, Language, and Cognition in Human Evolution.* Cambridge: Cambridge University Press.

Gibson, K. R., and Ingold, T. (eds.). 1993. *Tools, Language, and Cognition in Human Evolution.* Cambridge: Cambridge University Press.

Gigerenzer, G. 1997. The Modularity of Social Intelligence. In A. Whiten, and R. W. Byrne (eds.), *Machiavellian Intelligence II.* Cambridge: Cambridge University Press.

Goldman, A. 1993. The Psychology of Folk Psychology. *Behavioral and Brain Sciences* 16: 15–28.

Golinkoff, R. 1986. The Preverbal Negotiation of Failed Messages. In R. Golinkoff (ed.), *The Transition from Prelinguistic to Linguistic Communication*. Hillsdale, N.J.: Erlbaum.

Gomez, J. C. 1990a. Primate Tactical Deception and Sensorimotor Social Intelligence. *Behavioral and Brain Sciences* 13: 414–415.

Gomez. J. C. 1990b. The Emergence of Intentional Communication as a Problem-Solving Strategy in the Gorilla. In S. T. Parker and K. R. Gibson (eds.), *"Language" and Intelligence in Monkeys and Apes*. Cambridge: Cambridge University Press.

Gomez, J. C. 1991. Visual Behavior as a Window for Reading the Mind of Others in Primates. In A. Whiten (ed.), *Natural Theories of Mind*. Oxford: Blackwell.

Gomez. J. C. 1994. Mutual Awareness in Primate Communication: A Gricean Approach. In S. T. Parker et al. (eds.), *Self-Awareness in Animals and Humans*. Cambridge: Cambridge University Press.

Gomez, J. C. 1996a. Second Person Intentional Relations and the Evolution of Social Understanding. *Behavioral and Brain Sciences* 19: 129–130.

Gomez, J. C. 1996b. Ostensive Behavior in Great Apes: The Role of Eye Contact. In A. E. Russon et al. (eds.), *Reaching into Thought*. Cambridge: Cambridge University Press.

Gomez, J. C. 1997. On the Nature and Origins of Meaning: The Humpty-Dumpty Hypothesis. Manuscript.

Gomez, J. C. 1998a. Do Concepts of Intersubjectivity Apply to Nonhuman Primates? In S. Braten (ed.), *Intersubjective Communication and Emotion in Ontogeny*. Cambridge: Cambridge University Press.

Gomez, J. C. 1998b. Some Thoughts about the Evolution of LADS. In P. Carruthers and J. Boucher (eds.), *Language and Thought: Interdisciplinary Themes*. Cambridge: Cambridge University Press.

Gomez, J. C., Sarria, E., and Tamarit, J. 1993. The Comparative Study of Early Communication and Theories of Mind: Ontogeny, Phylogeny, and Pathology. In S. Baron-Cohen et al. (eds.), *Understanding Other Minds*. Oxford: Oxford University Press.

Goody, E. N. 1995a. Introduction. In E. N. Goody(ed.), *Social Intelligence and Interaction*. Cambridge: Cambridge University Press.

Goody, E. N. (ed.). 1995b. *Social Intelligence and Interaction*. Cambridge: Cambridge University Press.

Gopnik, A. 1996. The Scientist as Child. *Philosophy of Science* 63: 485–514.

Gopnik, A., and Meltzoff, A. N. 1997. *Words, Thoughts, and Theories*. Cambridge: MIT Press.

Gopnik, A., and Wellman, H. M. 1992. Why the Child's Theory of Mind Really Is a Theory. *Mind and Language* 7: 145–171.

Gopnik, A., and Wellman, H. M. 1994. The Theory Theory. In L. A. Hirschfeld and S. A. Gelman (eds.), *Domain Specificity in Cognition and Culture*. Cambridge: Cambridge University Press.

Gordon, R. M. 1995. Simulation without Introspection or Inference from Me to You. In M. Davies and T. Stone (eds.), *Mental Simulation*. Oxford: Blackwell.

Greenfield, P. 1991. Language, Tools, and Brain: The Ontogeny and Phylogeny of Hierarchically Organized Behavior. *Behavioral and Brain Sciences* 14: 531–551.

Happé, F. 1994. Communicative Competence and Theory of Mind in Autism. *Cognition* 48: 101–119.

Happé, F., and Frith, U. 1992. How Autistics See the World. *Behavioral and Brain Sciences* 15: 159–160.

Harcourt, A. H. 1988. Alliances in Contests and Social Intelligence. In J. W. Byrne and A. Whiten (eds.), *Machiavellian Intelligence*. Oxford: Oxford University Press.

Harris, P. 1989. *Children and Emotion*. Oxford: Blackwell.

Harris, P. 1991. The Work of Imagination. In A. Whiten (ed.), *Natural Theories of Mind*. Oxford: Blackwell.

Harris, P. 1993. Pretending and Planning. In S. Baron-Cohen, S. Tager-Flusberg, and D. Cohen (eds.), *Understanding Other Minds*. Oxford: Oxford University Press.

Harris, P. 1994. Understanding Pretence. In C. Lewis and P. Mitchell (eds.), *Children's Early Understanding of Mind*. Hillsdale, N.J.: Erlbaum.

Harris, P. 1996. Desires, Beliefs, and Language. In P. Carruthers and P. K. Smith (eds.), *Theories of Theories of Mind*. Cambridge: Cambridge University Press.

Heyes, C. M. 1998. Theory of Mind in Nonhuman Primates. *Behavioral and Brain Sciences* 21: 101–114.

Hickman, M. 1987. The Pragmatics of Reference in Child Language. In M. Hickman (ed.), *Social and Functional Approaches to Language and Thought*. New York: Academic Press.

Hirschfeld, L. A., and Gelman, S. A. (eds.). 1994. *Domain Specificity in Cognition and Culture*. Cambridge: Cambridge University Press.

Hobson, P. 1993a. Understanding Persons: The Role of Affect. In S. Baron-Cohen et al. (eds.), *Understanding Other Minds*. Oxford: Oxford University Press.

Hobson, R. P. 1993b. *Autism and the Development of Mind*. Hillsdale, N.J.: Erlbaum.

Hobson, R. P. 1994. Perceiving Attitudes, Conceiving Minds. In C. Lewis and P. Mitchell (eds.), *Children's Early Understanding of Mind*. Hillsdale, N.J.: Erlbaum.

Hofer, M. A. 1987. Early Social Relationships: A Psychobiologist's View. *Child Development* 58: 633–647.

Howes, C., and Matheson, C. C. 1992. Sequences in the Development of Competent Play with Peers. *Developmental Psychology* 28: 961–974.

Hume, D., 1756. *A Treatise of Human Nature*. Edited by L. A. Lelby-Bigge. Oxford: Oxford University Press, 1888.

Humphrey, N. K. 1986. *The Inner Eye*. London: Faber and Faber.

Humphrey, N. K. 1988. The Social Function of the Intellect. In R. W. Byrne and A. Whiten (eds.), *Machiavellian Intelligence*. Oxford: Oxford University Press. Originally published in 1976.

Ingold, T. 1996. Social Relations, Human Ecology, and the Evolution of Culture. In A. Lock and C. Peters (eds.), *Handbook of Human Symbolic Evolution*. Oxford: Oxford University Press.

Janicki, M. G., and Krebs, D. L. 1998. Evolutionary Approaches to Culture. In C. Crawford and D. L. Krebs (eds.), *Handbook of Evolutionary Psychology*. Mahwah, N.J.: Erlbaum.

Jolly, A. 1988. Lemur Social Behavior and Primate Intelligence. In R. W. Byrne and A. Whiten (eds.), *Machiavellian Intelligence*. Oxford: Oxford University Press. Originally published in 1966.

Karmiloff-Smith, A. 1992. *Beyond Modularity*. Cambridge: MIT Press.

Kummer, H. 1988. Tripartite Relations in Hamadryas Baboons. In R. W. Byrne and A. Whiten (eds.), *Machiavellian Intelligence*. Oxford: Oxford University Press. Originally published in 1967.

Kummer, H. 1995. Causal Knowledge in Animals. In D. Sperber, D. Premack, and A. J. Premack (eds.), *Causal Cognition*. Oxford: Oxford University Press.

LeDoux, J. 1996. *The Emotional Brain*. New York: Simon and Schuster.

Lehrer, K. 1997. *Self-Trust*. Oxford: Oxford University Press.

Leondar, B. 1977. Hatching Plots: Genesis of Storymaking. In D. Perkins and B. Leondar (eds.), *The Arts and Cognition*. Baltimore: Johns Hopkins University Press.

Leslie, A. M. 1988. Some Implications of Pretense for Mechanisms Underlying the Child's Theory of Mind. In J. W. Astington et al. (eds.), *Developing Theories of Mind*. Cambridge: Cambridge University Press.

Leslie, A. M. 1991. The Theory of Mind Impairment in Autism. In A. Whiten (ed.), *Natural Theories of Mind*. Oxford: Blackwell.

Leslie, A. M. 1994. ToMM, ToBy, and Agency. In L. Hirschfeld and S. A. Gelman (eds.), *Mapping the Mind*. Cambridge: Cambridge University Press.

Leslie, A. M. 1995. A Theory of Agency. In D. Sperber, D. Premack, and A. Premack (eds.), *Causal Cognition*. Oxford: Oxford University Press.

Leslie, A. M., and Roth, D. 1993. What Autism Teaches Us about Metarepresentation. In S. Baron-Cohen et al. (eds.), *Understanding Other Minds*. Oxford: Oxford University Press.

Levinson, S. 1995. Interactional Biases in Human Thinking. In E. N. Goody (ed.), *Social Intelligence and Interaction*. Cambridge: Cambridge University Press.

Lewis, C. 1994. Episodes, Events, and Narratives in the Child's Understanding of Mind. In C. Lewis and P. Mitchell (eds.), *Origins of an Understanding of Mind*. Hillsdale, N.J.: Erlbaum.

Lewis, D. 1969. *Convention*. Cambridge: Harvard University Press.

Lewis, D. 1972. Psychophysical and Theoretical Identifications. *Australian Journal of Philosophy* 50: 249–258.

Lloyd, D. 1989. *Simple Minds*. Cambridge: MIT Press.

Loar, B. 1981. *Mind and Meaning*. Cambridge: Cambridge University Press.

Lock, A. 1980. *The Guided Reinvention of Language*. New York: Academic Press.

Lock, A., and Peters, C. (eds.). 1996. *Handbook of Human Symbolic Evolution.* Oxford: Oxford University Press.

Low, B. S. 1998. The Evolution of Human Life Histories. In C. Crawford and D. L. Krebs (eds.), *Handbook of Evolutionary Psychology.* Mahwah, N.J.: Erlbaum.

Lunzer, E. A. 1979. The Development of Consciousness. In G. Underwood and R. Stevens (eds.), *Aspects of Consciousness.* New York: Academic Press.

Luria, A. R. 1979. *The Making of Mind.* Cambridge: Harvard University Press.

Mandler, J. 1988. How to Build a Better Baby. *Cognitive Development* 3: 113–136.

McGinn, C. 1982. The Structure of Content. In A. Woodfield (ed.), *Thought and Object.* Oxford: Oxford University Press.

McGrew, W. C. 1993. The Intelligent Use of Tools. In K. R. Gibson and T. Ingold (eds.), *Tools, Language, and Cognition in Human Evolution.* Cambridge: Cambridge University Press.

Mead, G. H. 1934. *Mind, Self, and Society.* Chicago: University of Chicago Press.

Mead, G. H. 1963. *Selected Writings.* Edited by Andrew J. Reck. Indianapolis: Bobbs-Merrill.

Mellor, D. H. 1978. Conscious Belief. *Proceedings of the Aristotelian Society* 78: 87–101.

Meltzoff, A., and Gopnik, A. 1993. The Role of Imitation in Understanding Persons and Developing a Theory of Mind. In S. Baron-Cohen et al. (eds.), *Understanding Other Minds.* Oxford: Oxford University Press.

Messer, D., and Collis, G. 1996. Early Interaction and Cognitive Skills. In A. Lock and C. Peters (eds.), *Handbook of Human Symbolic Evolution.* Oxford: Oxford University Press.

Mitchell, P. 1994. Realism and Early Conception of Mind. In C. Lewis and P. Mitchell (eds.), *Origins of an Understanding of Mind.* Hillsdale, N.J.: Erlbaum.

Mithen, S. 1996. *The Prehistory of the Mind.* London: Thames and Hudson.

Moore, C., and Dunham, P. J. (eds.). 1995. *Joint Attention.* Hillsdale, N.J.: Erlbaum.

Morillo, C. 1995. *Contingent Creatures.* Lanham: Rowman and Littlefield.

Mundy, P., Sigman, M., and Kasari, C. 1993. The Theory of Mind and Joint-Attention Deficits. In S. Baron-Cohen et al. (eds.), *Understanding Other Minds.* Oxford: Oxford University Press.

Nelkin, N. 1995. *Consciousness and the Origins of Thought.* Cambridge: Cambridge Univerity Press.

Nelson, K. 1996. *Language in Cognitive Development.* Cambridge: Cambridge University Press.

Newell, A., Rosenbloom, P. S., and Laird, J. E. 1989. Symbolic Architectures for Cognition. In M. Posner (ed.), *Foundations of Cognitive Science.* Cambridge: MIT Press.

Ninio, A., and Snow, C. E. 1996. *Pragmatic Development.* Boulder: Westview Press.

Olson, D. 1988. On the Origins of Beliefs and Other Intentional States in Children. In J. W. Astington et al. (eds.), *Developing Theories of Mind.* Cambridge: Cambridge University Press.

Ozonoff, S., Pennington, S. J., and Rogers, S. J. 1991. Executive Function Deficits in High-Functioning Autistic Individuals. *Journal of Child Psychology and Psychiatry* 32: 1081–1106.

Papprote, W., and Sinha, C. 1987. Functionalism and Language Development. In M. Hickman (ed.), *Social and Functional Approaches to Language and Thought.* New York: Academic Press.

Parker, S. T., and Gibson, K. R. 1979. A Developmental Model for the Evolution of Language and Intelligence in Early Hominids. *Behavioral and Brain Sciences* 2: 367–408.

Parker, S. T., and Milbrath, C. 1993. Higher Intelligence, Propositional Language, and Culture as Adaptations for Planning. In K. R. Gibson and T. Ingold (eds.), *Tools, Language, and Cognition in Human Evolution.* Cambridge: Cambridge University Press.

Perner, J. 1991. *Understanding the Representational Mind.* Cambridge: MIT Press.

Perner, J., and Lang, B. 1999. Theory of Mind and Executive Function: Is There a Developmental Relationship? In S. Baron-Cohen, S. Tager-Flusberg, and D. Cohen (eds.), *Understanding Other Minds*, 2nd edition. Oxford: Oxford University Press.

Piaget, J. 1936. *La naissance de l'intelligence chez l'enfant.* Neuchâtel: Delachaux et Niestlée.

Piaget, J. 1960. *The Psychology of Intelligence.* Totowa: Littlefield.

Piaget, J. 1964. *Six études de psychologie.* Geneve: Editions Gonthier.

Piaget, J. 1967. Les données génétiques de l'epistémologie physique. In J. Piaget (ed.), *Logique et connaissance scientifique*, Encyclopédie de la pléiade. Paris: Gallimard.

Piaget, J. 1974. *Understanding Causality.* New York: Norton.

Pipp, S. 1993. Infants' Knowledge of Self, Other, and Relationship. In U. Neisser (ed.), *The Perceived Self.* Cambridge: Cambridge University Press.

Poulin-Dubois, D., and Shultz, T. 1988. The Development of the Understanding of Human Behavior. In J. W. Astington et al. (eds.), *Developing Theories of Mind.* Cambridge: Cambridge University Press.

Povinelli, D. J. 1996. Chimpanzee Theory of Mind? In P. Carruthers and P. K. Smith (eds.), *Theories of Theories of Mind.* Cambridge: Cambridge University Press.

Povinelli, D. J., and Eddy, T. J. 1996. *What Young Chimpanzees Know about Seeing.* Monographs of the Society for Research in Child Development, vol. 61, no. 3. Chicago: University of Chicago Press.

Premack, D. 1988. 'Does the Chimpanzee Have a Theory of Mind?' Revisited. In R. W. Byrne and A. Whiten (eds.), *Machiavellian Intelligence.* Oxford: Oxford University Press.

Premack, D. 1990. Do Infants Have a Theory of Self-Propelled Objects? *Cognition* 36: 1–16.

Premack, D., and Premack A. 1995. Intention as Psychological Cause. In D. Sperber, D. Premack, and A. Premack (eds.), *Causal Cognition*. Oxford: Oxford University Press.

Pylyshyn, Z. 1978. When Is Attribution of Belief Justified? *Behavioral and Brain Sciences* 4: 592–593.

Pylyshyn, Z. 1984. *Computation and Cognition*. Cambridge: MIT Press.

Pylyshyn, Z. 1989. Computing in Cognitive Science. In M. Posner (ed.), *Foundations of Cognitive Science*. Cambridge: MIT Press.

Quiatt, D., and Reynolds, V. 1993. *Primate Behavior*. Cambridge: Cambridge University Press.

Reiss, D., McCowan, B., and Marino, L. 1997. Communicative and Other Cognitive Characteristics of Bottlenose Dolphins. *Trends in Cognitive Science* 1: 140–145.

Reynolds, P. C. 1993. The Complementation Theory of Language and Tool Use. In K. R. Gibson and T. Ingold (eds.), *Tools, Language, and Cognition in Human Evolution*. Cambridge: Cambridge University Press.

Rogoff, B. 1990. *Apprenticeship in Thinking*. Oxford: Oxford University Press.

Rosenthal, D. 1986. Two Concepts of Consciousness. *Philosophical Studies* 94: 329–359.

Rosenthal, D. 1993. Thinking That One Thinks. In M. Davies and G. W. Humphreys (eds.), *Consciousness*. Oxford: Blackwell.

Rozin, P. 1976. The Evolution of Intelligence and Access to the Cognitive Unconscious. In J. M. Sprague and A. N. Epstein (eds.), *Progress in Psychobiology and Physiological Psychology*. New York: Academic Press.

Rumbaugh, D. M., and Savage-Rumbaugh, E. S. 1996. Biobehavioral Roots of Language. In B. M. Velichovsky and D. M. Rumbaugh (eds.), *Communicating Meaning*. Mahwah, N.J.: Erlbaum.

Russell, J. 1996. *Agency: Its Role in Mental Development*. Hove: Erlbaum (UK) Taylor and Francis.

Russell, J. (ed.). 1997. *Autism as an Executive Disorder*. Oxford: Oxford University Press.

Sacks, O. 1994. A Neurologist's Notebook: An Anthropologist on Mars. *The New Yorker*, Dec. 27, 1993–Jan. 3, 1994.

Savage-Rumbaugh, E. S. 1986. *Ape Language*. New York: Columbia University Press.

Savage-Rumbaugh, E. S., and Lewin, R. 1994. *Kanzi*. New York: Wiley.

Sellars, W. 1963. *Science, Perception, and Reality*. New York: Humanities Press.

Siegler, R. S. 1991. *Children's Thinking*. Englewood Cliffs: Prentice-Hall.

Simon, H., and Kaplan, C. A. 1989. Foundations of Cognitive Science. In M. Posner (ed.), *Foundations of Cognitive Science*. Cambridge: MIT Press.

Sinha, C. 1996. The Role of Ontogenesis in Human Evolution and Development. In A. Lock and C. Peters (eds.), *Handbook of Human Symbolic Evolution*. Oxford: Oxford University Press.

Slobin, D. 1990. The Development from Child Speaker to Native Speaker. In J. W. Stigler, R. A. Schwede, and G. Herdt (eds.), *Cultural Psychology*. Cambridge: Cambridge University Press.

Sorce, J. F., Emde, R. N., Campos, J., and Klinnert, M. D. 1985. Maternal Emotional Signalling. *Developmental Psychology* 21: 195–200.

Sperber, D. 1994. The Modularity of Thought and the Epidemiology of Representations. In L. A. Hirschfeld and S. A. Gelman (eds.), *Domain Specificity in Cognition and Culture*. Cambridge: Cambridge University Press.

Sperber, D. 1997. Intuitive and Reflective Beliefs. *Mind and Language* 12: 67–83.

Sperber, D., and Wilson, D. 1986. *Relevance*. Cambridge: Harvard University Press.

Stich, S. 1983. *From Folk Psychology to Cognitive Science*. Cambridge: MIT Press.

Stich, S., and Nichols, S. 1993. Second Thoughts on Simulation. In M. Davies and T. Stone (eds.), *Mental Simulation*. Oxford: Blackwell.

Swettenham, J., Gomez, J. C., Baron-Cohen, S., and Walsh, S. 1996. What's Inside Someone's Head? *Cognitive Neuropsychiatry* 1: 73–88.

Tager-Flusberg, H. 1993. What Language Reveals about the Understanding of Minds in Children with Autism. In S. Baron-Cohen, S. Tager-Flusberg, and D. Cohen (eds.), *Understanding Other Minds*. Oxford: Oxford University Press.

Tian, P. 1996. The Modularity of Thinking and the Problem of Domain Inspecificity. Ph.D. thesis, Tulane University.

Tomasello, M. 1993. On the Interpersonal Origins of Self-Concept. In U. Neisser (ed.), *The Perceived Self*. Cambridge: Cambridge University Press.

Tomasello, M. 1995. Joint Attention as Social Cognition. In C. Moore and P. J. Dunham (eds.), *Joint Attention*. Hillsdale, N.J.: Erlbaum.

Tomasello, M. 1996. The Cultural Roots of Language. In B. M. Velichovsky and D. M. Rumbaugh (eds.), *Communicating Meaning*. Mahwah, N.J.: Erlbaum.

Tomasello, M. 1998. Uniquely Primate, Uniquely Human. *Developmental Science*.

Tomasello, M., and Call, J. 1997. *Primate Cognition*. New York: Oxford University Press.

Tomasello, M., Kruger, A. C., and Ratner, H. H. 1993. Cultural Learning. *Behavioral and Brain Sciences* 16: 495–511.

Tooby, J., and Cosmides, L. 1990. The Past Explains the Present. *Ethology and Sociobiology* 11: 375–424.

Tooby, J., and Cosmides, L. 1992. The Psychological Foundations of Culture. In J. Barkow, L. Cosmides, and J. Tooby (eds.), *The Adapted Mind*. New York: Oxford University Press.

Trevarthen, C. 1979. Communication and Cooperation in Early Infancy. In M. Bullowa (ed.), *Before Speech*. Cambridge: Cambridge University Press.

Trevarthen, C. 1993. The Self Born in Intersubjectivity. In U. Neisser (ed.), *The Perceived Self*. Cambridge: Cambridge University Press.

Trevarthen, C., and Logotheti, K. 1989. Child and Culture: Genesis of Cooperative Knowing. In A. Gellalty, D. Rogers, and J. A. Sloboda (eds.), *Cognition and Social Worlds*. Oxford: Oxford University Press.

Trivers, R. 1985. *Social Evolution*. Menlo Park: Benjamin Cummings.

Van der Veer, R., and Valsiner, J., (eds.). 1994. *The Vygostky Reader*. Oxford: Blackwell.

Vauclair, J. 1984. Phylogenetic Approach to Object Manipulation in Human and Ape Infants. *Human Development* 27: 321–328.

Vauclair, J. 1996. *Animal Cognition*. Cambridge: Harvard University Press.

Vygostky, L. S. 1981a. The Genesis of Higher Mental Functions. In J. V. Wertsch (ed.), *The Concept of Activity in Soviet Psychology*. Armonk: M. E. Sharpe. Originally but posthumously published in Russian, 1960.

Vygotsky, L. S. 1981b. The Development of Higher Forms of Attention in Childhood. In J. V. Wertsch (ed.)., *The Concept of Activity in Soviet Psychology*. Armonk: M. E. Sharpe. Originally published in Russian, 1929.

Vygotsky, L. S. 1986. *Thought and Language*. Cambridge: MIT Press. Originally published in Russian, 1934.

Wellman, H. 1990. *The Child's Theory of Mind*. Cambridge: MIT Press.

Wertsch, J. V. (ed.). 1981. *The Concept of Activity in Soviet Psychology*. Armonk: M. E. Sharpe.

Wertsch, J. V. 1985a. *Vygotsky and the Social Formation of Mind*. Cambridge: Harvard University Press.

Wertsch, J. V. (ed.). 1985b. *Culture, Communication, and Cognition*. Cambridge: Cambridge University Press.

Whiten, A., (ed.). 1991. *Natural Theories of Mind*. Oxford: Blackwell.

Whiten, A. 1993. Evolving a Theory of Mind. In S. Baron-Cohen et al. (eds.), *Understanding Other Minds*. Oxford: Oxford University Press.

Whiten, A. 1994. Grades of Mindreading. In C. Lewis and P. Mitchell (eds.), *Origins of an Understanding of Mind*. Hillsdale, N.J.: Erlbaum.

Whiten, A. 1996. When Does Smart Behavior-Reading Become Mind-Reading? In P. Carruthers and P. K. Smith (eds.), *Theories of Theories of Mind*. Cambridge: Cambridge University Press.

Whiten, A. 1997. Evolutionary and Developmental Origins of the Mindreading System. In J. Langer and M. Killen (eds.), *Piaget, Evolution, and Development*. Mahwah, N.J.: Erlbaum

Whiten, A., and Byrne, R. W. 1988a. The Manipulation of Attention in Primate Tactical Deception. In R. W. Byrne and A. Whiten (eds.), *Machiavellian Intelligence*. Oxford: Oxford University Press.

Whiten, A., and Byrne, R. W. 1988b. Taking (Machiavellian) Intelligence Apart. In R. W. Byrne and A. Whiten (eds.), *Machiavellian Intelligence*. Oxford: Oxford University Press.

Whiten, A., and Byrne, R. W. (eds.). 1997. *Machiavellian Intelligence II*. Cambridge: Cambridge University Press.

Whiten, A., and Perner, J. 1991. Fundamental Issues in the Multidisciplinary Study of Mindreading. In A. Whiten (ed.), *Natural Theories of Mind*. Oxford: Blackwell.

Williams, G. C. 1966. *Adaptation and Natural Selection*. Princeton: Princeton University Press.

Wimmer, H., Hogrefe, J., and Sodian, B. 1988. A Second Stage in Children's Conception of Mental Life. In J. Astington et al. (eds.), *Developing Theories of Mind*. Cambridge: Cambridge University Press.

Wittgenstein, L. 1953. *Philosophical Investigations*. Oxford: Blackwell.

Wynn, T. 1988. Tools and the Evolution of Human Intelligence. In R. W. Byrne and A. Whiten (eds.). *Machiavellian Intelligence*. Oxford: Oxford University Press.

Wynn, T. 1993. Layers of Thinking in Tool Behavior. In K. R. Gibson and T. Ingold (eds.), *Tools, Language, and Cognition in Human Evolution*. Cambridge: Cambridge University Press.

Zimmerman, R. R., and Torrey, C. C. 1965. Ontogeny of Learning. In A. M. Schrier et al. (eds.), *Behavior of Non-human Primates*. New York: Academic Press.

Index